WILL YOU **BELIEVE** TO THE POINT
THAT IT **CHANGES YOUR STORY?**

RELEASED

BY MELISSA LLOYD

DEDICATION

*Above all else, this book is dedicated
to the One Who gave it to me,
that One Who is my Kinsman Redeemer,
the Hero of this story, the Love Who is my life.
I will always be completely undone by how
He crashed the gate in my place
with His extravagant grace and gave me
this chance to believe to the point
that it radically changed my story.*

*Secondly, I would have never known
how kind, sensitive, funny
and courageous my God is
had He not given me
such a beautiful picture
in such a beautiful man,
my husband, David,
who chose me for his love
almost 40 years ago.
You are my Boaz.
I will always love you like crazy.*

*These words are also dedicated
to the two little girls God gave to me
by bringing them through me,
my amazing daughters
who grew up to be my best friends,
Brittany and Kiley.*

*And finally, this book is for
Morgan, Penelope,
Marley and Rhys.
I love you more than
any words can ever say
and I wanted to write this book
for you most of all.
My prayer is that, one day,
as you read about Nana's passion,
each of you will believe to the point
that it changes your story,
and this passion will become your own!*

ACKNOWLEDGMENTS

*These words would have never
found their way onto these pages
without the trust of some amazing friends
who opened their hearts, as well as their homes,
so that I could teach this in a Bible study,
life group or disciple-making group;
who sat with me over lunch or coffee
while I babbled on about some new discovery;
or read drafts of these pages while I was still
in the process of finding the words
my heart had to say. You nurtured this dream
from infancy with your friendship.
Your belief in this project means everything.
Thanks for riding shotgun on
this incredible journey with me!*

CONTENTS

With her two daughters-in-law
she left the place
where she had been living
and set out on the road
that would take them back...

(Ruth 1:7 New International Version)

Introduction

Life is either a daring adventure, or nothing.
— HELEN KELLER, LET US HAVE FAITH

BETHLEHEM OR BUST

I was only three years old when Martin Luther King Jr. stood on the steps of the Lincoln Memorial crying out to a Holy God for an impossible dream called freedom. His were words so passionate that, by the mere speaking of them, they refused to accept the way things were and clung to a vision of something much more real to him than the hatred on the steps of the schools in Alabama, or the oppression in the streets of Mississippi, or the segregation on the buses in his own Atlanta, Georgia. Such picturesque words could only gush forth from a heart that had tasted a different reality and once walked there, if only in a dream. They ushered in a far different day than that of this historic moment, nothing more than a vision, nothing less than a prophecy, nothing else but freedom, "free at last." Some might say that Dr. King never lived to see it. Yet could it be he was already living in the midst of it, right then, right there, though surrounded by hatred, oppression and discrimination, as the sounds of misunderstanding and bigotry filled the streets? Could it be that he was miraculously transported to another place, dancing to a different song? Was that "beautiful symphony of brotherhood" more real to him than the clamoring intent on denying him such freedom?[1]

Corrie Ten Boom's God-born compassion for her Jewish neighbors in the midst of the Nazi holocaust ultimately took her to a place that quickly became infamous for its indiscriminate cruelty and brutality, the Nazi extermination camp known as Ravensbruck. Packed like livestock into a freight car, deprived of water, forced to live in their own excrements, Corrie and her sister, Betsie, were transported to a place she could only describe as hell. Freedom had no reasonable place in their vocabulary. Freedom was no obvious element of their existence. Yet in her autobiography entitled, *The Hiding Place*,[2] amidst vivid imagery of their hideous oppression there, Corrie described a burning light that illuminated the darkness of their prison barracks. She and

Betsie had miraculously smuggled in a copy of God's Word. They shared that hidden treasure at every opportunity with the other women who were held prisoner in that torturous nightmare. This is how Corrie explained it,

> I would look about us as Betsie read, watching the light leap from face to face. More than conquerors...it was not a wish. It was a fact. We knew it, we experienced it minute by minute – poor, hated, hungry. We are more than conquerors. Not "we shall be." We are! Life in Ravensbruck took place on two separate levels, mutually impossible. One the observable, external life, grew every day more horrible. The other, the life we lived with God, grew daily better, truth upon truth, glory upon glory.[3]

Corrie became enfolded by another life, unobservable yet irrepressibly true. Swept up into the very presence of God, Corrie was empowered to conquer what most of us could barely survive.

The Lord set apart Paul as His chosen instrument to carry God's name to the Gentiles. Illuminated by a dramatic vision of a man from Macedonia pleading for his help, Paul and his companions received this experience as a calling from God. This vision immediately defined reality for them. So they set sail for the leading city of Macedonia known as Philippi, expecting to find a group of seekers to encourage and instruct. Upon their arrival they found a prayer gathering and, among the worshippers, a woman named Lydia. She anxiously opened her heart to the Lord and her home to Paul and his companions. With her simple act of hospitality the church of Philippi was born. God had flung open the doors to Paul and Silas, setting the stage for this vision to come to life in their midst.

Then opposition arose. This vision met resistance. Their belief was tested. Before long, Paul and Silas were held in the clutches of an angry mob. They were stripped of their clothing, publicly humiliated, beaten and thrown into jail. Guards locked them into the innermost cell, the darkest place in that prison, where their feet were fastened into stocks that held them with an iron grasp. By all indications every bit of their freedom had been taken from them. They were no longer free to move about the city making disciples, no longer free to help the Gentiles come to know their God, no longer free to live out this powerful vision, this destiny that God had revealed in calling them to Macedonia.

Or were they? You see, at about midnight, in the pitch black darkness of that prison cell, something supernatural began to stir. Though every element of their surroundings pressed hard against their hope, Paul and Silas clung to the vision that their circumstances denied. Despite the pain of their physical wounds and the tremendous unfairness of their imprisonment, they began talking to the One who first spoke that vision into existence. I have no idea what sort of prayers they spoke into that darkness. Maybe they were asking God how all this fit into His plan. Perhaps they were questioning whether that vision was simply the result of wild imagination. Surely they cried out for God's strength to sustain them in the midst of such powerful opposition. We may never know what they were saying, but soon they were singing, and, defying the distance the darkness created around them, all the other prisoners could hear their song.

Then, within that atmosphere of unbounded worship, God's presence was manifest in such a way that the walls that held them captive began to tremble. Suddenly the doors to their prison cells swung open. Not only Paul and Silas, but every prisoner in that place, felt the chains fall from around his feet. Right there in the darkness, right there in that jail, still surrounded by the hatred, skepticism, misrepresentation and false accusations that sent them there, still bearing the marks and the pain of their wounds, they were free! These men, sent on mission by God, were free to go, to run into the streets, to return to Lydia's house and once again experience the safety of having their friends on every side. Yet theirs was a transcendent freedom, one neither easily understood nor contained, because once unchained they refused to run. These apostles felt no need to flee to a place of self-protection, no compulsion to hide from the ones who inflicted their injuries, kept them confined and misjudged their hearts. Paul and Silas were so free that they chose to stay, to courageously trust in the Source of true freedom so that others could believe in Him too.

The Bible does not say it, I have no way to scientifically prove it, but I believe within the darkness of that innermost prison cell what started as only a flicker of light became a burning flame that miraculously, inexplicably, escaped through every crack and crevice in those thick walls of rock and mortar. I believe that light could be seen, overcoming the darkness, pushing back the night, walking back the enemy, taking back what had been stolen, setting free what had never been created for a cage. (Acts 16 New International Version paraphrased)

If we meditate long at all on these stories, and scores of others like them, if we ponder such paradox, if we consider this mystery, then we must reexamine what freedom looks like. We must re-determine how reality is defined. We must ask ourselves, and more importantly our Vision-Caster, if anything remains that is so powerful, so devastating, so pressing that it can prevent us from moving toward what He says is already true, who He says we already are, the purpose He has called us to fulfill while we are on this planet. If not, then why have we allowed so much to stand in our way for so long? You see, these stories of release give us a tip-off that truth is not defined by circumstances, that our freedom has very little to do with humanity's empowerment, that our identity is far too important to the One, in Whose heart we were first conceived, to ever be left to chance.

God speaks to each of us in His words to Jeremiah, *"Before I formed you in the womb, I knew you. Before you were born, I set you apart;"* (Jeremiah 1:5 NIV). His desire is to reveal the sheer passion and delight that He feels for who we are right where we are, in order to release us to run with complete abandon toward our awaiting destiny. Perhaps God gives us the clearest definition of what it looks like to live in such freedom as He goes on to say, *"They will fight against you but will not overcome you, for I am with you and will rescue you"* (Jeremiah 1:19 NIV). Or, as Corrie Ten Boom expressed it, 'We are more than conquerors. Not 'we shall be.' We are!"[4]

That is Ruth's story, a story of intimate relationship that brought about her beautiful redemption and her unstoppable release. Ruth's life too "took place on two separate levels, mutually impossible,"[5] yet incredibly undeniable. This young woman who refused to be defined by her circumstances or defeated by her wounds, came to the end of the road and stepped across that threshold to freedom. If she could be released to run with such complete abandon, surely so can we!

And so it begins, as deep calls to deep, and our spirits are invited to answer. How we answer, how we find ourselves in this story and begin to make this journey our own, will change everything. My prayer is that you will meet God here, that this encounter with Him will release you to run your particular race with unbridled passion, completely unhindered by where you have been or anything you have been through, free to fall in love with this One who refuses to let you settle for anything less. God is wooing you at this moment, urging you to take this chance, inviting you to believe to the point that it radically changes your story as you come to realize He has woven your story into His.

Chapter 1

Sometimes you don't know when you're taking the first step through a door until you're already inside.

— ANN VOSKAMP, ONE THOUSAND GIFTS: A DARE TO LIVE FULLY RIGHT WHERE YOU ARE

THE DANGERS OF WATER BALLET

When I was a little girl, my family and I became charter members of the Alice Bell/Spring Hill Aquatic Center. I admit that this was an awfully big name for a small community's swimming pool, but, hey, this was an awfully big pool — an Olympic-sized pool to be exact. This was also an awfully big deal to all of us who had previously been recreationally confined to plastic wading pools in our backyards or a splash in the puddles on a rainy day. I loved the water and I loved summer. So, as far as I was concerned, we might as well have decided to recreate heaven a few blocks from my house.

I went to the pool every day of the summer. When I was 9 years old, the thing I loved to do the most was to position myself on one end of that pool, then dive in and swim my heart out down the officially marked lane toward the opposite end. All the while, I was competing in the Olympics in my mind and halfway to the front of a Wheaties box. I hit the water with tremendous intensity and tenacity, pretending that no one else could come close to competing with my pace. All the while the sound of an imaginary crowd roared in my head, frantically cheering me on. I could almost picture the throngs standing there on the sidelines, nudging and nodding in amazement at my extraordinary speed and skill. I pushed my endurance farther and farther each day until finally I could swim over 20 laps without stopping. That feat is truly amazing, considering the fact that today even one lap would probably leave me frantically gasping for air. In those sweet days of childhood, that imaginary swim meet was my favorite pastime, my singular passion. No one had to coax or convince me to jump in. There was such satisfaction gained from adding even one lap to my record that it totally overshadowed the sheer exhaustion

I felt as I finally heaved my body out of the water at the end of the afternoon. An actual walk to the concession stand or to the car would find me pretending to make my way to an imaginary platform where I would receive my gold medal, cover my heart and relish the playing of the national anthem over the loudspeaker.

It was right in the middle of this scenario of serenity that the announcement was made that the Alice Bell/Spring Hill Aquatic Center would soon be offering water ballet classes. Though I might have spent hours envisioning myself as a true Olympic champion, I have to admit that, on some level, I should have suspected that water ballet might not be my strongest event. My style has always been characterized by a lot more passion than poise, if you know what I mean. Still, my older sister, Susan, who from day one in my young life had pretty much been recognized as the queen of the world, had already signed up to take the water ballet classes. So, that settled it. The way it was done in my family was that whatever Susan did, baby sister would tag along. It was expected. It was a given, or, at least, I thought it was. If Susan was going to become a water ballerina at the young age of 13, then somehow I would learn to do the moves at age 9, or die trying. Without even stopping to consider it, I signed up for the class. Apparently, so did every other girl in the community, especially those whose families comprised the exclusive charter membership of the Alice Bell/Spring Hill Aquatic Center. As a result, the class was soon filled to capacity.

On the first day of instruction we all lined up on the side of the pool to learn the rules. Class would be held in the diving well, which was twelve feet deep and, for the entire one hour class period, no budding water ballerina would be allowed to touch the side. That meant I would be required to paddle like crazy to keep my head above water while at the same time making an attempt to do silly little flips and turns and tricks that were way out of my league. On top of it all, I had to wear a nose plug throughout the entire miserable experience. This would be agony. Not only would I become exhausted from the tremendous physical exertion, but, thanks to that nose plug, I would be suffering from a serious lack of oxygen!

I spent that first sixty minutes of precious water time expending an incredible amount of energy, doing all kinds of unusual contortions that I am not sure any creature was ever intended to do. Just as I suspected, I was literally and frantically fighting for my life every minute, gulping in much needed air whenever I could get my mouth above the water line. Only when at long last the hour came to an end, could life, as I knew and loved it, get back to normal. I could finally return to something I really loved to do. As soon as the lifeguard's whistle blew, announcing the end of that first class, I dragged myself over to the long forbidden side of the pool and pulled my aching body out of the water. Then I hurried over to get in position for another beloved race. This was my moment to finally get to do what I was there for, to finally be free to enjoy what makes me soar. Carefully positioning myself, I got ready to dive in. Then suddenly I was overpowered with an unexpected but prevailing thought, "I need to go home and take a nap." Sadly, I turned away from the race and went home that day, flopping myself down on the couch where I slept for the rest of the afternoon.

The next morning I learned that "soar" can be spelled another way. Nevertheless, I got up and went back to the water ballet class where we did the same thing all over again. Insanity has been defined as doing the same thing over and over while expecting different results.[6] If that is true, then I must have temporarily lost my mind. I did the flips, wore the nose plug, and could hardly wait for the class to end so that I could get back to my Olympic training. Then, the minute we were finished, I hurried over to jump in, but again I was too exhausted. My knees were weak and I was feeling a little sick. I had no choice but to go home for another nap.

Before long I realized there was something wrong with this picture. (See, I told you it was only temporary insanity.) This was no fun for me at all. I was just going through the motions, more accurately, paddling like crazy to keep from drowning. At last I realized that this experience was just not worth it because it cost me what I loved. I may have been merely a child but somehow I found my way clear to retire from water ballet without regret.

Yet I discovered a very important truth in that experience. I learned that when you are trying to be who everybody else thinks you should be, trying to do whatever you think is required in order for you to fit in, when you are running hard after what everyone else is seeking, you can so easily lose who you are. Soon you realize that you have allowed those things that really matter to you to slip right through your fingers. You completely miss out on the life that you were created to live when you get caught up in trying to be some version of a water ballerina.

I suspect there may be a few water ballerinas reading this now, those who are constantly struggling to keep their heads above water, trying desperately to meet expectations that have nothing to do with their true identities. That is a scary place to be and it will definitely prove to be exhausting.

Yet at the heart of all that effort is an authentic, God-given desire to live out our own stories and live them well. Each of us is on a quest to find out that we are enough, maybe even beautiful, to discover that our story is infused with a purpose that equips us to make a real difference in the lives of the people around us. We are desperate to confirm that the authentic version of who we are was profoundly meant to be.

I am convinced that our God really cares about that too. In fact, that desire was born in His heart. You see, I know that there were no crowds of people actually standing, watching, applauding as I limped away from my once-in-a-lifetime opportunity to be a water ballerina and opted, instead, to sell out to my personal passion for racing to the other end of the pool. Then again, Hebrews 12:1 does mention that we are surrounded with a cloud of witnesses. So I think that my Daddy God may have had a whole crowd of people somewhere, gathered around Him to watch me and applaud my efforts every time. I imagine Him nudging one and nodding to another to say "Look at her go!" He is delighted when we discover the truth of who we are and what really makes us soar (as opposed to that other kind of sore). It thrills Him when we choose to embrace our truth, saying, "Yes" to His idea of who we were meant to be and "No" to anything else. The thing about it is — we can never pull off being anybody else anyway. Oh, we might be able to fake it for a short amount of time but then we have to go home and take a nap.

God tells us through His prophet, Jeremiah, *"Before I formed you in the womb, I knew you"* (Jeremiah 1:5 NIV). What a great place to start. How can I possibly uncover the vision of who I was created to be if my quest does not begin with my Vision Caster? I had no idea I would hate water ballet. He already knew. In this experience of allowing me to try something on, that He knew would never fit, He was helping me tap into the truth of who I was made to be and what it looks like for me to live authentically. My God was inviting me to catch a glimpse of the vision long ago born in His heart for my life. The God, Who knows who I am, longs to unveil that one-of-a-kind creation for the world to see. As we lay a foundation of truths that this study will build upon, Fact #1 has to be this: **God knows who I am better than I do.**

This God, who perfectly knows who I am, longs to unveil that unique creation and release me to run with abandon in all of the freedom He has waiting for me to experience. The key that will unlock that freedom is revealed in these words of Jesus, *"Apart from Me you can do nothing"* (John 15:5 NIV). It is in intimate relationship with Him, doing that dance of faith in which He gets to lead, that I am able to discover, and fully become, who I was created to be in the first place. No one else can take me there and I will certainly never find my way stumbling through life on my own. What a waste of time to try to force myself into a mold that is not at all to my liking, when, instead, I can submit to the shape and form of God's perfect design under the gentle pressure of His guiding touch. In our foundation of truths Fact #2 is this: **God will reveal who I am in the context of my personal, intimate relationship with Him.**

After all, only in the purity of His design can I find my greatest purpose. Paul's letter to the church in Ephesus reveals that each of us was *"chosen, having been predestined according to the plan of him who works out everything in conformity with the purpose of his will, in order that we, who were the first to put our hope in Christ, might be for the praise of his glory"* (Ephesians 1:11-12 NIV). Put in everyday terms, this means that my greatest purpose is to tell, in my life, the story of Who He is. We were made to be God carriers, to be the ones through whom He has chosen to bring His life into the world. What an awesome task! I can only accomplish this purpose, I can only achieve the contentment found in knowing that I am doing the will of My Father, carrying Him faithfully into my world, when I am living the life that He predestined specifically for me, and no one else. My personal fulfillment rests in the extent to which I experience the perfect freedom to be who He knew me to be when I was still in my mother's womb. In the simplicity of that particular life, lived out in the boldness of radical faith, He has tucked away beautiful secrets of His character, just waiting to be released for a longing world to see. Fact #3, as we lay our foundation, is this: **My purpose is to carry God into this world, to unashamedly tell the story of Who My God is, with the boldness of one who truly knows and walks with Him.**

The problem with all of this is that God is so huge, so awesome, so colorful and complex, beautiful and rare, that I am sure I will never possibly be able to take all of Him in or fully grasp every facet of His being, much less deliver Him faithfully to those who watch my life each day. I am a flawed mirror at best, not a perfect reflection of His light. Yet that never takes Him by surprise nor hinders His purposes to use me in that way. In fact, Paul explains,

> *Now the Lord is the Spirit, and where the Spirit of the Lord is, there is freedom. And we, who with unveiled faces all reflect the Lord's glory, are being transformed into His likeness with ever-increasing glory, which comes from the Lord, who is the Spirit* (2 Corinthians 3:17-18 NIV).

God gives me the freedom to let go of the impossible dream of being perfect in order to take up the cause of simply being who I am right where I am on the way to fully becoming who I was created to be. The key to this verse is found in this word translated, "likeness." You see, if I wanted to show you the likeness of my husband, I could never fully accomplish that by carefully choosing just the right descriptive words or even picking up a pencil and sketching out what he looks like. I could certainly never accurately communicate the complexity of his personality through a simple pantomime or charade. That is not at all the idea that this word, "likeness," conveys in this verse. Whatever I could create might look somewhat like David but, as hard as I worked on it, it would never be more than a picture of this man that I love. However, if you would look into the eyes of my oldest daughter, Brittany, or see her passion for leadership and order...if you could see all the freckles spattered on the face of my youngest daughter, Kiley, or get just one taste of her light-hearted outlook on life, then you would see the likeness of my husband. You would see traits of his character displayed in each of theirs. My girls carry the likeness of their father because each is his daughter. They not only carry His DNA but they live in intimate relationship with him.

In just that same way one can grasp what is meant by this word, "likeness," when you see the sun reflected in the water. The reflection looks like the sun because it comes from the sun. All you see there, the colors, the basic form, the placement against the blue of the sky, is a product of relationship that captures the essence of the sun so much more than any description or sketch ever could. In the Greek, this is the specificity suggested in this term.[7]

Therefore, the likeness of God that you were created to hold is released in the context of your connection with Him. Anything less is merely a picture, a rough sketch, a charade. You carry His DNA. Then you become increasingly like Him in the context of intimate relationship that you experience with Him. Ultimately His likeness is the beauty in you. It is the fullness of your personal expression. You look like Him because you come from Him. You were born in His heart and specially designed to see Him and reflect Him in your own particular way. Your own flaws do not diminish that any more than the beauty of the sun's reflection is diminished by the distortion that the imperfect texture of the water brings. You carry the color of His character, the intensity of His light, the perfect wisdom of His intellect, in direct correlation to the measure that you experience those traits in intimate relationship with Him. You look like Him because you come from Him, and, in growing relationship with Him, you reflect His heart more and more. Your continual transformation is not a hindrance to that reality. Rather, it is the measured revelation that God has prepared for you to unveil piece by piece. He is the Alpha and Omega, the Beginning and the End of this process, the Eternal One who conceived and created you to be just who you are and is meticulously molding you, transforming you into the completeness of the one He already sees you to fully be. So our final foundational truth rests in Fact #4: **I am empowered to tell His story simply by living out my true story in continual, intimate relationship with My Maker.**

This is as simple as the hand mirror that is stored in the left hand drawer of my bathroom vanity. That mirror has been with me for years. You can tell because the handle is taped together and it has a couple of melted spots in the plastic, scars of a couple of close encounters of the curling iron kind. What you may or may not realize, just by looking, is that this mirror plays a very significant role, influencing how I present myself to the world every day of my life. That mirror must be intentionally turned in my direction so that it can accurately reflect who I am. Basically the goal of that mirror's existence is to let me see myself in it, especially when it comes to the back of my hair. You see, I made an investment in that mirror years ago for just that reason. I selected it to serve that purpose, not just for me, but for those around me, especially that lady that sits directly behind me in church or follows me in the check out line at the grocery. Tragically, that purpose is lost if that mirror is out of my hand. If that mirror is lost or out of place then it will never be what it was created to be. If the face of that mirror gets marred and covered with hairspray, then sadly too, its ability to function the way it was created to function is greatly diminished. All that mirror has to do is stay reasonably clean and connected to me and the rest completely depends on me. How sad it would be for my trusty hand mirror to spend day after day trying to be a brush or a comb, or, heaven forbid, some kind of volumizing hair product. It is absolutely beyond my understanding why it would ever try to distort itself in that way. That mirror, just as it is, is just what I need it to be, as long as it rests in my hand. There is just no telling how many lives have been affected by the faithful, simple way my mirror has continued to serve me through the years. It is not gold plated or ornate, but I love it. I use it with great confidence and pride. I would never want to face a day without it. That mirror has become a precious part of my daily routine.

So, you see, you cannot possibly be who you were created to be if you are disconnected from the One you are meant to reflect. You cannot possibly fulfill your purpose apart from walking this journey with Him. He formed you, knowing your form. You can never accomplish what you were made to do in this world apart from Him. He has chosen you and predestined your circumstances to release you to carry that part of Him, that dimension of His character, which He has given you eyes to see and has opened your heart to experience, so that this light will bounce off of you and be put on display for those you have been entrusted to touch and to know. That is what your life is supposed to be about, nothing more and surely nothing less. Finding that is all wrapped up in finding Him, in knowing Him, in pressing in for a deeper, more intimate relationship with the One Who loved you first and created you to relate to Him in the safety of that pure love. There is just no other way to get there.

As we step into Ruth's story, this is precisely what makes hers a story of freedom. Nothing in her circumstances pointed her toward release. Yet, like Abraham, the father of a faith yet unproven to her, she hoped against all hope. She transcended the destiny that her circumstances would dictate to discover the freedom released in the context of intimate relationship with the Author and Finisher of every life's story. That is the only true freedom there is. God is the only One who has the power and the vision to release us to be. We will see as Ruth comes into being, that when He does, nothing can snatch that freedom away.

Still, on the surface, the setting and backdrop of Ruth's saga from the very outset screams anything but freedom. Her situation really does not seem to hold much possibility for release. That is what makes this account so much more than merely her story. It is undeniably God's story because what God unfolds in her life is so beyond the natural, the expected, or the norm. We should keep that in the forefront of our minds as we examine Ruth 1.

> *In the days when the judges ruled, there was a famine in the land, and a man from Bethlehem in Judah, together with his wife and two sons, went to live for a while in the country of Moab. The*

man's name was Elimelek, his wife's name, Naomi, and the names of his two sons were Mahlon and Kilion. They were Ephrathites from Bethlehem, Judah. And they went to Moab and lived there. Now Elimelek, Naomi's husband, died, and she was left with her two sons. They married Moabite women, one named Orpah and the other Ruth. After they had lived there about ten years, both Mahlon and Kilion also died, and Naomi was left without her two sons and her husband. When she heard in Moab that the LORD had come to the aid of his people by providing food for them, Naomi and her daughters-in-law prepared to return home from there. With her two daughters-in-law she left the place where she had been living and set out on the road that would take them back to the land of Judah (Ruth 1:1-7 NIV).

From the start this does not look like freedom's story. In fact, Ruth's circumstances seem devastating, especially for a woman in her times. The first thing we learn about the background of her story is that it takes place "in the days when the judges ruled." According to the book of Judges, this was a time when enemy nations lived right in the middle of the land that was supposed to be possessed solely by God's people. Though God had commanded His people, under the leadership of Joshua, to go in and take possession of this land with the promise that He would drive out the enemy before them, when the Israelites entered into that land, they dropped the ball. Even after several tastes of victory, as they found themselves living among this powerful enemy, their eyes fell upon the iron chariots that seemed to make those opponents invincible, or at the very least, a whole lot of trouble to defeat. In the face of such formidable opposition, the Israelites abandoned the cause. They forgot about God. They failed to remember what He had promised. They became convinced that they could not drive this powerful enemy from the land and fully possess this lavish homeland God had provided. The strategic fact God's people apparently missed is that God never said that they could drive their enemies out, He said that He would. That is a completely different thing. Their fear displaced their desire to live out their destiny. God's people abandoned the vision of who they were created to be and the power of God to accomplish their transformation into that identity, allowing circumstances to shape their identity instead of the Word of God. They opted for compromise, deciding to let the enemy occupy that land with them, deceived into thinking they had no other reasonable choice.

In fact, in their unbelief, the people of God gave up even more than that. You know how ornery enemies can be, especially having won such an easy victory without striking a single blow. These warring nations had no motivation to share and would not be content to simply live there among the people of God. They went on to oppress the Israelites, stealing their food, ravaging their harvest. The enemy adopted strategies to torment them until the Israelites were found in Judges 6, living in caves, hiding out in fear, a defeated people. By beginning Ruth's story with the words, "In the days when the judges ruled" God is giving us a heads up that this was a time of conflict, a time of terror, a time of defeat, and a time of unbelief, as God's people opted for far less than what God had in mind for them. What kind of setting is that for freedom's story?

In the days when the judges ruled there was also a catch phrase that we find throughout the book of Judges, "everyone did what was right in their own eyes" (Judges 17:6 NIV). There was a leadership void. There was an absence of vision, a scarcity with respect to clarity of purpose. Nobody was asking God for direction. Everyone basically did whatever they wanted to do. A whole generation had grown up that did not even know who God was or what He had done in the past for His people and, therefore, had no chance of knowing who they were meant to be as His chosen ones. It was an every-man-for-himself society and the morality of the day reflected that self-serving perspective. Purpose had been abandoned for survival and the enemy was right there to take advantage of the vulnerability of such a desperate climate.

During this time in Israel's history, the experiences of the nation also followed a distinct and repetitive pattern, sort of like that often quoted definition of insanity. There was a cycle of behaviors repeated over and over by the people of God. The Israelites would forget about God, choosing rather to do their own thing. Their selfish pursuits had no capacity to bring the fulfillment they longed for because it left them disconnected from the bigger picture and the One whose vision it describes. Instead their self-centered strategies left them vulnerable to the enemy's tactics as he pressed in to take advantage of their weakness. Oppressed and defeated, the Israelites would then cry out to God. In mercy, God would answer, by raising up a leader supernaturally empowered to drive out the enemy and lift his people out of oppression and despair. As a result of God's mercy, the Hebrew people would soon feel better. With the pressure off, they would forget about God and start living however they pleased again. Then the whole cycle would be repeated over and over. This nation, born to carry in her the very identity, the heart and passion and power of their God, was reduced to a selfish, defeated victim who could never break free from the destructive behavioral patterns that held her captive and denied her vision. Is that the setting one would expect for freedom's story?

Yet this is pretty much the scenario in the society in which Ruth's story begins, except for one significant thing. You see, this is the description of life for God's people, the ones who had actually tasted His power, the ones who actually had access to His promises, the ones who had been set apart to carry His life and light to the nations around them. Ruth was not one of God's people. Ruth was a woman, in contrast, who grew up in her native country of Moab among a people who had no knowledge of anything pertaining to the One True God. Oh, they did have their own cheap substitute. They served a false god named Chemosh who was believed to require child sacrifice in return for his protection in war. So Ruth's only hope of knowing the True God, her only hope of finding His vision for her life, lay in the hands of a people from outside of her nation who were created to show Him to the nations like hers but who had forgotten all about Him, had forgotten who they were created to be, and had left Him totally out of their lives, except in fleeting moments of desperation.

The only flicker of hope at the beginning of this story of freedom is in the heart of God for a young woman who longed for something more than the life her pagan society and her empty circumstances would offer. The only flicker of hope at the beginning of this story of release is that the plans of this passionate God would be to move heaven and earth in pursuit of her precious heart and her priceless destiny. So, though His people forgot about Him, God refused to forget His people. He refused to do anything but stay the course and use the faithless nation of Israel to carry His light and the love of His heart to one woman who lived not so far away and yet who seemed to reside light years from any chance of knowing Him.

Ruth was that young woman. One Jewish family unconsciously carried that love to her doorstep as they traveled to her country in a vain attempt to feed their undying hunger. These people came to her land out of unbelief. These were not pinnacles of faith, standing out in contrast to those unbelieving people. They had become immersed in their culture of fear. They had forgotten that God had said that they would never be hungry. They had fled from the land that He had promised would flow with milk and honey. They had abandoned their home in the city of Bethlehem, which in the Hebrew language means

"House of Bread,"[8] in hopes of feeding their hunger among a people who knew nothing of God's provisions and had a history of denying food to His people. Still this family carried a light that the darkness of Moabite culture could never extinguish. Even their faithlessness could not prevent God from using them for His glory as He pursued Ruth's heart through the intimate connection she would make with this feeble Hebrew family.

So Elimilek, his wife and their two sons came to "sojourn" in Moab. How ironic that the Hebrew wording indicates that they saw this as just a temporary departure.[9] They never intended to stay, yet this story will soon reveal that three out of four of them would never return to Bethlehem. Ruth met one of their sons and married him. His name was Mahlon, which in the Hebrew language means "sick,"[10] Can you imagine having him as the man of your dreams? His brother's name was Kilion which is a form of a word that means means "pining, devastation."[11] Okay, so this is a family issue. Ruth quickly finds herself married to a sickly guy while his brother, left pining because of his devastation, marries another Moabite girl whose name, Orpah, comes from a Hebrew Word meaning "stiff-necked."[12] So now we have a stubborn sister-in-law thrown into the chaos. Ruth just cannot seem to catch a break. To top it all off, Ruth's mother-in-law, Naomi, whose given name meant "pleasantness or delight,"[13] (finally!) announces before the first chapter of Ruth's story is through, "Don't call me Naomi, call me Mara" which means "bitter."[14] Are you getting the picture? When Ruth married, her ailing husband was part of a package deal that included a bitter mother-in-law, a stiff-necked sister-in-law and a weak brother-in-law. Both of the surviving men of the household were unsatisfied and sickly until the day they died. In other words, Ruth has married into a family that was a picture of dysfunction and weakness, not unlike many of our families in the every-man-for-himself culture in which we live today. These people, set apart by God to carry His light into a dark world, had so allowed their culture and their fears to distort their personalities that they hardly looked different from any native Moabite that Ruth had ever known, except for a strange light that their God had placed within them that could not be denied. I believe it had to be that unusual light, though flickering and frail, some sort of indistinguishable quality about them, that pulled Ruth's heart toward it, attracting and inviting this young girl from Moab to something more.

Upon her husband's death, the best Ruth could realistically hope for in her society was to scrape by in poverty. A widow in her world could not make a way for herself. She was destitute, destined to beg for her food. There was nothing that she could do to drastically improve her situation. She was forced to try to find her own way through the death, grief, poverty, and hopelessness. In the midst of that hopelessness and grief, Ruth had absolutely no background with God, except for the little taste she had received from this fearful, misplaced Hebrew family. She must have felt so disappointed and alone. Still God's pursuit of her heart continues in Ruth 1:8,

> Then Naomi said to her two daughters-in-law, "Go back, each of you, to your mother's home. May the LORD show kindness to you, as you have shown to your dead and to me. May the LORD grant that each of you will find rest in the home of another husband." Then she kissed them and they wept aloud and said to her, "We will go back with you to your people." But Naomi said, "Return home, my daughters. Why would you come with me? Am I going to have any more sons, who could become your husbands? Return home, my daughters; I am too old to have another husband. Even if I thought there was still hope for me-even if I had a husband tonight and then gave birth to sons-would you wait until they grew up? Would you remain unmarried for them? No, my daughters. It is more bitter for me than for you, because the LORD's hand has gone out against me!" (Ruth 1:8-13 NIV)

Ruth stands at this fork in the road, in the midst of these devastating circumstances, with all of her loss and need pressing in on her, faced with a life-changing decision. What do you think her instincts told her to do?

In one of the most poignant scenes from the second installment of *The Lord of the Rings Trilogy, The Two Towers,* Princess Eowyn perhaps expresses the emotion that would be in most of our hearts under these circumstances and what most certainly could have been in Ruth's. The hero of J. R. R. Tolkien's saga, Aragorn, finds Princess Eowyn training for battle with extraordinary prowess as this conversation comes to life upon the screen.

"You have some skill with a blade." Aragorn observes.

Princess Eowyn explains, *"The women of this country learned long ago that those without swords can still die upon them. I fear neither death nor pain."*

"What do you fear, my lady?"

"A cage…to stay behind bars until youth and old age accept them and all chance of valor has gone beyond recall or desire." the princess admits.

To which Aragorn replies, *"You are the daughter of kings, a shield maiden of Rohan, I do not think that will be your fate."*[15]

Surely Ruth's internal conflict could not have been much different than that of Princess Éowyn. Her circumstances threatened to confine her. What viable options did she have? I suspect she thought she had no other recourse than to learn to take care of herself, to become a survivor, perhaps her own savior, to make sure that she was equipped to keep herself safe by preventing the walls of her situation from closing in around her. What did she fear most? Perhaps the same thing Princess Eowyn feared, a cage, getting stuck in the prison of her circumstances. If anyone ever had a right to feel trapped, it must have been Ruth. The losses she had experienced must have seemed overwhelming. How could hers possibly be a story of freedom after all of this? What could she reasonably do but follow Orpah as she turned to walk away from hope, from believing that anything good could come from her situation, expecting nothing more than what life had dropped into her lap. Yet Ruth chose a different road.

At this they wept again. Then Orpah kissed her mother-in-law good-bye, but Ruth clung to her. "Look," said Naomi, "your sister-in-law is going back to her people and her gods. Go back with her." But Ruth replied, "Don't urge me to leave you or to turn back from you. Where you go I will go, and where you stay I will stay. Your people will be my people and your God my God. Where you die I will die, and there I will be buried. May the LORD deal with me, be it ever so severely, if anything but death separates you and me." When Naomi realized that Ruth was determined to go with her, she stopped urging her (Ruth 1:14-18 NIV).

Ruth came to the end of the road with Naomi insisting, "Look at everything that has happened to us. Look at everything we have lost. You have no other choice but to give up now." Yet Ruth refused to give up. She would never abandon the vision that God had deposited in her heart of a life she was born to experience. Instead Ruth planted her feet, grabbed hold of Naomi and denied that those circumstances would dictate her destiny. Like a warrior, she fought for the dream God had planted within her and refused to be relegated to a cage. Instead, with everything in her, she held on, stubbornly insisting, she would not go down to defeat in this pivotal moment.

The prophet, Micah, speaks of a relationship that transcends our circumstances, a presence that will light our path toward freedom. God's voice through Micah echoes the undaunted determination that Ruth exhibited at this moment of decision, *"Do not gloat over me, my enemy! Though I have fallen I will rise. Though I sit in darkness the Lord will be my light"* (Micah 7:8 NIV). In the face of seemingly inevitable defeat, Ruth chose to fight on. Neither the darkness of her surrounding culture nor her dismal future prospects would be given the power to define her. She was determined to rise by reaching out to the God she was convinced could change everything.

It is not where you are that matters, even when your circumstances look darkest and everything you hoped for seems lost. It is not what you might be going through at this moment that will ultimately determine your destiny. Ruth defied her circumstances with a radical resolve to pursue a relationship with Naomi's God.

Through this defining moment in Ruth's story, God presents us with a question that we must answer with Ruth as we join her on this journey, "Will you believe? Oh, but not only believe, will you believe to the point that it changes your story?"

Ruth's answer was a resounding, "Yes!" What's yours? You see, what matters so much more than where you are or what you are going through, is who you are moving toward and whose voice you will trust to guide you to where you belong. You get to choose between living your life caged by your own limitations and circumstances or released to run with abandon, holding fast to a dream that was born in the heart of God, carrying the very essence of Who This One True God is within the truth of being just who you are, right where you are in your journey, flaws and all. The choice Ruth made, at this all important crossroad at the edge of all she had ever known, is the choice you and I will make, not just once, but over and over again, every day. Will you choose to stay in Moab or step out in search of Bethlehem? Will you save yourself, or die trying, or will you fling yourself out on the limb of trusting everything to God? Every day, at every fork in the road, you must settle this question, "Will I stay where I am or will I move closer to God? Will I merely say I believe, or will I radically believe to the point that it changes my story?"

There are going to be times in every life when it seems like all is lost. As God has deposited His words of destiny in my own heart, words holding that vision of who I was created to be, you must know that everything the enemy could think of has broken out against it. Circumstances have pushed intensely in opposition to every promise, and all kinds of barriers have stood in the way. Yet God has placed a hope within me that has much more to do with His faithfulness than my own. His Spirit whispers at every crossroad when my circumstances threaten to turn me around, "What I've said about you is already fully true! Even though you may not be able to see it from this stop on the journey, you will rise so far above where you are, if you just keep moving toward Me!" So, awkwardly stumbling forward, as I often do on this uphill climb of life, my confidence is found in the reality that I do not walk this God-chosen path alone. I have God's promise, *"If the Lord delights in a man's (or woman's) way, He makes his steps firm; though he stumble, he will not fall, for the Lord upholds him with His hand"* (Psalm 37:24 NIV).

Ruth faced incredible odds, seemingly insurmountable circumstances. She could have given up and walked away and no one would have blamed her. Yet she became like those people the psalmist speaks for in Psalm 126 saying,

> *When the Lord brought back the captive ones to Zion, we were like men who dreamed* (Psalm 126:1).

That word translated here as "dreamed" can also mean "to be pregnant" in the Hebrew language. This passage describes people who for seventy years had been oppressed by their enemy, held captive, displaced. Now they were on the way home again with a dream in their heart, with a job still to do, with a vision of who they were destined to be. This was their chance to begin again, to believe again, but not just believe, to put feet to their faith by believing to the point that it changed their story. They refused to be defined any longer by what they had been through or anything that might have been done to them, and you can too. This is the moment when you can choose to allow everything you have been through to define you or you can rise by reaching out to God, believing to the point that your story is forever altered.

God's people set out from the land of their oppression, the only life some of them had ever known, to meet their God right back in their land and be the people He had called them in the first place. The dream they carried would begin as they rebuilt the temple of God, set up a place where they could hear from the Lord again. After all this time, they so needed to hear from Him again. He held the truth that would restore and release them to live their destiny. He never forgot who they were and only He could speak that vision into their reality. Seventy years of oppression had not killed it. Though they had fallen, still they would rise from the ashes of their failures to discover that what God said about them was forever true. These people, on their way out of slavery, simply set out on the road that would move them toward their God, and, even while still on the way, they were pregnant with dreams, and pregnant with hope, and pregnant with desire. Theirs was freedom's story simply because, before creation, God planted the seeds of that freedom to one day be birthed within their wombs. Theirs was a story of destiny because it would never rest on their shoulders or depend on their faithfulness. It had always rested in the heart of their God and all they had to do, in order to rediscover it, was to walk in intimacy with Him.

In much the same way, Ruth's vision of her destiny as an adopted daughter of this King, had now taken on a life of its own. It would not be denied by race or rejection or the ruins of her circumstances. She was leaving Moab and all that had happened there behind, with a hope in her heart and a song on her lips, pregnant with the dream of the woman she was destined to become, carrying the seed of the life she was born to experience. With such a diehard grip on this vision, what was anyone to do but to release her to run with abandon in pursuit of her most unlikely but unstoppable destiny!

Several years ago I had an opportunity to share this part of Ruth's story with a group of single moms from an underprivileged neighborhood who were invited to have dinner once a month at a church nearby. As I prepared what I wanted to say I longed to find a tangible way to communicate the daring of Ruth's choice, especially in light of the fact that her only exposure to the God of the Israelites had come through a frail and embittered old woman who feebly carried a flickering light of God in her heart. I longed for these women to see that maybe all they would need in order to make just as radical a choice to move toward God would be a simple taste, a passing glimpse, of another's freedom. As my idea came together I realized that I was missing one element of my illustration. So I stopped at a grocery store on the way to the church to pick up some slices of cake. Much to my surprise not one pre-sliced cake was available for purchase. So hurriedly I made a decision to go with brownies and I was back in the car to drive to the dinner where I was scheduled to share. As I came to this part of Ruth's story I held up a brown paper bag, declaring that within that bag I had a luscious brownie that would be given to the first person whose hand went up to claim it. Much to my surprise as I looked around the room, not a single hand was raised. Finally, one woman threw her hand up carelessly. Punctuating her decision with an expletive she blurted out, "I guess I'll take it!" She was obviously only half-convinced that she had made a wise decision. Still she took the bag from my hand and hesitantly peeked inside. Instantly pleased with her decision, she looked up at the other women, grinning from ear to ear, to announce with undisguised surprise in her voice, "It is a brownie!" Then immediately she took a big bite for everyone to see. Reaching down to pick up an entire box of brown paper bags, I sat them on the table in front of her now envious friends and repeated my offer to give one to anyone who raised a hand. This time every hand shot into the air instantaneously. Women all around the room willingly reached out to receive the treat that I promised. So I asked them, "What made the difference from the first time I offered the brownie to the second?" The certain answer was that once they witnessed what happened in another woman's life they were emboldened to believe that it could happen for them as well. Their willingness to risk everything for what was simply promised, yet still unseen, was the testimony of a friend about what happened for her when she did. Interestingly enough, as we sat there enjoying our brownies around the table the first woman who took the risk in hopes of a brownie spoke up again saying, "Well, God answered a prayer for me today!" We all sat up a bit with interest as the facilitator of the group asked her to share. She went on to explain that a few weeks ago these same women had been served delicious brownies as a part of the dinner the church had provided for the group. "Today, I was thinking about those brownies," she explained. "So I just asked God if we could have brownies again tonight. And we did!" she told us with a shining pride. What she did not know was that I had intended to use slices of cake for my illustration. Had the grocery store had any sort of cake that would have been already cut and ready to be placed inside brown paper bags I would have opted for that. God answered her prayer, by making sure she had her brownie and that every woman in that room understood that sometimes our invitation to radical faith is simply prompted by the evidence we see of what God has done for someone else. I wonder what other prayers went up that night after this woman shared her story.

When you think about it, that is really all Ruth had ever seen of God. Naomi certainly did not have it all together. In fact, she was pretty much of a mess. Yet, like the sun's reflection in the water, she still carried the light of God, though rippled and distorted by the texture of her life. That glimpse of God was enough to send Ruth chasing after Him. In her world she had experienced rejection, oppression, fear, failure and loss. Her decision, to abandon her own efforts to restore what was broken, in order to embrace a love like no other, promised true release to live the life of her dreams. Ruth made the choice to simply move toward a relationship powerful enough to protect her, passionate enough to satisfy her, perfect enough to define her. Through meager glimpses into God's heart through Naomi, Ruth got caught up in God's story and it became her own.

The closing scene of *The Lord of the Rings: Two Towers* contains a conversation between Frodo and Sam that illustrates Ruth's expectation for playing a role in the much bigger, more magnificent story of God.

> As they climb a hill through the forest Sam speaks his own dreams aloud, *"I wonder if we'll ever be put into songs or tales…I wonder if people will ever say 'Let's hear about Frodo and the ring!' And they'll say 'Yes, that's one of my favorite stories! Frodo was really courageous wasn't he, Dad?' 'Yes, my boy, the most famousest of Hobbits and that's saying a lot.'"*

> Then Frodo chimes in, *"You've left out one of the chief characters, Samwise the Brave. I want to hear more about Sam. Frodo wouldn't have gotten far without Sam."*

> *"Now Mr. Frodo, you shouldn't make fun. I was being serious."* Sam protests.

> *"So was I."* Frodo admits, as Sam's face is overtaken by an expression of hope that his story could become part of a much bigger adventure saga. Sam murmurs the

name his precious friend had bestowed upon him once more, this time with a flicker of that dream in his eye, *"Samwise the Brave ..."*16

I believe a little bit of Samwise lives in each of us. We each have a desire to live a great story, one that matters and means something to somebody else along the way. That desire was put in our hearts by God because it flows out of His own. He created us to live lives that matter, that are worth remembering and cherishing, that carry the beauty of His very heart. Often buried by disappointments, pressures and rejections along the way, that desire leads us to pursue the heart of the One who holds our promise of release. We need Him. He holds our destiny in His hands. Even a chance to get caught up in His amazing story is worth the risk. It is our only hope of freedom. So we must take this risk, to abandon all we have known, to discover how well He knows us.

Perhaps you have lived your life, until now, in a place where God is completely left out. You no longer have to stay there. This moment can change everything, the same way it did for Ruth. She chose to abandon every effort of self-protection, and every lie she had been force fed all of her days, in order to fling herself recklessly into the arms of the Only One Who truly knew her and could release her to be the woman she was created to be. In this one defining moment, a story that streamed directly out of the heart and imagination of God was set in motion and nothing would be powerful enough to stop what God had begun, not only in Ruth's life but also in yours. Are you ready? Which way will you choose, to stay in Moab or risk everything to get to Bethlehem? It really is just that simple. Everything rests on your answer to this question, "Will you believe, not just believe, will you believe to the point that it changes your story?"

Chapter 2

I know now, Lord, why you utter no answer.
You are yourself the answer.
— *C. S. Lewis, Till We Have Faces: A Myth Retold*

THE COURAGE TO CLING

Your story matters to God because it holds the key to fulfilling your unique assignment on this planet. The God Who knows you intimately, loves you desperately. He wants your story to be told, so much so, that He has woven it together with His. As the object of His affection, you can be sure that God will fight for your story.

Nevertheless, like every other great story, not all of your life is going to be smooth sailing. The minute you decide, with Ruth, to choose Bethlehem, to choose the path that leads toward God, even if it means abandoning all that has been familiar to you, there are going to be some bumps in the road and even craters to fall into. This is why, in Princess Eowyn's world, it was described as a choice between a cage and a sword, to be imprisoned by her circumstances or run to the battlefield to fight for what is rightfully hers. God tipped us off to this through the Old Testament prophet, Jeremiah,

> *"They will fight against you but will not overcome you, for I am with you and will rescue you,"* declares the Lord (Jeremiah 1:19 NIV).

The fight is a given. God says it is, in black and white, *"they will fight against you."* Yet a more significant fact, that you need to be sure of, is that God is down for that fight. He is fighting for your story to be told, in all the fullness and the beauty with which it was first conceived. He will be there waiting for you the second you jump into the battle. God wants us to know, from the outset, so that we will not be taken by surprise, that great stories do not get told without a struggle. To live the truth of your destiny is going to demand that you cultivate a warrior mentality, an unflinching determination to never settle for that cage.

Remember Moab was the only life Ruth had ever known. It was everything that was familiar, the environment that had pretty much shaped her up until this point. Moab may have been ugly, but it was her ugly, and she knew how to manage it. The decision to leave had to come with a certain amount of struggle. It is difficult to imagine why she would even consider such a drastic life change. Yet God used one family, an incredibly flawed, messed up, out-of-place people of faith, to pull back the curtain of what His heart held for Ruth if she threw caution to the wind and made that change. Once Ruth caught a glimpse of that flicker of light Naomi's family carried within them, once Ruth got a chance to taste and see how good this God of the Hebrews was, she was ruined for Moab. She had to choose Bethlehem. No matter how many reasons she could find for Moab's side of the equation, this hope against all hope, that this incredible God could be her God and she could be His child, outweighed every single factor that could make her stay. As Ruth turned to see her sister-in-law, "old stiff-necked one," turn to go, Ruth fought through her doubts and made her decision to simply move to where she knew God was. Ruth did not just believe, she believed to the point that it changed her story. She stepped away from the way her life had always been to fight for a life that could be. So a new question now hangs in the air like the mistletoe waits for two lovers to kiss...not only, "Will you believe to the point that it changes your story?" but, "Will you believe when believing gets hard?"

> WILL YOU
> **BELIEVE**
> WHEN
> **BELIEVING**
> GETS HARD?

To be fair, before you answer, we must add one more critical certainty to our foundational truths upon which our belief system must rest. Fact #5: **The unfolding of your story will undoubtedly face obstacles and opposition**. So, as we head down that road to our Bethlehem, we must travel with a realistic expectation, a clear plan of action and a warrior's resolve. Did I ever find this out the hard way, when I found myself quite literally stuck by the side of the road several years ago.

As I was driving back from an overnight visit with my precious friend, Gayle, who lived in Louisville, Kentucky at the time, the engine of my car started making terrible noises. This was some sort of rattling that I had never heard before, yet as soon as the sound hit my ears I knew it meant that something had gone terribly wrong with my engine.

This keenness of perception might have been influenced by the fact that, almost simultaneously, the whole car began shaking vigorously, right before it stopped suddenly, just as I pulled onto the shoulder of Interstate 75. There I found myself stranded on that highway, between nowhere and who knows where, about seven miles north of Jellico, Tennessee on the border between Tennessee and Kentucky.

It is important to note that just before I left home on the previous day I had ironically asked my husband, David, what I should do if something like this happened. He had, in turn, given me some very specific instructions. Four simple rules to follow:

> Get out of your car and open the hood
>
> When someone stops, do not let them look at the car, simply ask them to call the high way patrol.
>
> Absolutely <u>do</u> <u>not</u> get in a car with anyone.
>
> <u>Never</u> stop at a rest area.

Now all of that information might look good on paper, but in the real world, where events are unfolding in rapid-fire 3-D, little details like previous instructions tend to get a little fuzzy. Not only that, but ever etched into my brain are my mother's immortal slogans that seem to replay on a loop whenever I get stressed. One of her favorites was the maxim "Rules were made to be broken." With my mental acuity heightened by terror at the thought that these rules would not apply, and with pure adrenalin rushing through my veins, this was pretty much a perfect storm.

Still, as soon as my car broke down, I immediately ran through a mental checklist of David's instructions, in hopes that this information would inform my decisions in the midst of this crisis. Rule #1 - Get out of the car and open the hood. Now when David offered me this tidbit of guidance I had actually questioned him about whether or not it would be safe for me to get out of the car in order to open the hood. His unfiltered response was to laugh at me, followed by a smug explanation that nothing could possibly happen to me in the little bit of time it would take for me to open the hood of my car. Clearly, this man had no idea of the skill level we were dealing with, nor just how long it would take a terrified novice in auto mechanics to accomplish what might seem to him to be a simple task. Sadly, I do not think, at that point in my life, I had ever actually attempted to open the hood of any car. Having viewed this task as so very elementary, David never thought to do any type of practice run nor provide a more detailed set of step by step instructions. So this was my maiden voyage and I was virtually on my own. As a result, I soon discovered that there were critical aspects involved in the successful completion of the task that my husband had failed to mention. For instance, there is a thing-a-ma-bob that you have to grab hold of through the front grill of the car to release the hood so that it can be opened. I was completely unaware of what turned out to be a crucial element of Hood Opening 101. Add to that complication, terror, which seems to supply an inherent degree of added difficulty by facilitating what can only be described as cognitive chaos. In this case, it manifested itself as I attempted to accomplish the task at hand while constantly checking over my shoulder to keep an eye on every passing vehicle. You see, I figured if David could be so wrong about the simplicity of this task, then he could be dead wrong (and I use the term intentionally) about my security in doing it. So there I was, tugging with all my might on the unreleased hood one second, while practically giving myself whiplash as I suspiciously peered over my shoulder in the next, in a futile attempt to cover my own backside and merely get through rule #1.

As impossible as it may seem, I did eventually manage to get that hood open. This achievement, however, was of very little comfort to me when I found myself locked safely back inside my car only to realize that the occupants of those passing vehicles, whom I had been eyeing as potential attackers, were now my only chance of rescue. Trust me, it was not pretty! I actually remained somewhat calm at first, but as time goes by one's mind tends to wonder, and even to dwell on unpleasant thoughts, and in this particular instance, time seemed to be going by in slow motion while my mind was racing ever faster with each passing Ford F-100 truck.

As you may have guessed, someone did stop, and I, through an infinitesimal crack of the window, pleaded with the poor man to simply call the highway patrol (See Rule 2). Instead he audaciously stuck his head under the hood and, to my horror, began to fiddle with things. Now since I cared very little, at this point, about what David had told me to do, there was just no way I was getting back out of that car in order to try to stop this stranger from doing that. So you can imagine the sick feeling I had in the pit of my stomach as I watched helplessly while this man actually poured some unidentified liquid into an unverified vessel within the unknown recesses of my engine. The next thing I knew I was getting into this stranger's red truck (See Rule 3). I positioned my body as close to the window as I could and held with a white knuckled grip to the handle of the door as this farmer type of guy, his adult daughter and I pulled out into the traffic, quickly leaving my car in our dust. The only thing I remember from our short ride together were these awkward words of comfort this stranger offered saying, "You know, lady, you're a whole lot better off in this old truck with me than you would be on the side of that mountain with your head cut off." After that, everything in my memory is pretty much a blank until the moment we reached our destination...A REST AREA! (See Rule 4) No wonder I finally ended up at the Jellico police station, I had already broken every one of my husband's useless rules. Besides, when a husband is as mad as I expected mine to be, a woman might need armed protection.

You know, I knew I was in a place that David never wanted me to end up and I suspected that somehow this was all going to turn out to be my fault, despite any excuse of ignorance I might offer. I had done the exact opposite of everything my sweet husband had lovingly instructed me to do before I ever left home and, in my current state, I was pretty much of a basket case. So, suffice it to say, this was not my most attractive look. Still, the first moment I laid my hands on a pay phone (because, as hard as this will be for some of you to believe, and as tough as this is for me to have to admit, this all took place before cell phones were a common accessory) but still, the first moment that I laid my hands on that pay phone at a rest area somewhere in the hills of southeastern Kentucky, whose number do you think I dialed? It was David's. You see, I knew David. Even though at that point we had been married a relatively short number of years, we already shared an intimate relationship built on what began as a beautiful friendship. We had been walking our journey together for a considerable amount of time and now shared an eternal commitment to each other. We had spent a lot of time one on one and, in the context of our shared moments, I had come to know his heart. I knew how He felt about me. He had whispered that at least a time or two in my ear. So, despite everything I had done wrong and all it would cost him, I knew that he would come for me. And he did.

All I wanted to do when I faced that crisis was to reach out to the one person whose heart I knew best, that one I was convinced loved me like no other, then hang on for dear life in a desperate effort to survive. In a world, where unforeseen obstacles seem to lurk around every bend in the road, that is the same kind of safety you and I can cling to within the intimacy of our relationship with God. He wants you to walk with Him, to know His heart, to understand exactly how He feels about you, to begin to grasp what you mean to Him, and how passionately He cares that your story gets told. In that knowing, you will be able to trust that, no matter where you find yourself along the road and despite everything you might have done wrong, you can reach out to Him without fear and be certain that He will come for you. When troubles come and your journey gets complicated by all sorts of circumstances that press hard against hope, He will be there to hang onto. You will find that His unusual love, which will prove both faithful and unbounded, will be more than enough to get you through whatever comes your way.

That is what the unfolding of Ruth's story conveys with such intricate detail as we rejoin Ruth and Naomi on that road to Bethlehem.

> *When Naomi heard in Moab that the Lord had come to the aid of his people by providing food for them, she and her daughters-in-law prepared to return home from there. With her two daughters-in-law she left the place where she had been living and set out on the road that would take them back to the land of Judah. Then Naomi said to her two daughters-in-law, "Go back, each of you, to your mother's home. May the Lord show you kindness, as you have shown kindness to your dead husbands and to me. May the Lord grant that each of you will find rest in the home of another husband." Then she kissed them goodbye and they wept aloud and said to her, "We will go back with you to your people." But Naomi said, "Return home, my daughters. Why would you come with me? Am I going to have any more sons, who could become your husbands? Return home, my daughters; I am too old to have another husband. Even if I thought there was still hope for me—even if I had a husband tonight and then gave birth to sons— would you wait until they grew up? Would you remain unmarried for them? No, my daughters. It is more bitter for me than for you, because the Lord's hand has turned against me!" At this they wept aloud again. Then Orpah kissed her mother-in-law goodbye..."* (Ruth 1:6-14a NIV).

Once Ruth made the decision to pack her bag and follow Naomi out of town, circumstances got tougher. Just consider the challenges a common sense analysis would identify within this passage. First, Ruth had to contend with the physical challenge of merely making the trip from Moab to Bethlehem. This was a journey of forty to fifty miles. It would take them two to three days on foot. The terrain would be rough, culminating in an uphill climb that would lead into the city of Bethlehem. Add to the physical hurdles, the emotional struggles that would naturally come from leaving everything Ruth had ever known in order to try to assimilate into a culture so drastically different from anything she had ever experienced. Undoubtedly there was the pull of home, and of family, as the two Moabite girls kissed their mothers goodbye and turned to leave with Naomi. Just imagine all the familiar sights, sounds, and smells that began to tug at their heartstrings with every additional step toward the outskirts of their town.

Having overcome that initial pull of all things familiar, having arrived at the edge of their village, these two Moabite girls were confronted with an intense argument from Naomi in an attempt to persuade them to turn back. The mother-in-law they had come to love and trust almost insisted that there was absolutely no positive future waiting for them in Bethlehem. Naomi offered no hope of a husband, children, prosperity or peace. She did everything she could to discourage these girls from traveling on. Blinded by her own loss and hopelessness, she had lost sight of any opportunity for these two young women to find shelter with God and His people. Naomi presented seemingly insurmountable evidence that following her would only lead to further disappointment and hardship. Then, as if to place the final nail in the coffin prepared to imprison Ruth's dreams, Orpah changed her mind and turned to go back home. Who would have blamed Ruth if she had chosen to go with her? Every argument made sense. She would be turning her back on everything she had ever known, for what? She would be leaving to follow an embittered woman to a place where Ruth would be an outcast, to a people who would only see her as a foreigner, a beggar, maybe even an intruder. Yet Ruth was unyielding. This was her response waiting at the end of verse 14,

> *At this they wept aloud again. Then Orpah kissed her mother-in-law goodbye, but Ruth clung to her* (Ruth 1:14 NIV).

Ruth came to what most observers would accept as a reasonable end of this road and her mother-in-law, the one person she knew that could lead her to the more of God, to this Drink her very heart was made to thirst for, urged her to turn back, to give up, to continue to live in the empty, godless, mess of a world she had always known.

Is there anyone telling you that today, that your story is not worth the fight, that you have no choice but to submit to the inevitability of your predicted outcome? Perhaps you even say such words to yourself when you look into the mirror at the end of a brutal day. Ruth could have accepted her fate, as defined by Naomi. She could have dismissed her dreams, explained them away as nothing more than silly fantasies. Yet Ruth emphatically refused. Instead of turning back, Ruth grabbed hold. She clung to her belief that there was a God Who loved her enough to promise more to her than what her circumstances might dictate and to keep that promise. She did not necessarily know all the details of what it would look like, but she knew that what she had seen with eyes of faith she could not let go of now.

So, through her story, God asks each of us another question...not only "Will you believe to the point that it changes your story?" but "Will you believe when believing gets hard?" Will you press past the obstacles and endure the resistance that stands between you and your destiny? Ruth was about to move into very unfamiliar territory, to step out on a dangerous adventure, to travel to a place where nobody knew her or even wanted her there, to become immersed in a culture where there might possibly be no willingness to receive, much less embrace, a young widow from Moab. She was about to leave everything that she found comfortable and normal and familiar behind, to run with abandon toward an intimate relationship with the God of the Hebrew people, to pursue with all her heart this vision of who only He knew she could be. So is it any wonder? Does it come as a surprise that we find this woman on the precipice of her destiny, at this crucial crossroads, clinging for dear life, literally, physically, holding on with both hands and refusing to let go?

Imagine, for a moment, that you stand at one end of a dark and unfamiliar room, a room, nonetheless, that you must cross in order to obtain a priceless treasure. This room is fraught with obstacles that have been strategically placed there intentionally to trip you up. Not only that, but you cannot see a thing, you do not know what barriers might block your path or cause your peril, because there is no light in that room and, to make matters worse, you are blindfolded. As you take your first precarious step, in a feeble attempt to cross to the other side, you realize you are being pursued by a relentless intruder who is determined to keep you from the treasure that awaits you on the other side. How do you feel? Terrified? Hopeless? Paralyzed? How difficult would it be to simply take that first step, and then the next? How hard would it be to believe that you were going to make it to the other side?

Yet what if, in that room, there is someone who knows the way, sees the obstacles, has the power and authority to remove them, and defeat that treacherous enemy? What if you discover He loves you like crazy and, though you can hardly see Him in the darkness, you become aware of His presence and feel the touch of His hand? Would you turn away, insisting to go it alone or would you grab hold and cling tightly to that person, taking every step, from that point on, with His hand in your firm grasp?

You see, clinging is not for cowards. Clinging is not an act of passivity. When Ruth grabbed hold of Naomi with both hands and refused to let go, it was an aggressive act, even forceful. This was not weakness on display. Clinging is an act of strength. It requires great courage. Clinging is also an act of desire. It is a product of desperation. Clinging is an outward expression of an internal decision that says, "I just got a taste of that thing I want more than anything else and I will not turn back, I will not give up, I will not let go until it is poured out fully and freely and running down all over me, until I am completely saturated with it!" Ruth was saying with her whole body "You have Him, I want Him, and nothing you say or do will convince me to turn back now."

Once we make our own decision to take the path that will get us closer to God, we soon run into resistance and become aware of the barriers that stand in our way. God is not asking anything more of us than what He asked of Ruth. He is not expecting you to step out into unknown territory, to have the courage to surrender to an uncommon intimacy with a God Who may have been little more than an acquaintance until now, with no assurance of His presence along the way. He is not asking you to work out some sort of extraordinary destiny on your own and present it impressively to Him at the end of this journey. No, all He asks is that you have the courage to cling. No courage delights God's heart more than this, that I have the radical faith to abandon my own efforts and the futility of the lesser gods who have ensnared and enslaved me in the past, to sell out, full out, to the idea that this One True God, and whatever He brings, is and always will be enough to overcome every obstacle and walk me safely through each storm.

In the movie, *I Am Sam*, the little girl at the center of this poignant story has been taken from her developmentally disabled daddy and placed in foster care. In the eyes of this world the love she has found in him is hopelessly inadequate to protect her or give her everything she needs. Yet every night, in utter defiance of what this world's system dictates, this child sneaks out of her bedroom window and makes the journey home to an apartment, where her daddy lives, not far away. It is an unquenchable longing in her heart for the peculiar relationship they share that drives her, a passion to rest in the embrace of his unusual love that refuses to be denied. Upon arriving at his window, immediately the child begins to chatter, making plans, maneuvering to secure her place there, where she feels safe and loved in the familiarity of his presence. Yet humbly, this wise and welcoming father picks her up and carries her back to the place the courts have designated as, at least, a temporary haven for her. Despite his unmistakable desire to protect her and be with her, no anger is evident in his response. He offers no defense, only a patient confidence, only a diligent commitment to allow his own deep love to be tested and proven against the standards of this world. As the caring foster mother opens the door to find the dedicated pair standing there once again, the extreme compassion of this tender father is displayed as he takes the time, not only to return the child, but to provide the woman with his secret, the inside information as to how she might be able to create a more comforting environment when his daughter awakens in the middle of the night. He explains it this way, "Sometimes if you rub her belly and then read her two stories and give her half an I-Hop corn muffin then sometimes she sleeps when she can't sleep." In those simple words all, who are willing to see, can see why this little girl clung so desperately to her father, why she could not stifle her longing, why she relentlessly pursued the comfort of his arms. He was the one who knew her best. He was acquainted with the intricacies of her personality. He understood so completely the longings of her heart. In the context of their intimacy she had found that he knew just what to say and do to make her feel secure because, really, security is all about having a place to be who you are right where you are in the knowledge that you will always be loved. In his knowing this father loved her deeply, he loved her well. In truth, her endless pursuit to be near him had little to do with an I-Hop corn muffin and much more to do with that knowing that attends to each tiny detail of life because it flows so freely out of such genuine, unconditional delight and fascination.[17]

What a picture this secular work of art paints for us of the heart of our Father. Certainly questioned by the world around us as enough, yet so focused on the object of His affection that He barely notices the scrutiny of the skeptics and wastes no energy on a defense against their doubts. The One and Only is so enraptured by His bride that He pays careful attention to every detail of her being from the number of hairs on her head to the dreams tucked inside the inner chambers of her soul. Knowing you is His priority. Boldly His love speaks, *"Before I formed you in the womb, I knew you"* (Jeremiah 1:5 NIV). He knows exactly what it takes to make you feel loved and secure, be that an I-Hop corn muffin, a raspberry chocolate chip bagel with a warm cup of coffee, or something completely different and individually you. The menu of our secret longings is as distinctive as our fingerprints and it was knit into our souls by a meticulous Creator. In the context of our intimate relationship, God begins to communicate that He knows, even better than we do, those things that we long for and cherish and He wants to release us to live in the truth of what they are. That is why He is our safety. He is our destiny. He is our life. Embraced by His truly unconditional love, one so holy, so "other than," we are released to simply be, without pretense or hesitation. In this peculiar relationship, we are loved just as we are.

Could Ruth have been merely clinging to Naomi, thinking Naomi was the answer? I hope not. Was she holding fast to what she knew for sure about her future? That would have been impossible. Was she just that desperate to take a road trip? Not hardly. Could there have been something much deeper inspiring her unflinching grip? Ruth's own words reveal what she was clinging to so tightly,

> *"Look,"* said Naomi, *"your sister-in-law is going back to her people and her gods. Go back with her."* But Ruth replied, *"Don't urge me to leave you or to turn back from you. Where you go I will go, and where you stay I will stay. Your people will be my people and your God my God. Where you die I will die, and there I will be buried. May the Lord deal with me, be it ever so severely, if even death separates you and me"* (Ruth 1:15-17 NIV).

That is the concept Ruth grasped as she came to the end of the road and refused to walk away. She clung to the vision of her story woven into God's. She could not know everything about what the future would look like, as she grabbed hold of it with both hands, but she knew that an intimate relationship with this God Who knew her, with this God Who loved her so well, would be enough. It would be enough, even if God's people refused to accept her in Bethlehem. It would be enough, if she had to go through the rest of her life alone. It would be enough, even if she never had children. It would be enough, if she had to beg in order to survive. It would be enough if she always remained an outsider, if she had to leave everything she knew and live the rest of her days far from her home. It would be enough, if it cost her life itself. Yes, that is precisely how far Ruth took the possibilities as she spoke of her conviction saying *"far be it from me if anything but death…"* Ruth had made up her mind that clinging to God was more valuable than even clinging to her own life. He was her destiny and all of the other details were simply wrapped up in holding onto Him. Ruth's act of clinging to the garments of her mother-in-law was an outward expression of this inner passion for the life she was created to experience with the One True Lover of her soul.

So it was decided. There was no more debate. In fact, Ruth 1:18 tells us clearly that *"When Naomi realized that Ruth was determined to go with her, she stopped urging her"* (Ruth 1:18 NIV). Even Naomi knew there was no talking Ruth out of this. Ruth had a death grip on a dream, on a vision of how her life was ordained to play out. Moving forward, taking that road, as risky as it might prove to be, was the only option Ruth was willing to consider.

Such determination is not achieved by accident. In fact, the Hebrew word translated "determined" in this verse means "to be courageous, to be strong, to be increased, to be hardened, to be established."[18] No one becomes strong, hardened or established overnight. This is a journey. I can just imagine that Ruth had watched Naomi pray, that, as they walked to the well for water, she may have asked her seasoned companion to tell her what life was like in this place called Bethlehem. Ruth must have seen glimpses of Who this God of the Hebrew people was, scattered throughout the day like stars scattered across the night sky. Perhaps she had even found within her the boldness to ask Naomi outright to teach her about this Hebrew God. Orpah may have laughed at her inquisitiveness, or even called such curiosity a silly waste of time, but Ruth persisted. Little by little God must have wooed her, whispered His truth, sung over her in the songs she heard Naomi singing when she thought no one could hear. Ruth's hunger had been stirred by so many things on the road to this life-changing decision. Now all of the bread crumbs God had left for her led her to this path, to this invitation to leave everything for His "House of Bread."

Yet to complete this course would demand courageous persistence and resilience, cultivated by the thoughtful pressure of a Potter's hand. God allows that pressure because He is never content for us to have a flimsy hold on our destiny or remain in a place of weakness and immaturity in our relationship with Him. He wants us to move forward in life with the strength and beauty of deep conviction so that we can run, not walk, but run with abandon, released to be complete only in Him. So He makes the pathway clear, the decision stark, against the darkness of all we have ever known. Then, in perfect wisdom, He initiates, supervises and completes a process that will accomplish such fortitude and thoroughness of resolve in each of our lives that we too will be equipped to take up the sword, run to the battlefield, and fight for our freedom.

We see this principle illustrated in the animal kingdom. I have heard that when a baby giraffe is born he behaves much like a newborn colt as he struggles and stumbles around to get on his feet. At the end of this difficult and persistent process, when at last he has accomplished his goal of taking his first stand, his mother comes over and nudges him, knocking him down. Then he works and works to make it to his feet again only for his mother to bump him once more, putting him back on his haunches. Apparently the reason they go through this laborious process is very intentional. His wise mother is strengthening his legs, she is building his muscles. This is what a football coach might refer to as conditioning. By instinct and experience she knows that when that baby giraffe is out in the wild, with a predator lurking nearby, the little giraffe's very survival depends on his ability to be alert, to be agile, to be able to get up quickly, to stand strong in the face of that challenge. What might seem like cruelty is a beautiful act of loving preparation as the mother giraffe wisely sees what is up ahead and equips her child to face it, and overcome it, as only she can.

If I showed you a bag of loose rubber bands and told you this would be my weapon to fight against you, would you tremble? Would you run in fear? Most likely you might laugh at me for thinking I could do much damage with such flimsy ammunition. If I were to position one of those bands perfectly on the tip of my finger and pull it tightly with my other hand, I might be able to sting you, but the assault would most likely not result in any serious injury. However, if instead I begin wrapping one loose band around another, continuing layer after layer until together, over time, these pieces, that were once flimsy and unthreatening on their own, came together to form a solid ball of rubber, my rubber bands might get your attention. Those same rubber bands, layered until they are a solid hardened mass, would carry much more force and weight than they did individually. In the face of that type of force you might run. That is what this word "determined" describes. It is something that has been solidified through a process of adding one layer after another.

Not only was Ruth's conviction developed through successive exposures to the attractiveness of Naomi's God, it had also been solidified in the testing. I have to believe that this was not Ruth's first rodeo. This was surely not the very first challenge of her fledgling faith that Ruth had confronted and overcome. Just knowing she was a girl from Moab tells us that. She had grown up surrounded by dysfunction, paganism and cruelty. Yet she was still standing. She met and married a man whose very name conveyed his frailty, but she stayed. She had made the critical decision to follow the God of the Hebrew people, abandoning the pagan gods of her people and her homeland. Now she had chosen to pick up and move toward an unknown future, to walk away from her home and say goodbye to her family. She had heard her mother-in-law advocate for changing her mind, for abandoning this dream as crazy, even impossible. She had watched her sister-in-law take heed to that advise and turn back at the edge of town. Why would God allow her to endure all of these challenges on her way to her destiny? He was building her up, increasing her strength, developing her stamina, reinforcing her belief system, one layer at a time.

Her Father was not only strengthening her character but also her vision. With each obstacle she had to overcome, clinging desperately to God and His dreams for her future, she began to see herself differently. She began to recognize her transformation, from a girl who would have settled for the life she had always known, to the warrior who would battle her way out of that cage and into her freedom. Maybe her thinking sounded something like this poem God poured into my heart a few years ago in a similar season of heartbreak, yet ensuing resolve.

Becoming Brave

I have this picture, of me, becoming brave.
Can you imagine it? Me?
The one who never gave herself permission
To sing out without a sellout
To the braver ones who took pride in keeping her in her place?
The one who let the bullies
And the hecklers and the cynics
Make her turn and go another way
Or slink down the road they think they own
Shrouded in an apology?
Yeah, that's the one, that's the person I see

Suddenly different, somehow changed,
Surprisingly unhindered by what could have been,
Or what should have been,
Or even what will never be.

I have this vision,
If you'll pardon the fanciness of the expression,
Of me, becoming brave.
Stepping out of these long, dark shadows
In some fine, new, colorful garment
That I would have never had the courage
To wear out in public before.
Strutting my stuff with attitude
Right past the critics who think they could do better
But they never do.
And the liars who think they know better
When they never will.
In the face of all those opposing ones
Who can't stand to see me hit my stride
While I'm marching right past their window,
Marching right up that mountain of fears
That has kept me down, and kept me out,
And kept me convinced that I'd never climb out of here.

That's right, I can see me, becoming brave
A warrior, in fact,
Though I may never look like what you might
Expect a warrior to be.
Unstoppable nonetheless, undaunted,
Unashamed and unmasked.
Not quite, yet confident that I will be.

Refusing to be defined by the failures of my past,
Or the dim predictions of my detractors,
Or the ever empty promises of those pretenders
Who fain their caring because they think they have
A right to manipulate my destiny.

I may not yet know the way,
Nor the length of my journey,
Nor how many bruises of body and soul
I must yet endure,
But I am sure.

For I can see it coming,
I will move beyond where I am,
For I am ever held firmly,
Prodded gently, guided clearly
By That One,
The Word that spoke this into me and over me
Before anyone else knew anything about it.
I have this picture of me,
Finally, truly, becoming this picture of me,
Becoming brave.

When Jesus peered over the side of a dried up well to talk to a terrified guy named Gideon, this trembling man did not look much like a mighty warrior. Yet that is exactly what God called him, because that was the Gideon He knew, the man of God's pre-designed destiny. That was the Gideon He knew he would be in the end, after all the training and conditioning that began down in that well and would now continue all the way to a waiting battlefield. Jesus knew, with those words, He was speaking to that future Gideon that this terrified farmer was destined to become. (Paraphrased from Judges 6:11-14 NIV)

Do you ever wonder what God would call you if He came to where you hide when you are afraid? I think He would say, "She's a woman of exquisite beauty. She's a rock. She's a warrior! She's the one I have chosen to love without reservation!" Only He knows the exact words He would speak to you but I can assure you they would seem completely impossible and yet incredibly true. When He deposits them in your heart, from someone's lips, or someone's pen, or a song, or a verse, or a message, or a whisper, He is starting the process, He is calling out your destiny. Believe Him!

I love how Paul described this propensity of God to speak each destiny into existence, *"God calls things that are not as though they were"* (Romans 4:17 NIV). Not only are God's dreams for you bigger than those you dream for yourself, God's capacity to empower those dreams, to call what is not yet true in our experience as though it already is, to speak His vision of you into existence, is everything you will ever need to get there. He knows the end before the process even begins. He is showing you the last page of your story while you are just beginning to make your way through the introduction. That means you can trust that He knows the way and, if You cling to Him, He will get you there. A woman who starts out like that bag of flimsy, non-threatening rubber bands can become dangerously solid and powerfully sound, if she will only submit to the process.

As we will see in Ruth's story, this will require that we align ourselves with His movements, that we position ourselves intentionally to hear His voice. We must nurture an intimate relationship with Him so that, when obstacles threaten to turn us around or take us perilously off course, we will be close enough to grab hold of and hold on to The One who loves us like we have never been loved or could be loved by anyone else.

David and I live close enough to hear the voice of the announcer from one of the largest college football stadiums in the country, Neyland Stadium, which is the home of the University of Tennessee Volunteers. On crisp fall afternoons, we can hear the words, "Give him six!" each time one of our hometown heroes crosses the goal line. Yet no matter how close or how far that gifted athlete made that trek to the end zone from the line of scrimmage, I would contend that this moment in the spotlight began long before we knew his name or heard that victorious declaration of his success. This kid probably began with a pick up game in his back yard or perhaps an inglorious career in a youth football league. Somewhere along the way I would imagine this young athlete spent some hot afternoons not running the field but running the bleachers, perhaps completely alone, but certainly far from the cheering fans that now have a complete come apart over his most recent accomplishment. The point is that this young man never ran the bleachers in the heat because he merely wanted to make a name for himself as an ardent bleacher runner. He ran those bleachers, suffered through every concrete step in the heat of the afternoon sun, because he dreamed of running the touchdowns, he was training for this celebrated moment. The bleachers were a means to an end, a demonstration that this young man had made the decision to believe when believing gets hard, because the dream that he holds in his heart is worth enduring the pain to achieve it, not only for himself, but for his family, and for those poised to see the outcome of all that preparation.

In much the same way, there are going to be times when God says "Run the bleachers!" and run we must, because our Good Father sees us after we have weathered the storm, after we have pushed past the obstacles He is allowing now to strengthen us and cultivate a depth of character we could not achieve any other way. God sees you as you will be when this journey is finished. He knows precisely how much pressure is needed to bring out all the beauty He hid inside of you before you were born. God is not intimidated by anything you might face, or any question that circumstances might stir within your heart, because He knows that in those challenges you will find new strength, you will develop new courage, you will tighten your grip on His grasp. He already sees you becoming brave when with trembling legs you step out to take just one step closer. At each turn He will give you something else to hold to, another layer of understanding that will only add depth to what you had when you began on this road to your Bethlehem. Even when you get knocked down, when in weakness and immaturity you seem slow to take your stand, remember God is gracious. It is His unusual kindness and extraordinary grace that will get you back on your feet every time you fall. When life shakes you to the core, God's loving grasp remains invincible. Just the other side of your deepest heartache His outstretched arms will encircle you with a sweeter affection than pain could ever deny. He will show up for you right in the middle of whatever mess you are facing right now. I know He will because He has always shown up for me.

Anyone acquainted with David and me for long at all has heard about four little objects of our greatest affection. Our four grandchildren, Morgan, Penelope, Marley and Rhys have brought more healing and joy into our lives over the past nine and a half years than words could ever convey. I once said "Becoming a grandmother was like falling into a huge vat of dark chocolate with nothing but a cup of coffee and a spoon!" With their giggles, tickles, witticisms, hugs and kisses they have brought the beautiful heart of our Heavenly Father right to our doorstep and put it unashamedly on display.

What we do not get opportunity to talk about quite as often are the two little angels who carried our hearts to heaven. Our second grandchild lived only the first few weeks after conception. It will be one of heaven's sweet surprises to find out if that grandchild is a boy or a girl. I can just imagine the reveal party God will throw us when we get there. I so look forward to picking up that sweet baby boy or girl that God gave us briefly to forever love.

Julia Angela Puglisi, our third grandchild, died while still inside her mommy seventeen and a half weeks into that pregnancy. Our youngest daughter, Kiley, labored all day on a Wednesday in January of 2010 to deliver her. There are no words to describe what it was like to hold our tiny 1.1 ounce baby girl in our hands. Julia was just 4" long but the first words Kiley said were "Look, Mom, the baby looks like me...like I looked when I was born." It was true, even though she was tiny she favored her mom, even Kiley's husband, Tony, could see it. David and I could hardly miss the similarities in those two tiny girls.

Julia's birth was probably the most heart wrenching and sacred moment we have ever shared. We had all relaxed a bit when Kiley got through her first trimester without any problems. It was only the previous August when her first pregnancy had ended in a miscarriage in its ninth week. This time Kiley and her husband, Tony, had heard a strong heartbeat and were just a couple of weeks away from finding out their baby's gender. There had been no complications or concerns at all until Kiley woke up on that Wednesday morning at about 5 a.m. to discover she was bleeding, but only slightly. She called her obstetrician, a beautiful man named George Vick who ministers the Lord's care and healing through his practice, and he told her to lay down until she could meet him at his office at 8:30. At about 9:30 a.m., Kiley called with the devastating news none of us were expecting. After telling her that the baby had died, her sweet doctor went on to gently explain that she was too far along and the baby was a little too large for him to confidently recommend that any other type of procedure could be done safely. So he said that she would need to labor and deliver the child. All she said about it, as she shared that devastating news, was that she had given that baby to the Lord just after she woke up bleeding early that morning.

Everyone was blown away by the courage and grace with which Kiley and Tony endured the day's experiences. It was so obvious that they had been equipped with a special kind of grace for this significant moment. They would need it. The medications used to induce Kiley's labor were much stronger and more fierce than ones administered, when needed, at the culmination of a successful pregnancy. Kiley suffered just about every side effect they could bring...severe headache, nausea, fever, chills...not to mention the emotional trauma and shock of knowing that these labor pangs would not bring the usual joy that overshadows them at the birth. It was a horrifying experience to watch. Yet Kiley was a warrior. Even as tears ran down her face she said, "Mom, I'm not bitter but I still wonder why." To which I could only respond, "All I know is that this is an experience God has entrusted to you. We live in a broken and fragile world, babe, and if only the people who don't know God ever suffered pain or loss how would we know how to reach out to them?"

We were amazed and thankful at all the ways we saw the Lord surround our kids, and us, with His extraordinary love and graciousness. Every nurse, family member, or friend who showed up at the hospital brought a different piece of what we needed. Our other son-in-law, Drake, had a morning appointment unexpectedly cancel. So he was there to meet me at the hospital door when I arrived and helped me find my way through the unfamiliar halls to Kiley's room. When we reached the room we discovered a little sign and a bouquet of artificial violets had been hung on her door. Without my glasses ready, I could not read the inscription, so Drake read the beautiful message to me that was there to let anyone who entered that room know ahead of time that this was a different kind of birth experience, "A gentle hug goodbye." Some of the first words on the little note were "violets are for remembering," which particularly touched my heart because, nearly twenty-four years before this, Kiley's grandmother had purchased the Dogwood Arts Festival print for Kiley from the year she was born, 1986, and it was a picture of violets with those very words written beneath.

My sister, Susan, was somehow able to leave her busy workplace almost immediately upon hearing the news. She arrived to be with us only a few minutes later, though on most days it would have been very difficult to cover her responsibilities on such short notice in order to free her to meet us there. As a result she was already at the hospital when my aging parents arrived. However, as they were walking into the hospital, my mother fell. Since she was holding my dad's arm, as she lost her footing, she inadvertently pulled Dad over the top and he landed on the pavement on the other side. When they called us with the news of this mishap, Susan, and my son-in-law, Drake, were available to immediately go downstairs to be with them in the emergency room, freeing me to stay with Kiley throughout the morning.

Soon other family members arrived and joined the waiting room vigil. Kiley and Tony were not up to seeing anyone else but it was such comfort to know that so many were waiting and praying just down the hall. My husband, David, was in North Carolina on a business trip when we got the news. So he had a lonely two and a half hour drive before he could get to the hospital. Somehow, while God had arms to hold each of us, He still managed to accompany David on what must have seemed like the longest drive of his life.

Kiley's first really rough moments, physically speaking, came just as the nurse who had been with her since her admission had taken a short lunch break but the relieving nurse, Jennifer, was both compassionate and gentle. We could almost sense that there was a reason that her quiet way was appropriate for those harder moments. David arrived around

12:30 and he and I were permitted to stay in the room with Kiley and Tony for the rest of the time. Our older daughter, Brittany, joined us as soon as she could find someone to take over her class at a nearby elementary school.

As Kiley's daytime nurse's shift was about to come to an end we noticed the nurse seemed to be lingering in the room. It seemed as if she had something she wanted to say but was not quite sure of how or when to bring it up. Finally, she reached out to offer Kiley and Tony a list of funeral homes that they could use if they wanted to have a service. In response to their reluctance, she asked if they planned to see the baby. Tony responded "We don't really know." The nurse then encouraged them to consider it. With their permission she went on to describe to them what to expect, assuring them that the experience would not be scary and that she thought it would be really important for them to have that moment in order to say their "goodbyes." She chose her words carefully and spoke with such comfort and wisdom that could only be offered by someone who had bravely stood by many other couples struggling with those questions.

After that compassionate conversation, it was as if the nurse's words lingered in that hospital room, gently breaking through any sort of denial any one of us still held in our hearts. The reality of what was happening was at last sinking in fully and forcefully, releasing what was probably the most heartbreaking scene of that horrific day as tears signaled the acceptance that this little one had really died. Tony sat beside Kiley up in her bed as they held each other. David and I, though we were trying to be strong, could hardly help but feel the tears flooding our eyes and faces as well, not only for the loss of our grandchild but also for the grief that our kids were being called to endure.

For a while the four of us just sat with our grief. Then we all needed a moment to catch our breath before going forward. David and I went out to the waiting room to fill everyone in, as they had been waiting most of the day with little information. It was almost four in the afternoon and we decided to encourage our families to go on home because we knew Kiley's pain would only intensify for the rest of the day and they would not be able to see her. My Dad and Mom were out of the emergency room, each banged up a bit but with no serious injuries as a result of their tumble on the way in. Tony's co-workers had brought by a tray of sandwiches, chips, cookies and tea, giving all of us who had been waiting through this long day, a moment's distraction and a little more strength for the remaining hours.

Kiley's second shift nurse was a particularly tender and sweet woman. She seemed to hurt with Kiley as she endured another round of horrible side effects. She also always took the time to keep David and I fully informed anytime we had to step out of the room as the doctor and nurses did their examinations.

Finally, at a little after 8 p.m., Kiley began to give birth with Tony by her side. The doctors and nurses attended her while David and I waited right outside in the hall. Kiley said that she felt no pain at the moment of the birth. As soon as Julia was delivered Dr. Vick led in prayer. His wife had died of cancer only a few years before and he especially asked God to allow his wife, Nancy, to rock our little one in heaven for us that night. Then a nurse carried Julia out of the room and down the hall, being careful to turn so that we could not see what she was carrying as she left the room, but we knew.

It seemed like the whole floor and everyone who worked on it, held their breath in this moment. The activity was almost like a choreographed dance, as each person played their role, did their job, moved in concert with God. Just as we knew that the baby had been born, the voice of the hospital chaplain began to say the nightly prayer over the intercom. As the prayer came to a close, David reminded me of a Karla Worley song with the lyrics, "Somebody lost their baby...and the world turns a little slower tonight." It was almost as if the Lord even provided the soundtrack for our grieving, putting that song in our hearts many years before as Karla had sung that song in a Sunday night church service that we had never forgotten. Little did we know that those poignant words would someday speak the truth of our experience. Everything seemed to slow down in reverence as this tiny miracle was being ushered into the presence of God and released reluctantly from our loving grasp.

While nurses attended to Kiley, her doctor came out to tell us how she was, giving both David and I much needed hugs. Then the nurses brought the baby back for Kiley and Tony to say their goodbyes. Julia's tiny body was nestled in a little white crocheted cap and was surrounded with a little blanket. They spent about 15 minutes tearfully holding her close. Then the doctor and nurse returned to the room and soon Dr. Vick came to the door and motioned for us to join them. As we came into the room he said, "Kiley and Tony would like the two of you to see their baby."

As I wrote at the beginning of my story, there are no words to describe that moment nor fully express the emotion of that experience. The child looked perfect except for a tiny fluid-filled cyst on the back of her neck that I probably would never have noticed had the doctor not told us about it in advance. Kiley was holding her as she told us that they had chosen to give her a name that meant "little angel," Julia Angela Puglisi. Tony held her and then the doctor handed the child's tiny body to me. It was an unbelievable moment that nothing could ever prepare a mom to receive. It was true, she did look like her mom and, although she felt almost weightless in my hand, it was obvious that she was perfectly formed with such tiny little hands and feet. As I carefully handed her back, the doctor held her up and prayed with our family once again. Then the nurse took our precious child that fit so perfectly in one hand, stepping back into the corner, leaving us to wrap our arms around each other as we wept together. After a few moments she stepped forward to offer Kiley one more chance to see her tiny girl, assuring them that Julia would be just down the hall in the nursery for a while if Kiley and Tony decided that they needed to see her once more.

All that was left for the four of us to do was to simply wait through the several hours that it took for Kiley's legs to awaken again from the epidural anesthesia. During that time the nursing staff changed again and we were a little disappointed to see someone unfamiliar had come to join us. There was just something special about the one nurse who had stood with us as we spoke our goodbyes. However, this new nurse soon shared that she had gone through a stillbirth at only 18 weeks in her pregnancy. As a result she had a special understanding and compassion, information gleaned from her own tragic experience. She was equipped to prepare Kiley for physical changes she should expect, even though the birth took place so early in her pregnancy, as well as the emotional and hormonal upheaval that would come. This nurse connected with Kiley heart to heart and spoke with a knowledge that could never be gained from a textbook. By the end of our stay we understood why God had brought her into that room at that hour.

Finally, as we left the hospital to head home at about 3 a.m., our 22 hour journey of carrying Julia home was complete. As that now familiar nurse wheeled Kiley toward the door to leave, she suggested that Tony and David pull our cars up to the door. As they walked out toward the parking lot, the nurse and I each looked up to notice an ambulance waiting just outside with a sign that read "NEONATAL" taped to the side. Before I had time to fully process what that meant, this caring professional said "Let's back up out of the door," and as she did, she turned Kiley's wheelchair all the way around with only about a second to spare before three nurses rounded the corner of the hall with a tiny baby in an incubator headed for that ambulance. To distract from the passing commotion, the nurse began to have an especially lively conversation with Kiley about a small vase of flowers that had come from her co-workers and was now being held in Kiley's lap. Because of this nurse's sensitivity, Kiley never even knew that a tiny baby passed so closely that we could have almost touched it. I was amazed at all the ways God positioned people around all of us who were uniquely gifted and equipped to care and perform such acts of kindness on our behalf.

Since David had driven to the hospital from North Carolina we each took that quiet 3 a.m. drive to our home alone. Driving through those dark and mostly deserted streets I could not help but thank my God for all the different people He surrounded us with during this painful journey. I sensed the Lord whispering to my heart in response "That's because I wanted you to see that there are more with you than against you." How like God to think of me and even whisper words of comfort in the midst of my little girl's crisis. He knew that David and I had endured a recent experience within our church family that had left us wounded and raw. In the midst of betrayal and hurt, it had been easy to feel like we were all alone, to even conclude that everyone was against us. As a Master of Detail, God refused to miss this opportunity to touch my wounds as well. In the awareness of His unusual compassion to think of even me, I was overwhelmed.

Kiley and Tony had such a tough recovery time over the next few days. It broke our hearts to see such lively and naturally happy young people engulfed in their grief. Since their miscarriage in August, Kiley had been especially captivated by Hannah's story in the Bible. Sometime right after they found out she was pregnant again, Kiley and Tony were in a store where they saw a wooden figurine of an expectant mother engraved with the verse "I prayed for this child and the Lord answered my prayer" taken directly from Hannah's story recorded in 1 Samuel. Kiley had mentioned the statue to me several times and told me how much she longed to buy it. Then Tony confided in me secretly that he planned to buy it for her. At the beginning of the very week of their loss, late on the previous Monday night, Tony had, in fact, sent me an e-mail asking me to order the figurine for him, so that he could keep it a secret until Valentine's Day. I placed the order before going to bed that night, just two days before this whole experience. So as soon as I got home from the hospital, in the wee hours of that Thursday morning, I checked to see if there was still time to cancel the order. It was too late, the item had shipped. I decided not to mention it to Tony. I would place it on my closet shelf when it came and keep it for another day, when hopefully he might need it again.

On Friday morning I went back to Kiley and Tony's house to spend some time with Kiley. The pain she was in would crush any mother's heart, it certainly broke mine. Both of them just looked like little kids to me, not knowing where to turn to escape their agony. Their eyes searched mine for answers I did not have. I just brought food and sat beside them and did whatever I could think of at the moment. As we were talking through everything that had happened over the past forty-eight hours I did remind Kiley of that verse, of Hannah's story and how Hannah had to give her child back to the Lord too. I held out to her what little hope she might cling to in knowing that God gave Hannah other children after she brought Samuel to Him. Through sobs all Kiley could do was nod and say, "I know." It was all any of us could do.

Through the rest of that day I could hardly get that figurine, and the verse it held, out of my mind. All the way home, I was flooded with memories from 24 years before, when God introduced my little girl, Kiley, to the world 10 weeks before any of us expected her. Just as Kiley had clung to that verse from 1 Samuel, God had given me a verse to hang onto as I waited for her birth as well. So our conversation had taken my mind back to those days when I was in labor and delivery.

In the sixth month of my second pregnancy, I was on the way to a doctor's appointment, having been told at my previous check up that I was again experiencing pre-eclampsia. Pre-eclampsia was a condition which brought our first daughter, Brittany, into the world seven weeks before her due date. As I drove to the appointment at the University of Tennessee Medical Center, a sermon by Chuck Swindoll played on my car radio. I listened as he read these words from Ecclesiastes, "He hath made every thing beautiful in his time…" (Ecclesiastes 3:11 King James Version). Pastor Chuck elaborated in his radio message that "this loss of a job, this hospital stay, whatever you might be facing today, may not seem beautiful but it will be in its time." God gave me that promise that morning and David and I held onto that verse through several days of uncertainty and stress as we waited in the labor and delivery ward for Kiley to be born. Several times we were told that our baby would need to be taken by Caesarean section on that very day only to have doctors change their minds, postponing the surgery. One day my kidney function became impaired only to improve for no apparent reason. On another day lab tests that seemed to show that my blood was losing its ability to clot, as it had done in my first pregnancy, only fifteen minutes later were discovered to be in error. Every day brought new uncertainty about when our baby should be delivered. David and I continued to find pretty much our only comfort in that verse that read in its entirety, *"He hath made every thing beautiful in his time: also he hath set the world in their heart, so that no man can find out the work that God maketh from the beginning to the end"* (Ecclesiastes 3:11 KJV). As we waited for our baby's birth we knew that God held her in His hands and that He knew, like no one else could know, the precise moment when she would be born. At last Kiley was born on a Tuesday morning, 10 weeks prematurely, weighing just 2 pounds and 10 ounces, our own little miracle, such evidence of the brilliance of God. So surely you can imagine our awe and emotion when we realized that her birthday was March 11 (3/11) and the verse we had held to leading up to her birth was Ecclesiastes 3:11. God went out of His way to assure us that this was all a part of His plan. We named our little girl, Kiley Shannon, which meant "beautiful, small and wise" and we knew that God gave us this beautiful little one not early, but at precisely this perfect moment in time.

Now it was that beautiful baby, Kiley, who was holding on to God's promise, waiting on God to give her a child. At this moment in her story, the child came too soon to stay in this world, for her days had been planned for heaven. Even with Kiley's incredible birth story, that history with our God still cherished in our hearts, it was hard to know how to assure her that this would ever be beautiful. As I reflected on my memory of her birth, as well as her heartbreak now, I thought it would be so cool if there was some way that her verse, her promise, those words from Hannah's story that she and Tony had held onto for these months, could somehow correspond with Kiley's experience in a way that would give her comfort like His Word had given us as we waited for her birth twenty-four years earlier. Disappointed I realized that the verse they had clung to was 1 Samuel 1:27 and that their baby girl, Julia, had come on Wednesday, the 28th. I walked over to the computer thinking, "Well, maybe verse 28 says something great too." Then my eyes fell upon the calendar and I dropped to the chair. I realized that Wednesday was not the 28th. Julia Angela Puglisi's tiny body was born on 1/27 and that verse, as incredible as it seems, was 1 Samuel 1:27. The recognition of that fact literally took my breath away. I could hardly believe that such a thing would happen to us once, but there it was again. Instantly I knew God planned that day. God heard that prayer. God gave that child, just as He had promised. I may never know why that little one never got to run and play and give Kiley and

Tony, as well as us, all the hugs and kisses we dreamed of for her, but I know that at that moment, as we looked down at her tiny face and felt her almost weightless body in our hands, that Julia had finished her course and was now safely waiting to meet us again someday in the arms of God. I do not know why this loss was in God's plan. I cannot answer all of Kiley's questions or my own. Yet I am completely convinced that God was not taken by surprise, that before we knew Julia Angela Puglisi, our "little angel," God knew her name and the precise day that we would see her tiny face.

Those first few days after Julia's delivery were filled with additional "only God could do that" moments. I had no idea of what to do but hold Kiley's hand or hold the phone as she cried. I knew, even then, that as much as her sadness was an essential leg of her journey, it would not be the end of her story. It was just one heart wrenching moment on the way to her destiny. Since that season God brought Tony and Kiley two beautiful and healthy children, Penelope and Rhys. Even as more time passes and we do not hurt quite as badly as we did when our loss was new, we will always remember and love little Julia as much as when we held her in one hand. We may not talk about that experience often but she is such an important part of God's story in each of our lives. As Kiley left the hospital in those early morning hours after Julia's delivery, she was given a tiny padded box that contained Julia's treasures, two tiny hand prints that the nurses lovingly obtained for Kiley and Tony to cherish, the little crocheted cap that she lay in as we first saw her face, a note card containing hand written messages from each nurse that cared for Kiley through that day, a tiny blanket monogrammed in yellow letters "In Loving Memory," even a little measuring tape to remind us of just how tiny this miracle was, just in case we could ever forget. This box, along with a few photos taken by the nurses for us to keep, are all we have of Julia now, except for the memory of the all too brief time when we were able to hold her and say our "goodbyes." These keepsakes have been a comfort to all of us as we have moved beyond that moment.

The genetic testing showed that neither Kiley nor Tony carry any chromosomal abnormalities. So I guess, by some, this whole experience would be considered a fluke. Yet beneath the pain, and all the unanswered questions, lies a deep sense of knowing in all of us, that not one bit of this was an accident, that for some reason God invited us to a miracle, to a moment when His presence seemed more real and His Spirit seemed so much more alive in the people around us than ever before. Maybe Julia's little sister and brother, as well as her cousins,

Morgan and Marley, are loved just a little bit deeper and held with a bit more awe and wonder at the miracles that only God can make because of how our moments with Julia made a lasting impression on each of our hearts.

Someone who was not there that day might wonder where God was. They might ask why a loving God would allow His children to go through so much pain. They might struggle to understand why this was part of each of our stories. They might even bring questions for which I still have no answers or speak words of misunderstanding of a plan far too big for one as simple as I am to fully grasp or explain. I could simply tell them all the ways that I saw Him right in the midst of the horror, in the well spoken words and gestures of warrior nurses or the gentle prayers of a doctor who had been sensitized by a tragic loss of his own. I see His heart all the time in a deeper sort of love we share as a family since we went through that war together. I cannot miss His hand in that tiniest miracle I ever held, if for only a moment, in my own. I am forever changed by the instant I saw that date on the calendar and realized that once again God, in extraordinary kindness and grace, had shown up for me.

If you ask me why God let this happen I could give you so many reasons. I would say I am who I am today in great part because My Crazy Loving Heavenly Daddy cared about me enough to trust me with that pain. When all I could do was to cling to Him and hang on, He changed me forever. He pulled me in closer and gave my faith legs in ways I can hardly measure. On the 27th of January in 2010, when God came for Julia to take her to live with Him in heaven, He also pulled her Nana up so close to Him that she will never get over it and never be the same.

I guess that is why it means so much to me that, in this precious Old Testament story, there were two women who came to the edge of that village and paused for a moment on that road out of town: one whose grip was firm and established, but another whose grip seemed to be slipping and frail. In chapter 1, the latter circumstance is where we find Naomi but this is not who Naomi was. This is just a snapshot of her in the middle of her journey. This is just a painful portion of the much bigger process. This is just a moment when her fingers began to tire, when her grip began to weaken, when once again God allowed her faith to be mightily challenged that it might become stronger than it had ever been. Circumstances had powerfully come against her conviction. Yet God refused to let go of her. He refused to let the isolation and resignation satisfy the desires of her heart. He refused to let her own plans, to feed her hunger with detachment, bitterness and pain, work out for her. Instead, in the clinging hands of her young daughter-in-law, God tightened his grip on this embattled older woman once more.

In Ruth's faith declaration, not only was God establishing one young woman's courage, He was offering a desperately needed reminder of truth in response to the gnawing questions of another. Though Naomi's grip was slipping God's hold on her was firm and steadfast, as steadfast as the mind of this young woman who was determined to walk this out by her side. Like Ruth, Naomi's life held a beauty and a destiny that God cared about, even more than she did. He was not about to let her give up on His dreams for her now.

Consider the emotional turmoil Naomi must have been experiencing as she spoke these words,

> *But Naomi said, "Return home, my daughters. Why would you come with me? Am I going to have any more sons, who could become your husbands? Return home, my daughters; I am too old to have another husband. Even if I thought there was still hope for me—even if I had a husband tonight and then gave birth to sons— would you wait until they grew up? Would you remain unmarried for them? No, my daughters. It is more bitter for me than for you, because the Lord's hand has turned against me!"* (Ruth 1:11-13 NIV)

The essence of Naomi's words was that she had lost all hope. Too much had happened. She had lost too many precious loved ones, cried too many tears. She had been knocked down too many times just to struggle to her feet again. She had tried too hard to figure out how to make things work amidst their devastating circumstances. It was no wonder she was ready to give up because she had been depending so much on her own resources. As she came to the end of this road she was done. She was all out of answers and felt like she had no hope left at all.

The word translated "hope" in this passage is not the word that is most often translated as "hope" in the Old Testament. No, this word has an unusually descriptive meaning. This is the word, "tiqvah" in the Hebrew language which means "a cord."[19] It was as if Naomi was saying, "I have nothing left to hold onto. I am not only at the end of my rope, I stand here completely out of rope! I have nothing left to cling to." She never knew she had a God who could be her husband.

She had forgotten about His unusual capacity for extravagant love and had let His miraculous provision slip through her fingers long ago. So she uses this particular word to give those girls, and us, a picture of what it looks like when you know that you are losing your grip, when you have no more strength with which to get back up again. Yet God was speaking to her, through Ruth, the same message He offers us today. "There is always a hope available to you. You can hold onto Me. I am your Strength. I am the One you can cling to when there is nothing else in your life to hold onto anymore." As Ruth spoke of that hope, God was inviting Naomi to trust Him once more, to take that chance to believe again, to find hope against all hope in the One who is Hope, the Only True Hope of His people, the One who still held onto her and would never let her go.

Interestingly enough we find this same word in another story involving a woman in a desperate situation who made a radical choice to trust in God. Her story is found in the book of Joshua. The circumstances bear some ironic similarities to this story in Ruth. This woman too was about to have to leave her home and go on a journey that she never expected to take. Her town was under siege by an enemy nation. She was surrounded by an invasion of God's people into her world and she was not one of them. Yet when their spies came over the wall upon which her house was built, Rahab seized that opportunity to find hope in their God and to cling to His goodness. This is how the incident is recounted,

> *Before the spies lay down for the night, she went up to the roof and said to them "I know that the Lord has given this land to you and that a great fear of you has fallen on us, so that all who live in this country are melting in fear because of you. We have heard how the Lord dried up the water of the Red Sea for you when you came out of Egypt, and what you did to Sihon and Og, the two kings of the Amorites east of the Jordan, whom you completely destroyed. When we heard of it, our hearts melted and everyone's courage failed because of you, for the Lord your God is God in heaven above and on the earth below. Now then, please swear to me by the Lord that you will show kindness to my family, because I have shown kindness to you. Give me a sure sign that you will spare the lives of my father and mother, my brothers and sisters, and all who belong to them, and that you will save us from death."*

"Our lives for your lives!" the men assured her. "If you don't tell what we are doing, we will treat you kindly and faithfully when the LORD gives us the land."

So she let them down by a rope through the window, for the house she lived in was part of the city wall. Now she had said to them, "Go to the hills so the pursuers will not find you. Hide yourselves there three days until they return, and then go on your way."

The men said to her, "This oath you made us swear will not be binding on us unless, when we enter the land, you have tied this scarlet cord in the window through which you let us down, and unless you have brought your father and mother, your brothers and all your family into your house. If anyone goes outside your house into the street, his blood will be on his own head; we will not be responsible. As for anyone who is in the house with you, his blood will be on our head if a hand is laid on him. But if you tell what we are doing, we will be released from the oath you made us swear."

"Agreed," she replied. "Let it be as you say." So she sent them away and they departed. And she tied the scarlet cord in the window (Joshua 2:8-21 NIV).

That same word translated "hope" in Naomi's story is literally the "cord" of Rahab's.[20] In Joshua 2:21 Rahab's hope hung on that scarlet cord, the "tiqvah," that she displayed out her window, symbolizing her hope for a relationship with a God she hardly knew Who held out a promise of a better life and brought it right to her door through His people. If she could only find within her the courage to cling to that cord she would be safe.

Perhaps the most beautiful thing about her courage, surely the most profound discovery we might make in comparing these two passages in which this Hebrew word is found, is that Ruth was destined to meet a man named Boaz later in her story, who will become what the Bible calls "her kinsman redeemer." Disney would undoubtedly label him Prince Charming and, for us, he will not only become the hero of this romantic tale but, more importantly, a picture of our God. In an exquisite plot twist, Boaz is Rahab's son. Though she had previously lived her life as a prostitute among an ungodly people, this desperate woman found the strength, the courage, and the hope to cling to the One True God. Her uncanny faith would defy her circumstances and pave the way for another outsider to be brought into the family of God years later. How amazing that, by God's design, the very man that Ruth would one day stumble upon, in a field where she came to gather leftover grain, just happened to have a mom who had also come from a foreign land and a pagan nation to live among God's people. How incredible that this man, who would come to love and accept Ruth as His beautiful bride, already had a special love in his heart for a woman who had found the courage to cling to the gracious, loving heart of God and defy the destiny that her circumstances would have dictated. Boaz was predisposed to welcome Ruth, to treat her fairly. God knew that. That was His idea. He conceived all these details in His heart long before they played out.

There was an unseen hope waiting for Naomi and Ruth if they pressed past the obstacles and kept moving closer to God. As Ruth chose to cling to Naomi she could have never dreamed of what God had planned, had already done on her behalf, to set this beautiful story in motion. She was simply hanging on to God. He was her hope, this was the cord that would lead her to His heart. God had a beautiful story waiting to unfold, not only for Ruth, but Naomi as well. In Ruth's decision, in her words of belief and hope and courage, God was inviting each of them to hang on a little tighter, to refuse to stop believing that God's unlimited power and unusual passion would lead each of them to their glorious destiny.

Something incredible happens in the life of a woman who has become convinced of God's passionate love for her, of God's capacity to know her, of His power to release her to live her destiny, of His purpose for her to experience the life of her dreams. God orchestrates a process to establish a rare and unusual courage in each of our lives, unafraid of how circumstances will press hard against it, because He is committed to seeing our conviction strengthened and firm. Once that courage is cultivated, after layer upon layer of belief is established in the testing, there is a freedom in that woman's life that cannot be defeated nor denied. This is what we find in Ruth's story.

> *When Naomi realized that Ruth was determined to go with her,*
> *she stopped urging her* (Ruth 1:18 NIV).

This word translated "realized" seems so much stronger in the Hebrew language because it goes beyond Naomi's mere awareness to say that she was able to see, she was able to inspect, she actually experienced Ruth's determination.[21] No wonder the writer penned it just that way since she literally felt the tug of Ruth's ironclad grip pulling on her garments. Naomi got it. Ruth's determination could not be denied.

Know this, there is a definitive goal to all this conditioning. When God takes you through this process of building such tangible courage into your life, it shows. You speak differently. Your words are anointed with a wisdom born, not only of experience, but of an expectation that experience has cultivated. You act differently. You hold on to a hope that others cannot see. You walk differently. You carry with you a dignity and beauty that is only possessed by a woman who knows who she is, who knows that she is loved, and has been set free to pursue her own destiny. It becomes obvious to everyone around you. Others "realize" because they experience your determination. You are a warrior woman. You are a daughter of the King. The impact of your personal, vibrant, intimate connection with God will forever change you. You will have become undeniably brave.

In a later scene in the movie, *I Am Sam*, there is another late night knock upon the door. This time, the daddy, Sam, awakens to find the foster mother with his sleeping child draped across her shoulder waiting to see him. The woman explains through tears of realization,

> "She's okay…she fell asleep in the car…and I was going to turn back and tuck her in, in her room, you know that I, in her room that I made for her, 'cause I tried to make a really nice room for her, but I was afraid she'd wake up at our house and want to come home…I have to apologize to you, Sam, because I was going to tell that judge that I could give Lucy the kind of love she never had but I can't say that, because I would be lying…see you in court tomorrow. Save me a seat, Sam, on your side. Okay?"[22]

Certainly this must have been how Naomi felt as she watched Ruth grab hold of her with both hands, to say "I can't go back now. I just can't turn away from this God you have. I have to go with you to Bethlehem!" Like this foster mother in the movie, Naomi had to realize that, more than anything else, this girl she loved needed the greater love of her Father, needed the peculiar relationship that she could only have with Him. Recognizing His beautiful act of release that was unfolding in Ruth's life, she was able to walk this experience out with her. She was able to see that nothing else would ever be able to satisfy the cry of this young woman's heart except for this powerful intimate connection with the One who knew her and loved her so well. His love had taken Ruth through this harrowing process, given her this extraordinary courage that left her clinging with both hands to what she had tasted through Naomi. Only this God, who had chosen her for love, could take her all the way to all He had planned for her. It was so obvious, even Naomi, though immersed in her own bitter disappointment, could ignore it no longer. Touched by the passionate display of Ruth's craving, she had no choice but to relent and take her hand. Now as they turned to make their way together toward Bethlehem, this dramatic display of courage must have impacted even the grown-cold heart of an embittered woman, must have planted a tiny seed of believing, must have rekindled a little spark of hope that would smolder until it was fully ablaze within her too. Perhaps it was not yet strong, like Ruth's. Yet it was something she would carry away from this moment and take with her on the journey, something she could hold to, a tiny thread that would lead her back to the place where she had always belonged and give her too the courage to hang on.

We must never forget that this is not only Ruth's story. For the saga unfolding in Ruth is a foreshadowing of your journey and mine. The Maker of heaven and earth put on skin to walk into your world already predisposed to love a girl like you like crazy. He is wooing you now to abandon all that can never satisfy your deepest longing for this radical journey that will bring you ever closer to The Only One Who Can. He is unafraid of any disaster that might threaten your destiny whether it is a financial crisis, the loss of a job, the death of a spouse or a parent or a child, shattering news, a crumbling business, family dysfunction, addiction, abuse, rejection or fear, coping mechanisms that leave you exhausted, embarrassing failures, betrayal, emotional baggage or a messed up church experience that leaves you disillusioned and alone, everything from a disappointing set back to sheer exhaustion or the endless distractions that fight to keep you from really knowing His heart. No matter what sort of accusations or troubles surround you, they will become God's tools to refine you. He allows each struggle to strengthen your grip. He will never abandon your story. He will hold you when life gets messy and stand waiting beyond every heartbreak, poised to enfold you in His extraordinary love. When at last you rest in this sweeter embrace you will notice that you are different, forever changed by a deeper knowing that assures you that His promise to Jeremiah still rings true for you...

Today I have made you a fortified city, an iron pillar and a bronze wall to stand against the whole land—against the kings of Judah, its officials, its priests and the people of the land. They will fight against you but will not overcome you, for I am with you and will rescue you," declares the Lord (Jeremiah 1:18-19 NIV).

So it is at this crossroad in Ruth's story that God presents us with this second question, "Will you believe when believing gets hard?" and, how you answer will make the difference between a flimsy faith that falters or an established faith that endures. By divine design, the path to your destiny is strewn with obstacles. The enemy who seeks your destruction will not let you go without a fight. Yet once you have answered this question with a determined "yes," you will welcome that challenge, knowing that each struggle has been ordained to condition your faith, to strengthen your resolve, to get you to the life of God's dreams for you. Run to the battle, echoing the words of David, spoken as he stared into the face of a giant who had kept soldiers with flimsier faith paralyzed by fear,

"There is only one strong, safe, and secure place for me; it's in God alone and I love Him! He's the one who gives me strength and skill for the battle. He's my shelter of love and my fortress of faith, who wraps Himself around me as a secure shield. I hide myself in this One who subdues enemies before me" (Psalms 144:1-2 The Passion Translation).

It is at this place, this spiritual milestone where you make up your mind to believe when believing gets hard, that the journey to everything you long for comes face to face with the warrior that God has hidden within you. She runs courageously toward the battle, determined to fight for every ounce of the freedom that is rightfully hers.

Chapter 3

Your grace is relentless affection
independent of performance-a love that
we are not powerful enough to change.

— *WM. PAUL YOUNG, CROSSROADS*

SURPRISED BY LOVE

It has been 40 years since the day I first met my husband, David. I still vividly remember every detail of that jaw dropping moment when he first caught my eye. It was a Sunday morning in midwinter as 1978 spilled into 1979. I simply walked into my college and career Sunday school class on what I thought was just an ordinary Sunday morning. Hardly aware of any distinction among the group who normally met me there, I made my way to my regular seat on a couch that rested against the right hand wall. Then, there he was, seated directly across from me wearing a taupe pin-striped suit that bridged the gap beautifully between his curly dark brown hair and freckled-kissed fair skin. I found myself immediately drawn to this quiet soul almost as if I already knew the million little things I would come to adore about him. He looked across at me with this naturally shy half grin and I was completely taken by everything about him.

I guess if I had to single out the one characteristic that absolutely stopped me in mid-motion as I set my things on the floor at my feet, I would say it was a pair of the most alluring eyes I had ever noticed. Those eyes seemed to reflect a certain softness, an unusual sensitivity, even a daring playfulness. There was a message behind those eyes that seemed to carry an invitation, almost a dare, saying to at least one girl in that room, "There is more to be discovered and explored than what you see on the surface. This is a deep well but, if you are up for the challenge, I just might let you draw out what is hidden within."

Suffice it to say, I wanted a drink from that well. From our initial encounter I was totally intrigued by what I saw reflected in David's eyes as they captured mine unexpectedly from across that room. Now, after 40 years, his eyes still hold that same enchantment for me. I could not number how often I have looked across other rooms at other moments to catch a gaze that makes everything seem alright, no matter what kind of chaos is unfolding around me, or to dance around that familiar twinkle of amusement we share that long ago stopped having to bother with words.

It still took an agonizing three and a half months from that day for David to ask me out on our first date. This failure to make the most of such an incredible opportunity was in no way attributable to any lack of effort or enthusiasm on my part. I smiled at him, took up idle conversation with him at every opportunity, did everything, short of having my desire to date him tattooed on my forearm, but he would only offer that mischievous tilt of his head, that look of pure playfulness or some other polite but friendly response that left me interested but wondering if I would ever get my chance to win his heart, wondering, until the long awaited phone call finally came on a Monday night in April.

I was sitting at home, watching TV, when I picked up the phone to hear his voice on the other end of the line. He wasted only a moment on pleasantries before asking me if I would like to accompany him to see a play on the following Saturday night. In a matter of minutes I had covered my responsibilities to work with our youth group on that Saturday and broken a date with another guy who did not have those eyes, so that I would be free to say "yes" to the invitation I recognized so many months before in the soulful glance that I had been unable to forget.

When Saturday came there was magic in the air as I prepared for our date and waited for David's arrival. I chose to wear a lavender and beige flowered dress that I would never be caught dead in now but, at the time, was stunningly fashionable. He pulled into my driveway in his mom's sparkling white Ford Granada with maroon leather seats which he borrowed for the special occasion. As he stepped out of the car and approached the house I could see, through the slit in the shutters on my bedroom window, that he was wearing a navy pin-striped suit this time and looked so incredibly handsome that it was all I could do to wait for the doorbell to ring before making a mad dash to meet him. Once it rang, I held my breath, shot one last glance at myself in the mirror to make sure every hair was in place, and did my best to stifle all my inner hysteria as I greeted him with a calmness that showed not even a hint of the overload of emotion that had been building over weeks of anticipation.

We drove to the Westside Dinner Theater to see the musical, *Oklahoma*. On the way, the car was filled with the normal small talk and first date jitters, punctuated by those awkward pauses familiar to anyone whose mind has ever gone blank under pressure. After what seemed like a moment and an eternity all at the same time, we pulled into the parking lot in front of the theater. As we entered, the hostess promptly showed us to a table reserved for us by name. David pulled out my chair and, as I took my seat, I looked down to find a large crystal pig figurine resting in the center of my plate. As I witnessed this incredible gesture you have to understand that this object did not say "PIG" to me – it said, "I took the time to get to know who you are, I value what you care about, I celebrate you, I delight in the woman I see sitting before me." Now you have to admit that is quite a mouthful for an inanimate object, crystal or not.

To an outside observer I probably appeared to be just an average eighteen year old girl having dinner with a good looking twenty-three year old guy. Except for the fact that I had just received a pig on my plate, I am quite sure that it seemed like this was the same sort of date that a zillion other young people my age were probably participating in on that typical Saturday night in April. I was eating dinner, watching a play, making nervous conversation, and trying not to stare too much or allow even a trace of the food to get stuck between my front teeth. To anyone who might have noticed, it probably seemed like nothing out of the ordinary was going on at all.

What that observer could not see, what he had no way of knowing, is that this was not at all the casual occurrence it may have appeared to be. That night was a dramatic turning point in my story. I had come to the table looking for something, hoping for someone who would take the time to really know me, who would celebrate who I am, honor the life I have chosen, support the things I was striving for, protect and cherish all the things that really matter to me. So as we walked into that dinner theater, as David pulled out my chair and I sat down, before I had any time to make a great impression, before I said anything particularly witty or cast my own alluring look in his direction, before I had taken a single bite or done anything at all to win it or earn it or make it happen, as I glanced down at my plate and embraced this thoughtful gift, I realized that precisely what I was looking for, what I longed for and dreamed of, all I hoped someday I would be good enough to win, was already waiting there!

That experience is quite similar to Ruth's as we pick up her story to find her and her mother-in-law, Naomi, preparing to step foot on

Bethlehem soil. After making the incredibly gutsy decision to leave her homeland of Moab, Ruth had opted to set out on this arduous journey and embrace this vision of a different life than the one her godless surroundings could afford. Our examination of her decision, to leave the only life she had known to move to where she knew God was, presented each of us with a question, "Will you believe to the point that it changes your story?" In His brilliance, God had allowed Ruth's vision to be pressed against and challenged from the onset. Yet with each challenge, God strengthened her grip, giving her layer upon layer of new conviction as she faced every word of opposition, refused every chance to turn around. God used the example of her testing and determination to stir yet another question in each of our hearts, "Will you believe when believing gets hard?"

Ruth's categorical answer was "yes" as she literally clung to this vision, refusing to let go unless death pried her hands and heart from her earthly pursuit of God's beautiful dreams for her life. Now, having pushed past the obstacles, I can just imagine some of the questions that might have flooded Ruth's mind as she neared the end of her journey to this new home, questions that probably bear a resemblance to those I wrestled with on the way to the playhouse that night in the car: "Will I make a good first impression? Will I know the right words to say? Will I stumble? Is rejection waiting? Did I make the right decision to come? Is there any way that this journey could lead me all the way to true love?" Despite any doubts or insecurities that might have accompanied Ruth as they traveled toward Bethlehem, she and Naomi received a hearty welcome as they reached the edge of town,

> *So the two women went on until they came to Bethlehem. When they arrived in Bethlehem, the whole town was stirred because of them, and the women exclaimed, "Can this be Naomi?" "Don't call me Naomi, " she told them. "Call me Mara, because the Almighty has made my life very bitter. I went away full, but the Lord has brought me back empty. Why call me Naomi? The Lord has afflicted me; the Almighty has brought misfortune upon me." So Naomi returned from Moab accompanied by Ruth the Moabite, her daughter-in-law, arriving in Bethlehem as the barley harvest was beginning* (Ruth 1:19-22 NIV).

Just to look up and see those fields, ripe and ready for harvest, must have been like finding a crystal pig upon your plate at the beginning of a first date. As these two hungry travelers inched ever closer to their respective destinies this was like God running out to meet them, welcoming them with open arms, letting them know He knew them, understood their every inner longing, even before they arrived. Everything Ruth must have hoped to somehow win, all she came willing to work for and earn by the sweat of her brow, was boldly on display before she did a single thing to make it happen. The barley harvest was ready and waiting. Truly this road had led her to her Bread of Life, the answer to her deepest questions and longings, the One who would feed her and fill her and finally love her the way she always dreamed of being loved. Having been driven by their hunger to make this journey, can you imagine the exhilaration of seeing that harvest waiting in the field?

In the agrarian culture described in this passage, times of plowing, planting and praying for rain to water the crops were all significant but the prize the farmer sought, the desired result of all his labor was, of course, the harvest. It was the answer to all the unspoken, yet never forgotten, questions: Would God provide? Would He look upon us with His favor? Would He send enough rain to cause the crops to grow? Would He meet me at the place of my most basic need? As you think of what that first glimpse of a ready harvest must have meant to Ruth and Naomi, can you identify specifically what such a waiting harvest would look like and mean to you? What are you are hoping to find as you make your move toward God? What does your soul crave? Even if you have never put it into words, or truly struggle to do so now, you can be sure that God already knows and began planting the seeds of what will feed that hunger long before you planned to take this journey. It was no accident that Ruth and Naomi arrived at the edge of the town at this moment of celebration. God's willingness always stands waiting for those who will come seeking, ready to meet their trust with a feast of provision. If you will step out and take this journey toward His heart, your beautiful harvest will already be there as you arrive at your destination.

The very first grain to ripen was the barley. So this very beginning of the barley harvest was God's reemergence as Israel's Provider, His reestablishment of Bethlehem as His "House of Bread." Yet despite ten long years of waiting, and with no regard for their prevailing hunger, the people of God would not rush to the table. The Old Testament law instructed the Hebrew farmer to bring the very first ripened grain, gathered from various plants throughout his field, as a first fruits offering to God. This offering would be waved before the Lord, as a display of gratitude and celebration, as an expression of hope that this was only the beginning, that there would be more, so much more, to come. Every man, woman, boy and girl put their faith dramatically on display as they brought forth this offering of their first fruit to God.

So Ruth and Naomi arrived to find an abundant demonstration of the gracious heart of God coupled with a boisterous expression of His people's trust and worship. As the prodigal's father runs to meet his son at the first sight of his approach, God greeted Ruth and Naomi with barley fields ripe and ready and a city alive with expectancy. The barley harvest, the first taste of God's blessing, was received as just the tip of the iceberg. The Hebrew people opened their hands in a sacrifice of praise, thanking Jehovah, in advance, for the feast that would bring an end to their famine. The sights, the smells, the sounds must have washed over these two women as a sweet affirmation of their decision to come home to Him as well. This first glimpse of the grain coupled with the atmosphere of ecstatic gratitude, was only the beginning of what God had in store for them under the shadow of His wings of protection. This place to which He had wooed them would be the seat of His divine provision and the backdrop for His demonstrative passion. This was Bethlehem restored to her greatness, once again manifesting what she was created to be from the beginning, God's table set before His children and those grafted in by His grace, the fullness of God's passion poured out on His bride in His Bountiful House of Bread.

So Ruth and Naomi had at last arrived, and while everything Ruth was experiencing must have seemed new and different, Bethlehem, and all that was happening in her midst, must have had a bittersweet familiarity to Naomi. This was where she and her husband met, married, had children and made a life. For Naomi this was a different kind of homecoming with a whole different set of expectations and anxieties. Naomi had not gone so far, just far enough, just outside the boundaries of trusting God. So it was almost like she was trying to fend off the gossip by putting it out there herself, as she was greeted by those who knew her from so many years ago, when life was sweeter and the storms had not yet worn upon her disposition. Naomi's words betrayed how misfortune had distorted her perception of God. Now, though she still recognized His power, she believed His heart to be not only harsh, but even cruel.

Naomi's cranky introduction back into the Hebrew community that had once been her home clearly illustrates how we can easily miscast God in the mold of those who surround us. If our parents were abusive, we may tend to see God as angry and impossible to placate. An earthly Dad who was distant or weak, may cause us to picture God as uninvolved or feeble. Within a legalistic church culture we may develop a perception of God as demanding and hard to please, only caring that we continue to live under a prescribed set of rules and prohibitions. Each of us have probably had Naomi-like moments when we have allowed circumstances, an experience we have suffered through, or people who have dealt with us in a cruel manner, to mischaracterize the heart of God. Yet, given the chance to experience a healthy dose of kindness, unconditional love and acceptance, we are set free to experience the graciousness and compassion of God as He truly is.

No matter what sort of expectations Ruth might have brought with her from Moab, the atmosphere and culture of Bethlehem now provided her a chance to engage with God in the fullness of His beautiful truth. It did not take long for Ruth to recognize what a new beginning this could be for both her mother-in-law and her. Living among the Ephrathites, "the fruitful ones," heightened Ruth's anticipation and she put her hopes into words as the second chapter of Ruth opens,

> *And Ruth the Moabitess said to Naomi, "Let me go to the fields and pick up the leftover grain behind anyone in whose eyes I find favor." Naomi said to her, "Go ahead, my daughter"* (Ruth 2:2 NIV).

It would have been so natural for a girl from Moab to expect little of God. The false deity worshipped in her homeland was thought of as feckless and inept, demanding and cruel. Yet despite Naomi's frailty, God's presence within her had proven more powerful than her darkness. Naomi had walked into Ruth's world carrying the hope of Jehovah, a mere flicker of the One Who is the Light of the World. That Light reflected in Naomi, as imperfectly as the water reflects the sun, was enough to push back the darkness of Ruth's culture and open Ruth's eyes to a whole new reality. His gentle whisper wooed Ruth to step into that reality and embrace it as her own story. Ruth began to see herself as the bride of a Lover whose nature was one of extraordinary life-altering passion. Brought to this home she had never known by His heart's invitation, then welcomed by further evidence of a faith well-placed, Ruth had every incentive to step outside of her comfort zone fueled by hope, an untarnished expectation of a God who was completely unusual, "other than" anything she had ever experienced within the empty and enslaving religion of her upbringing.

Living in intimate relationship with this One who is Faithful and True will forever change your expectation of what He has for you to experience. Being set free from the skepticism and cynicism that disappointment always breeds will change who you are at the core of your being and change how you respond, what you choose, and what you expect to experience. Ruth now woke up believing God would be good because she saw His goodness in the grain that waved her into Bethlehem. Ruth now expected God to be kind because Naomi's kindness had nurtured her heart and brought her along on this journey back home. Ruth was free to accept the concept of a gracious God as she saw Him bring an end to years of famine and abundantly provide for His children once again. Her expectations were now shaped by who she had begun to tangibly experience as the One True God of the Hebrew people. Ruth woke up that morning ready to fully embrace what this God, Who is altogether lovely, would beautifully and bountifully pour into her outstretched hands.

On the surface, Ruth's words reveal some basic elements of her character, that she was willing to work, that she was neither lazy nor passive, that she was ready to get her hands dirty and bare the brunt of the heat of the sun to make sure their basic physical needs were provided. Just the fact that Ruth came to Naomi with this idea suggests that Ruth had a submissive spirit, showing respect in seeking her mother-in-law's blessing on her plans for that day. Her words also illustrate that Ruth was a woman of vision, that she was intentional in her actions, willing to take the required risks to see her dreams come true.

It is obvious that Ruth would not be satisfied to stay behind in the comfort of their home. Otherwise, why would she have ever left Moab in the first place? She would never settle for a life of destitution now that she knew she lived in a land that held such promise. Ruth refused to hide behind walls of self-protection and isolation. She took personal responsibility, to do what was within her power to do, to create the life that she desired and even envisioned as hers to obtain. She was clear about what she wanted and, by faith, determined to pursue it. This was not a young woman who was merely looking to get out of the house, she was going out with a purpose, with a specific goal in her view, and that goal was to pick up the leftover grain. This intention reveals that she was willing to do whatever it took to position herself to receive what she believed God intended to provide. She was neither proud nor rebellious about how to get there or what His provision must look like in order to meet her expectations. Ruth had a servant's heart. She felt neither entitled nor reluctant to share.

Ruth was also willing to properly align herself with the authority that was set up within her new community. You see, the system, already established within the Hebrew society of that day, was for foreigners who came to live among the people of God to be allowed to walk behind the reapers and pick up the extra grain that was left behind. So Ruth was not saying, "I want to get my needs met in another way" but rather she was willing to receive what she needed in the way that had been instituted to provide it. Her humility enabled her to operate within this system that was already in place, putting herself in a position to receive her sustenance from God and to trust Him completely with the outcome.

Beyond all that, her willingness to go out into the fields to work all day for a little bit of grain reveals most obviously, and perhaps most significantly, that Ruth was hungry. She was willing to spend the whole day out in the heat, expending her energy among people she did not even know. What would drive a woman to do that? Could it be she simply had nothing else to do? I think it was pure, undeniable craving.

What about you? Is there a hunger deep within your soul that can no longer be ignored? Have you reached a point where you are desperate for more of God? In the absence of desperation, you might deny your hunger or settle for less. You could procrastinate your gleaning a little longer. You could turn and walk away from the most significant moment in your life. Not Ruth, she was desperate. True desperation refuses to be pushed back or ignored. Desperation is relentless in the pursuit of the satisfaction of whatever it craves. Ruth asked to go, when she could have stayed home, because she was desperately hungry.

Yet bread alone could never satisfy Ruth's inner longing. The last part of this verse reveals that Ruth was looking for a little soul food as well. Her intention was to gather some barley "behind anyone in whose eyes I find favor." Ruth was hungry for more than bread. Her expectation had expanded beyond anything she had ever experienced in her homeland of Moab. That vision that God had planted within her had given birth to hope, not only for the satisfaction of her physical needs, but of her emotional and spiritual needs as well. She now believed that things would go well, that something good would happen. She did not say, "I fully expect to come home empty-handed. I am sure nobody will like me. These strangers will take the best for themselves. I will see what I can scrape up, even though it probably will not be enough." No, Ruth's words reflected her inner transformation and revealed that she believed that someone would be kind, that someone would choose to share with her out of sheer generosity, that God had brought her all this way to set her up for success. She was heading out looking for the place where she believed the blessing of God awaited her. She was looking for more than bread, Ruth was looking for favor.

Each one of us shares that desire. We too are hungry for more than bread. You may go to the office thinking you are just working there for money, perhaps driven by some sense of purpose, maybe just trying to get by the best you can. You may get up every morning and do whatever it takes to get your family through another day, thinking you have no other motive than their well-being or your survival. It does not really matter why you think you go where you go or do what you do, underneath it all there is this basic human desire that says, "I would love to find some favor." We hardly state it just that way. Favor is not a word we use in our everyday vernacular but, as we discover more fully what is meant by this term, I think we will find a great deal in Ruth's pursuit of it with which we can identify.

The Complete Hebrew Word Study Dictionary gives us a great start by identifying the meaning of this word translated "favor" as "favor."[23] Really? Oh, thanks for that clarification! Fortunately, the definition does not end there. The scholars go on to include additional words like "kindness, grace, loveliness, charm, preciousness."[24] As I read those words I realize so readily that I want some of all of those essential ingredients of healthy, fulfilling and fun experiences. In fact, as I go out to feed my other hunger, I am constantly driven by a desire for the very things these words describe. I want to encounter kindness in the people I meet. I want to find a place where I get more than I deserve, where someone is gracious to me. I want to go where someone creates and releases beauty in my life and recognizes the beauty that is already there. Beyond all that, Webster's dictionary defines the word, "charm" with the word, "magic."[25] We all want some magic in our moments, to experience miracles, and hear music, and see beauty in the midst of all that we experience! That is why little girls pretend to be princesses and little boys, superheroes. We are born hungry, for much more than bread! We want the magic that comes as we hear someone precious to us say, "I love you!" We want fireworks to light up the sky! We want to feel like what we do and who we are is valuable to somebody else in this world. We want to know that we are cherished and held as something precious and rare. As I have come to realize what favor looks like, I have come to understand that I go out seeking favor every day, that, like Ruth, I am hungry for bread and so much more. How about you?

I think that is why God tells us in Deuteronomy that *"man doesn't live by bread alone but by every Word that proceeds from the mouth of God"* (Deuteronomy 8:3 NIV). People can starve with food on their table and leftovers to spare, if they never hear someone say the words, do the things, that communicate what will satiate the hunger of a human heart. Users become trapped in a ravenous cycle of addiction in search of that elusive fix. This insatiable love hunger fuels strings of unfulfilling and unhealthy relationships that only deepen the wounds and intensify the pang of unfulfilled yearning. Homeless hearts try to chase away insecurity on treadmills, on websites or behind mountains of debt that will bury them alive under a heap of regret, when all they ever wanted flows freely and purely from the heart of God who is waiting to love us. We are a hungry people.

Thus, the theater of war is created. We get wounded before we even know we are in the battle, at the specific place of that deepest craving, by careless or harsh words and confounding or hurtful circumstances. The onslaught began on the day we were born. As a result, the very hope that was so alive in Ruth, this expectancy of finding favor and bread and experiencing the magic we were made for, all too often gets buried under mounting disappointments. We daily contend with an enemy whose agenda is murder. Most likely he fired the first shot at our hearts long ago and then reloaded to wound us again and again. While we were bleeding out, he whispered lies to us about God and about us, giving lots of supporting evidence for those lies in an effort to kill our expectancy, to destroy our dreams, to convince us that, all that happily ever after hope may come true for some folks, but surely not for us. We end up walking into our fields each day paralyzed with fear or limping from a landmine, loaded down with all of the extra baggage the enemy has heaped upon us, questioning whether or not God really is good, wrestling with whether or not He could actually accept us, much less love us, and wondering if He will really give us what we so desperately need. That is satan's step one in his strategy to shut you and me down completely.

This sly digression of believing can be as subtle and simple as this conversation depicted in a scene from one of my favorite movies, *Sleepless in Seattle,*

Annie: I heard it. This kid calls up and says "My dad needs a wife." And this shrinkette practically forces the guy onto the phone and says, "Do you want to talk about it?" And he says, "No, as a matter of fact, I don't." And then suddenly, for no reason at all, he begins to talk about how much he loved his wife and how he just fell in love with her, like he was just one of those cows in Michigan.

Becky: What cows in Michigan?

Annie: It was on sixty minutes. There were these cows that got zapped by stray voltage...no one knows why. Maybe it was Wisconsin. (Sigh) But anyway, I was listening to him talk about how much he loved his wife and suddenly I was crying. It's like what happens when I see those phone company ads. I don't have to see the whole thing, just the part where the daughter gives the mother the refrigerator...

(**Annie and Becky in unison**) with the big red bow.

Becky: Yes, or the Polaroid commercial. The two five year olds at their grandfather's birthday party...

Annie: they're making the album...

Becky: With all the glue...that kills me! (chuckles) **You should write something about this.**

Annie: About what?

Becky: Whatever it is.

Keith: I'll tell you what it is. Two thousand women calling a radio station for a husband. There are a lot of desperate women out there looking for love.

Wyatt: Especially over a certain age.

Keith: *Do you know that it's easier to be killed by a terrorist than it is to get married over the age of forty?*

Annie: That's not true. That statistic is not true.

Becky: That's right. It's not true. But it feels true.

Wyatt: It feels true because it is true.

Annie: There's practically a whole book on why that statistic is not true.

Wyatt: Calm down you brought it up.

Annie: I did not, Wyatt. Did you even read that book?

Wyatt: Did anybody read that book all the way through?[26]

Can you see how easily hope can devolve into skepticism as, first, a simple seed of doubt is planted. "Did you know it's easier to get killed by a terrorist..." With that, hope is wounded. Expectation is stripped away and replaced with a lie. Evidence is offered to support that lie, and, perhaps most significantly, "nobody even reads the book" that explains that this lie is not true. What a profound loss! There is an incredible book within which page after page depicts our Hero as good and His love for us, unwavering. The author of the greatest autobiography of all time calls you His bride from cover to cover. To our utter amazement His love is not based on a single thing we have done and it can not be erased by anything we do. While you and I were still sinners, total disasters, hopelessly broken, God reached out to love us, so much that He chose to die to buy back every single thing we have lost in this brutal war. He took our punishment and offers us His life in exchange. He thinks you are beautiful just as you are, right where you are. He desires an intimate relationship with you now, not when you get your act together. The Old Testament prophet, Zephaniah, tells us that He sings over you with His love (Zephaniah 3:17 NIV). Suffice it to say, He is just flat out crazy about you!

No wonder our vicious enemy uses all kinds of smoke and mirrors to distract us from reading that book. Believing in God's perfect love will make us fearless. A daily drenching in God's extravagant passion will make us dangerous. So satan employs tremendous cunning to pry that truth from our hands, our minds and our hearts. He knows that there is no denying the power of a woman who walks in the dignity of the knowledge of just how deeply she is loved.

Yet, despite satan's schemes to turn her back and wreck her story, as chapter 2 begins, we find that Ruth is still on course. As she heads out the door, having survived the deaths of her young husband, her brother-in-law and her father-in-law, now living in a land where nobody knows her nor has any reason to take an interest in her, she sets out to walk into the field of a stranger believing she will find favor, convinced that magic will meet her there.

Oddly, Ruth's hopeful attitude reminds me of all the shoppers who get up before the sun to stand outside in the cold, in the dark, waiting for the doors to open for a Black Friday sale. They do so because of what they expect to find there. Perhaps a friend, who has personally experienced such a sale, tells them the story of her dramatic savings. Maybe these diehard pursuers of bargains read an ad included in the newspaper on Thanksgiving Day and believe every word. No matter the source, something or someone creates an expectation that motivates their actions. So they say "yes" to the invitation. They set the alarm clock, make whatever sacrifice is necessary to take advantage of this opportunity, because they believe it will be worth it. They believe something good, maybe even life changing, awaits them. That is the kind of expectation that prompted Ruth to get up early and go out to glean. Perhaps someone told her about their experience. Maybe the Bethlehem Times ran a headline that gleaners were welcome that day. However the enticement was packaged, Ruth went believing that she would find bread and so much more.

Notice Ruth said "behind anyone in whose eyes I find favor." She did not say, "I want God to meet me in a field in just the way I have imagined." She reached up to God with an open mind, open hands and an open heart, willing to trust Him with the details. Though she was expecting His divine provision, she left lots of leeway concerning just what the delivery of that provision would look like.

Our lives intersect with Ruth's in this place of our desires. Deep within our souls we share her hunger for more than bread. Never deny your heart's desire. It is perfectly alright that you feel the way you do. Naomi knew that. She said, "Go ahead, my daughter." My paraphrase to you, "You go, girl!" Neither stifle nor deny your hunger for favor. Let yourself hope for, even dream about magical happy endings, because God placed that longing within your heart. If you will own that desire, if you will refuse to be talked out of what you were made to crave, that is the beginning of experiencing the provision God stands ready to pour out on you as you seek Him wherever, however, He wants to be found. Stay hungry! Stay expectant! Walk into your world each day looking for God to show up in incredible ways and He will.

God promised through the Old Testament prophet, Jeremiah, "*You will seek me and find me when you seek me with all your heart*" (Jeremiah 29:13 NIV). If you let disappointment or loss or ridicule rob you of your hope, cruelly crush your craving, you will miss the beautiful revelation that God has waiting for you to discover. With Ruth's decision to head out that day God whispers another question for you and me to answer, "Will you believe that God already loves you like no one else has ever loved you?" Stifling your expectations,

abandoning your hope, will inevitably cause you to settle for less. It reminds me of how the character of Annie Reed in *Sleepless in Seattle*[27] almost settles for Walter, her very nice, highly allergic and unexciting fiancé. Annie's heart longs for the magic of being loved like she has never been loved, but she stuffs that longing inside, until a segment on a call-in radio show taps into that secret yearning for more and releases it to be acknowledged and explored. Her best friend dismisses her feelings, accusing her of not wanting to be in love but "wanting to be in love in a movie." Yet Annie cannot stifle this gnawing question, "*What if this man is my destiny and I never meet him?*"[28]

In some ways, that is our question too. What if the beautiful, gracious goodness of God is your destiny and you settle for Walter? What if you talk yourself out of ever believing that such kindness, acceptance, and graciousness, that such passionate affirmation and, yes, even magic, can ever be true of your experience? What if God is simply waiting to love you like no one else has ever loved you but fear keeps you from seeking or ever receiving His love?

Walter can represent so many things, anything you talk yourself into because you are afraid you can not have what you want, what you were made to crave, the destiny that was born in God's heart the very moment He knit you into being. Even our closest friends, and those who love us most, can talk us out of longing for favor because they want to protect us from disappointment, from danger, from rejection, from failure, from all those things that they have become convinced are bigger than God. In contrast, Naomi encouraged Ruth saying, "Go ahead, girl." With Naomi's words, God is encouraging you to own your heart, your desire to be loved and affirmed. He is wooing you to go out into this world with great expectations, looking for Him to show up and amaze you!

There is still more to be discovered in this part of Ruth's story. Just as much as God invites you to identify with Ruth, to recognize your deepest longings in the words that flow from her soul, God invites you to see Him beautifully portrayed in the one she will meet in that field, who will embody the essence of true favor, a kindhearted landowner named Boaz. Consider what we find out about him in the first verse of Ruth 2.

> *Now Naomi had a relative on her husband's side, from the clan of Elimilek, a man of standing, whose name was Boaz* (Ruth 2:1 NIV).

The first thing we learn, as Boaz is introduced to us, is that he was a relative of Elimilek, Naomi's husband. Within the Hebrew culture the law of Moses established a person's family with certain specific obligations that would come into play in a season of hardship. Family members had the right to redeem, or buy back, whatever a relative lost due to suffering and need. If, in poverty, a family member was forced to sell a piece of land, a relative had the right to buy it back for them. If they sold themselves into slavery to pay a debt, a relative was obligated to redeem, or buy back, the one who was enslaved in order to set him free. If a family member was murdered it fell solely upon the shoulders of the family to avenge the death of their loved one. If a relative died without children, his brother, or another male relative, was designated to marry his widow and provide an heir that would carry on the name of the one who had passed away.

By identifying Boaz as a family member God is tipping us off that this is a redemption story and letting us know that Boaz is a picture of the One who identifies Himself by that same Hebrew word, "gaal,"[29] our "kinsman redeemer." Through the prophets of old, God makes it clear. Isaiah writes, *"This is what the Lord says—Israel's King and Redeemer, the Lord Almighty: I am the first and I am the last; apart from me there is no God"* (Isaiah 44:6 NIV). Jeremiah concurs, *"Yet their Redeemer is strong; the Lord Almighty is his name"* (Jeremiah 50:34 NIV). However, for the Old Testament "gaal," or kinsman redeemer, this was an obligation, a designated role in the family and defined by the surrounding culture. For our God, this was a choice. The Son of God, the fullest expression of all that God is, intentionally put on human skin and became known as the Son of Man on purpose, in order to position Himself as your Kinsman and mine. He is your relative, your family, so that He might be perfectly positioned to buy back everything you have ever lost in your poverty or pain. The Word became flesh to personally invite you into an intimate relationship that will preserve your name. This is how He fights for your story, the destiny you were created to fulfill. Though you were once a slave, your Redeemer came to set the captive free. Boaz's life, His character, His role in this story of passion and grace has been given to us so that we can understand God's heart that moves Him to become one of us.

For someone to be able to redeem he not only had to be positioned as a relative but he had to be able to do so. The duties of a kinsman redeemer required certain resources. That is the significance of this description of Boaz as a "man of standing." This Hebrew word, "chayil"[30] can also be defined as "a force." Boaz was a mover and shaker in Bethlehem. Just by showing up, he changed the atmosphere in the room. Various elements combine to make a man carry such weight in his community, wealth, influence, power, authority, wisdom, even dignity. As we read this description of Boaz as "a man of standing," we know Boaz has the strength, capability and resources to fulfill this redemptive role within the family. Boaz was a leader, someone people admired. Whatever the task, Boaz could get it done.

In choosing to embody this picture of Himself in the human flesh of an extraordinary Hebrew landowner, God invites us to grasp, not only His unique position as our relative portrayed in Boaz, but also His unequaled power, strength, ability and resources to do whatever it takes to bring about our redemption. God became a man to give you back every single thing you have lost in the war for your soul and every threat against your destiny, to buy you out of your spiritual poverty so that you are no longer enslaved by addiction or sin, to avenge every injustice, radically changing the outcome of every offense that has ever been committed against you and fight to the death to make sure that your story is told.

Then remember, most beautifully, there is another significant thing about Boaz that Ruth could not have even dreamed when she walked out of Moab, leaving everything behind. An essential element strategically written into Boaz's life story, that Ruth could not have imagined as she requested the right to go out into a field in search of favor, is that the kinsman must be willing. You see God, in His brilliance and His passion, had already prepared a heart to love her, to understand and accept her situation in a specific and unique way. Boaz's willingness was born in his relationship with his mother, Rahab, a harlot, a Gentile, who made a life-changing choice to abandon everything she had ever known to embrace the Hebrew God and His people, and was miraculously welcomed into their community. Surely his love for his mother gave him a tenderness that might have been missing in another man.

Boaz was Ruth's relative, a man of standing, who was distinctly predisposed in specific ways to be willing to care for her. God had positioned and prepared him to be her kinsman redeemer so that we might understand that God made Himself family, in order to offer everything He has and is, to demonstrate the extravagance of His love and grace for you and me. He gave us our craving, for more than bread, so that it would drive us to discover everything we want is found in Him.

You have this Lover of your soul, this One Who understands your deepest longings, into whose field you have been invited to walk, to come looking for favor. He too has a mixed blood line for He is the Son of God, born of a human virgin. His mother, Mary, was a girl, much like you. He is waiting to love you. His life experience has prepared His heart to understand whatever you are going through today and all you have struggled with in your past. This is the self portrait God paints in this man named Boaz, showing us the unique position, the unequalled power and the extraordinary passion of His beautiful heart.

Oh, but there is so much more that Ruth discovers as she goes out to glean.

> *So she went out and began to glean in the fields behind the harvesters. As it turned out, she found herself working in a field belonging to Boaz, who was from the clan of Elimelek.*
>
> *Just then Boaz arrived from Bethlehem and greeted the harvesters, "The LORD be with you!" "The LORD bless you!" they called back.*
>
> *Boaz asked the foreman of his harvesters, "Whose young woman is that?"*
>
> *The foreman replied, "She is the Moabitess who came back from Moab with Naomi. She said, 'Please let me glean and gather*

among the sheaves behind the harvesters.' She went into the field and has worked steadily from morning till now, except for a short rest in the shelter."

So Boaz said to Ruth, "My daughter, listen to me. Don't go and glean in another field and don't go away from here. Stay here with my servant girls. Watch the field where the men are harvesting, and follow along after the girls. I have told the men not to touch you. And whenever you are thirsty, go and get a drink from the water jars the men have filled."

At this, she bowed down with her face to the ground. She exclaimed, "Why have I found such favor in your eyes that you notice me—a foreigner?" (Ruth 2:3-10 NIV)

You see, when Ruth walked out into that field to pick up grain left behind by the reapers, she definitely found more than bread. At the end of this passage her own words reveal that she had stumbled upon exactly what she had hoped to find, kindness, graciousness, generosity, even magic. She called it favor. Consequently, we can conclude that everything we read, concerning how Boaz responded to her in these verses, illustrates for us what the favor of God looks like.

One of the significant acts that Ruth ascribes as descriptive of Boaz's favor is "that you would notice me, a foreigner." A more literal translation would say "that you would know me, an unknown."[31] That word translated "notice" also means "to scrutinize, to look intently at, it involves a taking the time to know, to understand and to honor."[32] That makes sense to me because a lover always becomes a student of the object of his affection. For instance, I can tell you even insignificant details about, the combined musical career of the Beatles, as well as the personal biographies of each member of this band that rocked the sixties, because the man I love is obsessed with everything there is to know about these four lads from Liverpool who came together to change musical history. There was also a season of my life when I could sing the theme song of Thomas and Friends without missing a single word because my little grandson, Rhys, would come running with excitement whenever he heard it. It is only natural that the Lover of my Soul endeavors to know every detail of my heart.

Yet what truly intrigues me is that Boaz knew what he knew about Ruth before he even approached her. That is the level of attentiveness that is attributable to God. Through Jeremiah He explains *"Before you were born I knew you, before I formed you in the womb, I set you apart"* (Jeremiah 1:5). God took the time to know you before you were known by anyone else, when you were a foreigner on this planet, just as Boaz took his time, made this effort to do his homework, to get to know all about this young Moabite girl who had happened into his field that day. As a result, Boaz knew all the positive words people might use to describe her but he also already knew everything about Ruth that she might expect to disqualify her from ever receiving his favor. He knew she was from Moab. That very fact is pointed out, not once, but twice in answer to his question. Ruth was not only a foreigner but she came from a pagan people that God had specifically warned the Israelites not to have anything to do with because of the inherent risk of becoming ensnared by their false gods. Boaz already knew that before he and Ruth ever met, before one word was exchanged between them. He knew Ruth was impoverished. Otherwise, she would not be there, gleaning behind his reapers in the heat of the day. This also means Boaz knew that Ruth was hungry, that she did not have everything she needed, that it was desperation that drove her to his field.

So apply that to your relationship with God. Take a second to identify that one thing that you think would most assuredly disqualify you for His favor, take you right out of the running for any possible fairy tale endings of your story, keep you from ever even getting this ultimate Prince Charming's attention, much less ever winning His heart. Do you have that one element of your story selected? I imagine you do. It only took me a split second to identify mine. Consider this: God already knew that about you, before you were ever born and, knowing that, He chose you for His love. Knowing that one thing you desperately wish no one ever had to know, He is absolutely crazy about you. No one has pulled anything over on Him. He is not ill-informed and the vote is not still out on how He feels. You do not have to change a thing to come into His presence and, the minute you come near Him, you will see nothing but crazy favor dancing in His eyes. Can you even imagine ever basking as long as you like in that sort of grace?

Now look back at the beginning of Ruth 2:8 where it says, *"So Boaz said to Ruth…"* Does that phrase, that act, hit you the way it hit me? Here was Boaz, arguably the most important man in town, owner of the field where Ruth was walking as a beggar, a man with a whole staff of reapers there who worked for him and took orders from him, yet he did not send word to Ruth through them. Instead he spoke to her directly, personally, one on one. Listen to me, never let anyone tell you that you have to hear from God through them, that will mess you up more quickly than any mistake you might make in your journey with God. It is great wisdom to sit under the solid Biblical exposition of your pastor, or an in-depth Bible teaching from someone more mature than you in their faith, but John 10 tells us *"My sheep hear My voice"*(John 10:10). When you open up the Word of God, when you bow your head to pray, the owner of the field will feed you, the Holy Spirit that lives in you will guide you into the truth. God does not choose to depict Himself here as somebody too important to take time to talk to you personally. Boaz was extremely accessible to Ruth, so willing to sit and talk with her and let her get to know his heart in their personal moments together, and Boaz is our picture of God. In writing this story in just this way, God is making it clear that He will speak to you directly, one on one, just as Boaz did to Ruth.

Then consider the rest of verse 8...

> *So Boaz said to Ruth, "My daughter, listen to me, Don't go and glean in another field and don't go away from here. Stay here with my servant girls"* (Ruth 2:8 NIV).

Boaz issued a very personal, very powerful, very purposeful invitation. He asked Ruth to stay close to him, to be exclusive in their relationship, to come back there every day expecting him to meet her there. Boaz was creating a place of belonging for Ruth. What a beautiful dimension of this picture of God's heart. This word translated "stay"[33] is a word we have seen before in this story. It is the same word used to describe how Ruth clung to Naomi at the edge of town, refusing to turn back. Now Boaz is saying to her, "Cling to me. In the same way you clung to your mother-in-law, now transfer that attachment to me." He was not inviting her to a casual relationship but to a committed and intimate one. His invitation to Ruth, to sit with him, even cling to him, expresses God's invitation to each of us. He stands at the door every day hoping you will open it and sit down with Him at His table.

Why do you think Boaz, this self-portrait that God has created on the canvas of His Word, wanted an intimate, exclusive, relationship with Ruth? This passage tells us. Boaz wanted Ruth to stay close so that he could protect her. In fact, as Ruth returns home later in this chapter to tell Naomi what Boaz said, her mother-in-law echoes her agreement, "It will be good for you, my daughter, to go with the women who work for him, because in someone else's field you might be harmed." The Hebrew word translated, "harmed,"[34] is a word that paints a picture of pushing and shoving for position, even violence. I can just imagine that because of Boaz's generosity there was no need for competition in his field. Everyone was empowered to succeed and to celebrate the successes of others. There was no need to jockey for a prime position because Boaz took special care of each one who walked in his field and his resources were sufficient to more than meet all of their needs. In urging Ruth to cling to him, he was sparing her the hurt that was so often characteristic of an atmosphere in which there was a shortage of resources. Boaz was rich and everyone who walked with him was made richer by the experience. Such an atmosphere of abundance would create safety for every woman who came to glean in that field.

Boaz wanted to keep Ruth close in order to protect her from harm. He also wanted her to return to his field every day because he knew what she needed before she even asked and had prepared in advance to provide for it. I can not conceive of Boaz running around frantically barking orders to his servants to go draw water after the workers came in from the field, parched and sweltering from the heat. This was not his first harvest season. He knew to have water ready and waiting. In fact, the Hebrew term for "jars"[35] carries the idea of "something prepared" in advance. Boaz had thought ahead and made certain that what would be needed would already be on hand when Ruth came in from the field. By urging her to cling to him he was not keeping her from some better situation. He was making sure that she had the best experience possible. How attractive! When God urges us to have no gods besides Him, His beautiful heart is wanting to protect us from the harm that comes in our every man for himself society and making sure we have every single thing we could possibly need.

Ruth 2:14 reveals even more about the heart of our Kinsman Redeemer.

> *At mealtime Boaz said to her, "Come over here. Have some bread and dip it in the wine vinegar." When she sat down with the harvesters, he offered her some roasted grain. She ate all she wanted and had some left over* (Ruth 2:14 NIV).

Boaz was inviting her to sit at his table, just as God is inviting us, offering Himself as the Bread that will feed our hunger, the Water that will quench our thirst. Yet Boaz was not merely giving Ruth the basic necessities or feeding her scraps, this was not Hamburger Helper at the noon hour, he was sharing with her the richest food he had. Wine vinegar was a delicacy.³⁶ He laid out the best for her and invited her to share it with him, just as a man would offer to the woman he loves.

Notice who else was seated at Boaz's table? The harvesters were gathered there. Boaz made no difference between this foreigner who simply happened into his field and his trusted staff who sat with him each day. There was no elitist mentality, no hierarchical separation, no in crowd versus outsiders. There was no snobbery toward the riff raff. Each person in Boaz's sphere of influence was treated with respect, spoken to with words of affirmation, and given a place to belong.

Yet perhaps the most box-shaking aspect, for me, of God's incredible character beautifully revealed in our introduction to Boaz is found in verses 15-16.

> *As she got up to glean, Boaz gave orders to his men, "Even if she gathers among the sheaves don't embarrass her. Rather pull out some stalks for her from the bundles and leave them for her to pick up, and don't rebuke her* (Ruth 2:15-16 NIV).

Boaz gave Ruth room to run. He said "if she gets off the path and gathers among the sheaves, do not wound her, never taunt her or even correct her, and, above all, do not embarrass her for being there." Is that the picture you have been given of God? Have you been told of a God that says "Now if she gets off the path, do not bug her, she will get back on track. I will gently woo her back with my kindness?" Does that sound like God, based on how this flawed world portrays Him, sometimes even the flawed church? Yet scripture tells us that it is "His kindness that brings us to repentance." How do we so easily miss that? This is God, portrayed in this picture He paints of Himself. This is the truth of His heart. Not that He encourages you to stray off the path, nor weakly enables you to continue in your sin, but, when you do sin, He will not condemn you nor prompt others to embarrass you. He forbids his servants from hurting you through harsh and insensitive correction. He knows that nothing can imprison you faster than the shame that comes through embarrassment. When you walk in intimacy with your Kinsman Redeemer, He compassionately walks you back to the path, without stifling your passion. So He says, "Give her some space. Give her some room to run, even room to make mistakes" He is that confident in His own ability to hold onto you.

Have you ever felt the sting of embarrassment in response to a mistake you made? Have you carried away the stench of shame after someone publicly pointed out your flaws or even laughed at you for them? Just as affirmation releases you to run with abandon in the fullness of who you are created to be, embarrassment, and the shame it will brand you with, will cause you to build walls that will keep you from your destiny. I remember the moment I built just such a wall, intending to stay behind it forever. I was 10 years old when my spirit was broken in a moment of harsh humiliation for a simple act of childishness. I gave myself a life sentence. I determined to wall off my heart from that moment on, to prevent myself from ever feeling that embarrassment again. Yet my Kinsman Redeemer came to give me back my freedom, to buy me back from that prison of shame! Jesus came to set captives like me free. He wants us to know that we are loved and cherished and that will never change, even when we mess up.

You see, God's enormous, unlimited capacity to love is determined by His character, not yours, nor mine. Do you understand how rich Boaz was? It is clearly revealed in what this wealthy landowner was saying here. He was saying that if this young beggar went over and began to pull the barley right out of a bunch the harvesters had already bundled up to be taken to the threshing floor for his own harvest, they were instructed to go ahead and pull some more out of that bundle, dropping it on the ground for her to take. Boaz was that rich. He would not be undone by her mistakes, or even her misbehavior. It seems unlikely Ruth could even do what is described in these verses by accident. It seems to me that Boaz is saying "If, driven by her hunger, Ruth actually deliberately tries to steal some of my harvest, as a reflection of my kindness I want you to give her even more!" I believe Boaz knew, even in that extreme hypothetical situation, that once Ruth truly grasped His willingness to provide her with such abundance, she would realize that she would never have to get it any other way!

Not only did Boaz warn his servants not to embarrass her, He instructed them to give Ruth ample and abundant resources. He told his workers to pull some extra grain out and throw it down for her. He surprised her with provision. Just as God takes the extra out of his pocket all the time and leaves it for you to find. So often we miss it, we may not even recognize it, because it is not what we expect Him to do, having our thinking distorted by the selfish mentality of our world. Such graciousness is so far outside our human experience that even believers may have no idea that this is the attitude reflective of our God's amazing grace.

As I first read the words describing how much barley Ruth was blessed with after a single day in Boaz's field, I became curious. I began to wonder what it looked like for Ruth to gather and take an ephah of barley home that day. So I did some research to discover how much barley an ephah represents. An ephah is "an ancient Hebrew unit of dry measure, equal to … about one bushel (35 liters)."[37] The dry weight of a bushel varies based on the substance being measured but a bushel of barley would weigh about 22 kilograms or about 22,000 grams. So I went to the store to see how much barley was in a single bag. The bag I found was about the size of a typical 32 ounce bag of corn meal which was only 850 grams of barley. That means it would take almost 26 normal-sized bags to make a bushel of barley, which is equivalent to approximately an ephah, the amount of barley Ruth carried home that day. Can you imagine that? Can you imagine seeing Ruth coming through the door at the end of the day not only with a load of barley that would equal about 26 small bags you would find at a typical grocery store and even a to-go box of leftovers from her lunch? What a take! It must have been so exhilarating to come back from the fields loaded down with such abundance. No wonder the first words out of Naomi's mouth were, "Where did you glean today?" This is God's extravagance! When they see you coming folks will know you have been with Jesus! No one else provides so much more than we ask or imagine!

Finally, Boaz released her. The words here say *"Don't rebuke her"* (Ruth 2:16 NIV). That Hebrew word translated "rebuke"[38] is also found in Psalm 106:9 where it is used to describe how God held back the Red Sea. God is saying, through this picture of Boaz, "Do not hold her back. Do not pen her in. Do not trap her. Release her and let her run with abandon."

What did Boaz see in Ruth that prompted such generosity? Boaz tells us what it was he saw in Ruth that motivated his graciousness,

> Boaz replied, *"I've been told all about what you have done for your mother-in-law since the death of your husband — how you left your father and mother and your homeland and came to live with a people you did not know before. May the Lord repay you for what you have done. May you be richly rewarded by the Lord, the God of Israel, under whose wings you have come to take refuge"* (Ruth 2:11-12 NIV).

When it comes right down to it, all Ruth did was believe to the point that it changed her story. She just put feet to her faith and believed, even when believing got hard, kept walking all the way to

Bethlehem when no one would have blamed her if she turned back. She grabbed hold of her mother-in-law and clung to that faint taste she had offered her of God. She walked in the footprints of Abraham, who simply believed God, period. He just took God at His Word and trusted Him and it was *"credited to him as righteousness"* (Genesis 15:6 NIV). In her hunger, in her desperation, Ruth went out looking for more than bread and here came Boaz with words that must have tasted like honey, and provision beyond anything she could have expected.

Perhaps no one else has ever noticed what you have hidden inside your heart but God already knows it, just as Boaz made these discerning observations concerning Ruth. Boaz said, "I see your courage, your sacrifice, your commitment, your dreams. I see what matters to you and those things are things I value too. More than anything, I see that you are hungry for God, that you are desperate to find Him here. I see that you are depending on Him to come through for you." You see, not only did Boaz see all the things that could have disqualified her but he also noted beautiful characteristics of her heart that were attractive to him. That is how God sees you too. He sees things you might not even know are in your heart that attract Him and cause Him to celebrate who you are, specifically and uniquely. He is over the moon for you! He loves you because of who you are, not in spite of it. All the while He is not put off by the things you think would disqualify you from ever experiencing such love.

This is favor…to be noticed, to be known, to be valued, to be protected and provided for like a bride, to be empowered through a relationship that gives you extra and overflow, resources and gifts, that sets you free to run and gives you space to try without fear of failure. Every person wants that. Yet many of us were unaware that this is what is already in God's heart for us, before we do a thing to earn it. We think that kind of love only exists in the movies, in the love stories concocted in man's imagination, when in reality *"no eye has seen, nor ear heard, no mind has conceived what God has prepared"* (1 Corinthians 2:9 NIV) for you! When God painted this portrait of His heart in this beautiful story of love, extravagant passion and delight, this is still only a taste, a foreshadowing of all He has in store for you, the one He has chosen to be His bride.

Just look back at verse 10 one last time to see Ruth's response.

> *At this, she bowed down with her face to the ground. She exclaimed, "Why have I found such favor in your eyes that you would notice me — a foreigner?"* (Ruth 2:10 NIV)

You see, this is the life-changing, heart-stopping point we must not rush past or overlook. Ruth's words reveal that all the favor you long for, the very things you crave and dream about, everything you hope desperately to one day experience, is already there, waiting to be discovered. She never said, "I made you love me." She said, "I looked and saw that favor I longed for was in your eyes." In other words, her discovery said nothing about her, but told her so much about Boaz. She just stumbled into his field and there it was, in the heart of the one who owned the field before she ever arrived that morning. It was his nature, his character, the very essence of who he was. How true that is of Your Boaz, your Kinsman Redeemer! The success of your quest for favor will never rest on the shoulders of your performance or your feeble attempts at reaching perfection. This is Who our God is. It always has been. You could not change it, if you tried. This is His story. When Ruth wandered into that field, the favor she was searching for was already there. It was the character of the man who owned the field and was waiting there to meet her.

Come to think of it, that is exactly what I experienced on my first date with David. You see, when David drove nearly forty miles one way to buy that crystal pig figurine because there was a running joke within the student ministry where I served about my love for pigs...when he drove almost sixty miles from where he bought that figurine to the dinner theater to arrange for the waitress to set it on my plate in advance...and then drove another eighteen miles back home to put on a suit, borrow his mom's car and get ready for our date...only to turn around and drive the eight miles to my home to pick me up...and then drive us back to that dinner theater another eighteen miles away from where he picked me up, just so I could walk in, sit down and see that he noticed me...that was not about me! That was a demonstration of who he was, who he is. The beauty of this man was already there waiting to be discovered. I had hardly had any chance to impress him by being particularly witty or cute or smart. I had done nothing to guarantee him that such effort would prove to be worth it. Yet when I walked into that restaurant, as our first date was only beginning, that crystal pig figurine said to me that the very thing I was longing for was waiting there for me already in the eyes and heart of the one who brought me to that place.

Perhaps Tom Hanks' character, Sam, in *Sleepless in Seattle*[39] describes it best when he says, "It was like coming home, only to no home I'd ever known. I was just taking her hand to get out of a car and it was like...magic."

There is a deeper passion, a more spectacular magic, a sweeter taste of favor than anything we have ever experienced. He is waiting for you to reach out and take His hand. The greatest love story of all time was never the plot of a movie or an epic tale of literature, it has never been fully captured in the beautiful intimacy shared uniquely between a man and the woman he has chosen to love for all of his life. Those are only pictures, morsels meant to invite us to the feast, to the field that holds the favor we have always longed to experience. There we find it waiting, our life written into God's story as the object of His affection. Will you believe that He already loves you like no one else has ever loved you? That magic is waiting for you as you take those first steps into God's field. God's unusual favor is there, you are extravagantly loved already. When you take your yearning there, He comes along and says, "Let me let you know me." Then piece by piece, little by little He does the convincing. Boaz said "Do not touch her." Boaz said "Give her a drink when she is thirsty." Boaz said "Give her something to eat." Boaz said "Stay close to me." Boaz said, "I know all about you." So do you think, when Ruth returned home that night, she said, "Let me tell about all the bread I got out there?" Oh no, verse 19 tells us, *"Then Ruth told her mother-in-law about the one..."* (Ruth 2:19). Take the risk. Let yourself believe that He loves you. The One Who has written you into His story will not disappoint. His unusual character, His extravagant passion for you is simply waiting on your open heart.

Chapter 4

Maybe this is how it always is, that we think we go into the
world alone and lose ourselves there until, at last, Love calls
our name and suddenly we remember the way home.
— BRIAN ANDREAS, REMEMBER HOME

THERE'S NO PLACE LIKE HOME

Perhaps no sweeter words were ever spoken in Houston's mission
control than the expression of profound relief that punctuated the end
of the dramatic reentry of Apollo 13, "Welcome home." Jim Lovell,
Jack Swigert and Fred Haise had undertaken an incredible adventure in
pursuit of a courageous dream — to blaze a new trail, make their own
mark on the pages of history, complete a mission so unique, so
dramatic that the whole world was poised and watching. Jim Lovell had
been here once before, to the moon and back. Now he was bringing
two brave young dreamers with him. They had received extensive
training, accumulated vast knowledge, and taken extreme risks. They
were fully aware of the great expectations that surrounded them, fully
informed of their detailed assignment and much of it was complete by
this point in their mission. Yet in the vulnerability of their precarious
position their ship had been damaged along the way and they carried
that wound with them, though it would not immediately be apparent to
those monitoring their mission from a distance. Forty-six hours and
forty-three minutes into the flight this trip had been so routine that
their contact on the ground in Houston expressed the sentiments of
everyone involved saying, "We're bored to tears." Then, just a little over
nine hours later, this same flight became the scariest ride of their lives
and had all who were waiting on their return poised on the edge of
their seats.

At this critical moment in the history of America's space program
it became obvious that the stunning photographs these astronauts had
taken, the significant scientific data they had collected, the unequalled
thrill they had experienced, would never be enough. It was not meant
to be. Their families prayed and watched through tears. Fellow

dreamers held their breath. As they came to the end of this journey, in this moment of crisis, they could not be, they would not be, satisfied with anything less than coming home.

Jessica Lynch's broken and battered body lay in a hospital in a tiny village called Nasiriyah in the midst of the Iraqi war in the spring of 2003. Despite her extensive injuries and the scarcity of effective pain medications, the Iraqi doctors and nurses made every attempt to care for her with compassion each day. One nurse sang to Jessica in the night to relieve her fears. Iraqi medical professionals even tried to return Jessica to American soldiers. They placed her in an ambulance and drove her to where the U.S. troops were stationed, but in an atmosphere where suicide bombings were the norm, they were unable to convince the soldiers of their true intentions and were forced to turn back. No one could question that these doctors and nurses cared for Jessica and wanted to provide a safe haven in which she could heal. Still, on April 1, 2003, as the story is told, a group of U. S. Special Forces stormed the hospital to take her out in a daring rescue mission. Some have disputed whether or not Iraqi forces really posed any threat at that particular location when the rescue unit arrived, but that is not the point. Regardless of the imminent danger or lack of any danger at all, it was not enough that Jessica Lynch was being well provided for there. It was not enough, that she was relatively comfortable and under no immediate threat. It was not enough that she was well hidden, protected from the enemy, even if the enemy was nowhere to be found. You see, as that first of the US special forces team came into her room, with an announcement offered to abate her fear that he was an American soldier, her initial response told him all he needed to know, "I am an American soldier too." With that clarity those soldiers knew their mission. They understood that they could never leave Jessica behind, even if the Iraqi doctors and nurses were well intentioned, even if she was being kept out of imminent danger, because Jessica Lynch did not belong there. The cry of her heart was for home.

Deep in the heart of every woman breathes a longing for more than this, for more than being bored to tears, simply meeting the expectations of others, staying relatively safe, accumulating vast amounts of knowledge or even experiencing some daring adventure. Deep within the heart of every woman there is a cry that says, "This is not enough, I want to be truly loved, I want to be completely free, I want to know who I am and have the chance to settle down in a garment that fits me to a tee. I want to relax, and laugh and know I am right where I belong." Deep within the heart of every woman breathes an undeniable cry for home.

That cry, that irrepressible desire, did not originate within her. No, that dream was first conceived in the heart of her Lover, her Creator, the One who took the time to know her before she was born, before she was ever known by anyone else. In the context of His perfect love, He alone has the capacity to release her to be that woman, to experience her destiny, live that singular life for which she was made. When Jesus said, *"I have come that you may have life"* (John 10:10), He refused to stop there. No, He revealed that it was for more than just a ticket to heaven that He would sacrifice His life. It was so that you and I could have a live-it-up life, that we would taste and see the answer to our heart's yearning. He came and gave His life for us, to us, so that we could live abundantly! He did not die on that cross to take us halfway there, He came to take us all the way to the answer to our heart's cry for home. So, in the context of an intimate relationship with Him, where you invite Him to speak His vision for you into your reality, where you depend upon Him to empower you to live that vision out, home is no longer a dream, it becomes a very "real, truly live place,"[40] as Dorothy described it in *The Wizard of Oz*. Before you leave these pages I believe you will be absolutely convinced that there really, truly, is no place like home.

In a beautiful dialogue from the movie, *The Gladiator*, Russell Crowe's character, Maximus, is asked by the Roman Emperor, Marcus Aurelius, *"Tell me about your home."* With a faraway look in his eye the weary warrior describes it,

> *My house is in the hills above Trujillo. A very simple place. Pinkstones that warm in the sun. A kitchen garden that smells of herbs in the day, jasmine in the evening. Through the gate is a giant poplar. Figs, apples, pears. The soil, Marcus, black. Black like my wife's hair. Grapes on the south slopes, olives on the north. Wild ponies play near my house. They tease my son. He wants to be one of them.*

The emperor then inquires, *"Remember the last time you were home?"*

Maximus responds as if he has already magically transported back there, *"Two years, 264 days, and this morning."*

"I envy you, Maximus. It's a good home. Worth fighting for!" the older man recognizes.[41]

At the center of Ruth's story is her longing for home. She refused to settle for the life she had always lived because her vision of the home she longed for was so different than the one she had experienced. She abandoned it all to run hard after God, stubbornly choosing to cling to the only person she knew who could get her closer to Him. She believed God would lead her to a place that would welcome her, a people who would accept her, an atmosphere that would release her to be the woman He created her to be.

Like Ruth, I am just not willing to settle for staying where I am. I refuse to be satisfied with simply collecting a head full of knowledge. I will never be content with just following a list of rules. I want everything that is coming to me, all the freedom I can experience. I want to make it to that place I dream of, fully experience that life I was uniquely created to live, completely relax in the garments of who God says that I am, as I lean back in the embrace of His unusual, incredible love and hear His voice whisper my name. To have a clear vision is one thing, but I want to get there. I want to make it all the way home, and I do not want to go alone. I want to bring some friends with me.

I know what it feels like to so intensely want to get home and how helpless you can feel when you find yourself far away from where you belong. Kiley, our youngest daughter, was in the first grade when she received her first invitation to the birthday party of a classmate from school. It was thrilling — not just for Kiley, but for me. I wanted her to be loved, accepted, to have a sweet circle of friends, to be part of the cool kid crowd. Everyone who was anyone in Mrs. Ballard's first grade class at Mount Olive Elementary School was going to be at this party. So I was going to do everything I had to do in order to make sure Kiley made it there. The celebration was set to take place at the hottest birthday spot any child could have imagined, Chuckie Cheese Pizza. Now bear this in mind, Kiley was particularly fond of pizza and amazingly fond of playing arcade games. I mean she was a gamer before anyone called them "gamers," and pizza and arcade games were the major attractions at this particular pizza chain. Basically the only drawback was that this Chuckie Cheese restaurant, and I use that term, "restaurant" loosely, was not all that close to our home. It was located at the Foothills Mall in the nearby city of Maryville, Tennessee.

The big event was planned for a Sunday afternoon which presented our little family with a critical obstacle because David is completely

THERE'S NO PLACE LIKE HOME

committed to his Sunday afternoon nap and not nearly as invested in his children's popularity. My oldest daughter, Brittany, who was in the fourth grade, and I were tasked with the chauffeuring duty, with the incentive that we could shop in the mall while we waited, instead of coming all the way back home. Just so you know, at this point in my chauffeuring career I had surprisingly never been asked, nor expected, to drive to the Foothills Mall in Maryville, Tennessee, even though it was only about 30 minutes from our home. In my defense, the Foothills mall had only been open a few short years at the time and I grew up in an area of our city that was much farther away from the nearby city of Maryville, making a visit to that mall impractical at best. Still, being one who easily embraces a new adventure, I dove into this challenge with little or no hesitation. Surely by the time you have made it to this fourth chapter you suspect that the sentence you just read is hardly the way things occurred. In reality, there was much hesitation on my part, and even whining and kicking of feet, before I set out on this journey.

When it became obvious that David was not going to change his mind, I basically grilled my husband on every turn that I would have to take and went over it a time or two to make sure I understood all the directions. For you younger girls, here is some shock and awe for you to absorb: there was no "Lady Tom Tom" to guide you, no iPhones with GPS, no google maps, not even a google back then. So think of me basically as a pioneer woman on the Oregon Trail. Those were the circumstances we faced as reluctantly the girls and I were left to our own devices, or should I say, lack of devices. Still I am happy to report that we arrived at the festive event without a hitch and the smiling faces of my little ones conveyed the satisfaction in my own heart, testifying unashamedly to the fact that I really am a world class wonder mom.

Foothills not being the largest mall in this area, Brittany and I were able to make the rounds a time or two before this festival of pepperoni and skee ball finally came to a close. So we were all pretty tired and more than ready to hit the road as soon as the party ended. As we climbed back into our car I had a tiny check in my heart that those directions I went over again and again with David were only for the trip to the Foothills Mall. I had made no preparation for a return trip and, to make matters worse, it was getting dark. I quickly reassured myself, without showing a hint of doubt to my trusting children, that I could turn those instructions around and make it home in no time.

I turned right out of the parking lot and made a left turn at the first light, knowing fully well that I had turned left into the lot as we arrived after turning right onto the side street. I drove for quite some time, expecting very soon to see a multitude of car dealerships that would point the way down Alcoa Highway to territory much more familiar to me. Yet those familiar car lots never materialized and it seemed to be taking twice as long as I expected to reach them. As we drove on, in the ever-increasing darkness, I was surprised to see instead a concrete structure of massive proportion approaching in the distance. As I got closer I realized — that was a dam. There had been no dam on the road that lay between the car lots and the mall as we drove to the party. I was certain of it. So immediately I felt that sick feeling one gets when they know they have messed up somewhere but cannot quite put their finger on the exact moment things went terribly wrong. Therefore, such a wanderer is rendered totally incapable of retracing their steps to make things right again. Instead I kept driving. In fact, I drove faster. Soon the road led us right over the dam. Not long after that we came to a small group of businesses in an area of someone's town I had never visited before and, if I had not known it already, as I surveyed those businesses, I knew that I was lost.

Once I made the clear determination that I had no idea where I was, all I could think to do was to pull up outside one of those buildings and use the pay phone, (Yes, once again, this was in those long ago pre-cellphone days). I found one that was mounted on the brick wall right outside the door of a video store (Yet another endangered species in today's streaming bliss). In irritation, now thinking that I had been obviously and totally ill-equipped to make this journey and that my husband had been completely rash in abandoning me in my time of need, what else could I do but call him? So I dialed his number and somehow found enough breath to utter between clinched teeth, "I'm lost. Can you tell me how to get home?"

What really annoyed me, even more than I was already annoyed, was the fact that this news did not seem to alarm my husband, David, at all. He seemed to take it rather calmly. Then again, who would not be relaxed in the comfort of home, having surely enjoyed a lengthy nap in an otherwise deserted house. So without getting in too much of a hurry or showing nearly enough impassioned concern, David simply answered my question with a question of his own, "Where are you?" obviously illustrating the fact that he was not really listening to me. Somewhere inferred in the word, "lost" is the idea that one does not have a clue as to where one is, right? So I said, even more clearly and slowly than before and in a slightly stronger tone to make sure that he understood the desperation of my situation this time, "I don't know.

I'M LOST!" Well, Mr. Smarty Pants then proceeded to tell me, with a smug chuckle that expressed complete insensitivity to my growing sense of panic, that there was no way that he could tell me how to get home unless and until I somehow found out where I was. This was utterly frustrating to me, even if it did make perfect sense. After all, I was on a pay phone, in an unfamiliar setting, between a convenient store and a video rental place and the guy that just walked by me had a rather stumbling gait and smelled a little funny. Was my husband actually suggesting that I should publicly announce my vulnerability by proclaiming my confused state of affairs? Why I would no more draw a large red target on my chest than I would tell these passersby that my children and I, having been totally deserted to make a perilous journey to a disappointing mall in a foreign town by an apathetic, but certainly not sleep-deprived, husband, were now easy prey and sitting pretty for the taking. Still, at this point, I did not have a lot of other options.

I sized up the next young man to get out of his vehicle, deeming him to be relatively harmless, and then, gripping the phone receiver much like I would a weapon, I asked, with the deadpan expression of a woman who had taken a long, hot ride on the PMS train, "Can you tell me what city I'm in?" With a complete disregard for the threatening nature of my stance, the man looked back at me, in much the same way that I had looked at the stumbling drunk that had passed me by only minutes before, and said "You're in Lenoir City, Lady!" Then he hurried away, shaking his head in obvious pity and bewilderment.

Now I know what you are thinking. I know exactly what you would have suggested, had you been there with me at that moment. It was now after dark. It was a school night. My kids were getting cranky and irritable and sleepy and they had not even had a bath. Lenoir City is probably an okay place to live. Not all the men who passed me while I was standing there at the pay phone were inebriated. Besides I was certainly not getting any help from my husband. So, why not? Why not just stay in Lenoir City? Why would I not be satisfied to land in such a picturesque and provisional spot where VHS movies, diet coke and candy are at my disposal for what few dollars I had left in my pocket? Why, surely no one would blame me if I had decided to just grab opportunity by the throat and settle down right there in good old Lenoir City, Tennessee.

Right?! No! Of course, I did not want to stay there. I did not belong there. This place was not right for me. No one knew me there. I did not feel loved or known or empowered there. I certainly did not feel safe or comfortable there! Surely this was not my destiny. I was not home.

My experience speaks to this foundational issue that Ruth and Naomi confront next in their story. There is a longing in every woman's heart for home. By now we are becoming very familiar with Ruth's back story. Ruth may have been born in Moab but it was not the place where her destiny could unfold. To live caged in this godless culture of dysfunction and conflict was not the life that Ruth was created to live. This woman, first conceived in God's heart and fashioned by Him in the womb of her mother, was destined to be a woman who would know that she was loved, who would know the God who thought her up, and who would have something of Him born in her and through her that would touch and change her world. Most significantly, everything I just said about Ruth is true for you, and true for me.

So God mounted a rescue mission. He issued an invitation for Ruth to know Him intimately so that He could release that woman she was meant to be to run with abandon in the freedom of His vision for her life. Strangely enough He chose to embody that invitation in a little Hebrew family, who, driven by hunger in the midst of a famine, left their home in a place with a name that literally meant "House of Bread" to seek food at the mercy of their enemy, a people, by the way, who had already refused to provide food to the Israelites as they made their exodus from Egypt. To me that decision would be tantamount to investing your life savings in a shop that carried nothing but merchandise promoting the University of Tennessee football team in the heart of Tuscaloosa, Alabama. Yet not even their frailty and their flaws, not even this bizarre decision, could prevent Ruth from seeing that there was something different in them, something completely unusual when compared with anything she had ever experienced, and she was drawn to that something, that God Who accepted them as His own. You see, this is what God does. In His brilliance and confidence He entrusts His very life to messed up, imperfect people, who rarely get it right. You are reading this now because of some of them who in their breakable, ordinary jars of clay existence carried His all-surpassing power right up to your door and held out His beautiful invitation for you to belong to Him too.

So the very second Ruth's mother-in-law announced she was leaving, Ruth made her choice, she chose Bethlehem over Moab. She chose to leave everything she had ever known. In fact, she grabbed hold with both hands and refused to let go, because, you see, despite all her failures Naomi knew the way, she knew the One that would change

Ruth's story, she was the only one left in Moab who could get Ruth home to Him.

How about you? You may know some messed up Christians who make stupid decisions but we are all you have to get you closer to God and, really, this is not about us anyway, it is about Who He is — He is that something different that you see somewhere in us. He is our only hope of getting this right, and, trust me, He is so much more than what we are, He is extraordinary! As soon as we arrived at the place in Ruth's story where she made her choice, God asked each of us this question, "Will you believe? Not just believe, but will you believe to the point that it changes your story?" He will, you know, He will change your story right this minute if you ask Him.

Well, once Ruth decided to go she was faced with another question, "Would she, would we, believe when believing gets hard?" As soon as Ruth chose to move toward God, her enemy got busy trying to turn her around, take her off course, slow her down or get her distracted. Pause and consider what that might look like in your life and mine.

Imagine yourself caught in the middle of a game of tug of war, holding to the center of a big, thick rope with the pieces of the rope extending to the right and to the left. This is your life and it is about to get hard. Just imagine that your enemy grabs hold of one end of the rope and begins tugging. At first it might be pretty easy for the enemy, all he has to do is give a little tug and away you go, in whatever direction he wants to pull you. Then imagine you meet someone whose life is going in the opposite direction. Instead of following the author of all the lies that seem to pull you in the wrong direction, this person follows the truth. Understand that this truth-follower is imperfect, but she is learning to separate truth from lies. She is broken, just like you, but she has found where to go with her brokenness. Her life gives you a tug in the opposite direction and the battle lines are drawn. Every time there is a tug in one direction, there is a pull from the other. She learns more truth and shares it with you but your enemy continues to try to unravel it all with his lies. So there is this back and forth, a pull one way and then another. It gets painful at times. You are constantly caught in the middle of this tug of war. How can you possibly break free? Simply make up your mind. Settle the question. Determine, once and for all, which way you will go and let go of the rope. Then the lies and the truth will still be in this constant conflict but you will no longer be pulled apart by the struggle because you will have chosen to run hard after God, to focus on Him and commit to only moving in whatever direction takes you closer to Him.

Ruth refused every excuse to miss out on what God had in store for her, and pretty much said to Naomi, "the only way I'm not going with you to Bethlehem is if you, or somebody we meet on the road, kills me before I get there." What was Naomi to do but take her along on the journey back to Bethlehem? In fact, the passage actually says that it was because of Ruth's determination, because Ruth made her choice and expressed it so definitively, that Naomi gave in and stopped arguing about it. No more tug of war.

Naturally, coming out of a famine and having taken this three day journey from Moab on foot, by the time these two women arrived in Bethlehem, they were famished. Soon Ruth went to a field to gather leftover grain behind the reapers, hoping to find more than just the makings of a tasty loaf of bread. From the very start she was hoping, as we learned in the last chapter, that she would find favor — this was her desire, just as it is yours and mine. We go out the door every day hoping things will go well, that folks will be kind, that we will get more than we deserve, and, even, that something magical will happen. We too are hungry for more than bread.

The Hebrew wording tells us that Ruth basically just stumbled into this field that was owned by a certain man named Boaz. What a man! God strategically placed Boaz into this story to present us with a picture of Himself. He is one of God's Old Testament self-portraits. Right off the bat, this man of great influence and affluence, noticed Ruth. Beyond a simple notice, Boaz took the time to know Ruth's whole story, even before she ever met him. In fact, he knew every single thing about Ruth that would reasonably disqualify her from his favor. His servants described her as the Moabite from Moab which was pretty much like saying, "The jerk from Jerkville." They did not hold back, like a lot of people who might take it upon themselves to tell your story when you are not around. Yet, without flinching, Boaz approached her. No kidding, this man, our picture of God, walked right over and spoke to her. That is the kind of God that is wooing you to a deeper relationship with Him. He will seek you out and even speak to you. You can open His Word and expect to hear Him whisper your name. Yet Boaz did not stop with a simple "Hello." He invited Ruth to sit with him. He fed her at his table. He protected her. He affirmed her. He had his men leave extra grain for her to pick up and instructed them not to embarrass her if she stepped off of the path. In fact, even if she walked right over and pulled some grain of out of the sheaths that had been gathered by his harvesters for Boaz Himself, he gave them direct orders not to hold her back. You see, Boaz was so rich, so full, he could easily absorb such a loss. This is what God wants you to know about Him. You do not scare God and neither does a single mistake you may have made or may make as you continue moving forward.

So when Ruth went home to Naomi at the end of her first day of gleaning, she was carrying an unbelievable haul of grain. The equivalent of twenty-six typical bags of barley you might purchase at any grocery store. Not only that, she also carried a to-go box from lunch under her arm. Yet it was not the grain Ruth was talking about, it was the one, the man she met in the field. She did not merely find the favor she hoped for, she was undone by the extravagance of his kindness. Who could have dreamed that this would happen to a young woman like her, this girl who is a picture of you and me. This kind and gentle man who lavished her, not only with his presence, but with all kinds of gifts and empowerment and grace, is just a reflection. Through Boaz, God is showing us His beautiful heart. This is the God Who is pursuing you for His love! He is not pushed away by where you came from or anything you have been through. He chooses you, every time, knowing every reason you might give Him not to ever choose you at all.

Then we learned that Boaz said something incredible to Ruth, something far better than anything she could have ever expected him to say, and this is where we pick up Ruth's story. This beautiful man, who showed her such extravagant favor, said, "I want you to stay."

> *Then Ruth, the Moabite said, "He even said to me, Stay with my workers until they finish harvesting my grain." Naomi said to Ruth her daughter-in-law, "It will be good for you, my daughter, to go with the women who work for him, because in someone else's field you might be harmed"* (Ruth 2:21-22).

Do you recognize what God acknowledges in this passage? There were other places Ruth could go to try to get her needs met. There are other places we can go to try to alleviate our hunger, to try to fill up our emptiness. Naomi knew all about those other fields. Remember this was a woman who had traveled completely outside of the loving boundaries set for her by God. She was driven by her cravings and all she got for her effort was disappointment, rejection, isolation, bitterness and tragic loss. In fact, she lost who she was in another field. She lost her sense of self, walked away changed. Her failure provides a teachable moment for each of us. Never think that you can try to get your needs met, silence that gnawing within you, stifle that endless craving for more than bread, on your own and not be changed? When you were created to live as the daughter of the King and, instead, you choose to live on the streets as a beggar, it is going to have devastating effects. Naomi had been down that road and it cut her deeply, cost her dearly. Her family stepped out from under God's provision and protection to stray not too far, just right outside of the land God had given His people, to seek to feed their hunger in the land of their enemy, and three out of four of the members of Naomi's family never got the chance to come back home. So Naomi told Ruth, that in another field, outside the boundaries of Boaz's protection and grace, she would get hurt because Naomi had made that mistake and learned that lesson the hard way.

You see, all the elements of favor we identified, all the benefits lavished on Ruth in Boaz's field, are not showered on the women who glean in other fields. Boaz was completely unusual. His extravagant generosity was not common place. The Hebrew wording actually indicates that there would be violence in other fields. To be sure, many more people go gleaning in those other fields. Those fields are crowded, and a scarcity of resources that results from that crowding, coupled with greed in an every man for himself culture characteristic of the days of the judges as well as today, creates bitter competition.

What made conditions so much better in Boaz's field? Simply this, Boaz was there. Boaz made the difference. He was the difference. His character, his graciousness, his generosity set the tone, created an atmosphere that was completely unique from anywhere else Ruth might have chosen to try to get her needs met. The benefits found in Boaz's field do not happen by accident. They are intentional, purposeful acts, products of his character, his desire to provide safety, sensitivity, abundance and freedom. These are the things every woman craves. If they were easy to come by, we would not be so conscious of our hunger for them. The fact that we go out looking for favor attests to the scarcity of it, it is all too often in short supply in our world, as it was in Ruth's. So there is a culture of competition, of pushing and shoving, an every man or woman for themselves attitude, in our society, just as there was in the days of the judges. Unfortunately, since violence runs rampant in the other fields, there is also fear, unrest, discontentment and unhealthiness that such a culture of self-centeredness breeds.

It seems so obvious, so clear cut, who would not stay, once she stumbled in, just happened by, this field characterized by such extraordinary generosity? Who would not choose to bask in that place where such grace flowed out to her and into her so freely? Ruth was filled up to overflowing while she was there. Who would not stay?

You would not stay. I would not stay. There have been countless times in each of our lives when you or I knew where God wanted us to be, knew what He most likely wanted us to do, knew what God would want us to say or not say, knew who God would want us to cling to, follow, connect with, pursue, but, if we have to wait, if we have to go without, if we think we might be missing something that looks so good from over here, before we know it, we are trying to get what we need our own way, in another field. We do not always stay. That is the tragedy of sin.

Yet the beauty of this story, Ruth's life, Ruth's destiny, is that it is a picture of everything we can experience, a beautiful incredible intimacy we were made for, a destiny that God invites us to embrace, if we stay.

We can know that every single gift, every joy, every incredible detail of Ruth's destiny can be ours, if we will believe enough to return day after day to His field, under the covering of His protection and provision, and plant our feet firmly in His House of Bread, even when famine comes. The Spirit leans down to whisper to us another question, "Will you believe to the point that you will stay?"

Sadly, we do not stay, not always. Sometimes we look a little more like Naomi, than we do Ruth. Naomi lived in a town called the House of Bread, but when life got hard, when she got hungry, she did not stay. She did not go that far, you know, just outside of God's promises, just outside of God's plan, just a few miles from God's people. Then she went through stuff. We all go through stuff, whether it is a financial struggle or a broken or struggling marriage. It may be a battle with cancer or a chronic disability. It could be a job loss, the betrayal of a friend, depression, family dysfunction, stress in the workplace, loneliness, shame, abuse, rejection, the loss of a child. We all go through stuff. When Naomi went through the stuff she went through, she went through it alone, because she did not stay. We do not know everything that happened in their ten years in Moab but we know this: we know she lived in a vile, godless culture. We know her sons' names meant "sick" and "pining." We know she lost her husband. We do not know everything Naomi went through but we know this: there was a last straw; there was a coming to the end of her rope; there was a coming apart at the seams that left her feeling like she did not even have a rope to hold on to anymore. We know she heard God was doing things in other people's lives, but she heard it from a distance, until she finally came to her senses and realized, "I'm not home! This place, where I am, this place outside of where God lovingly placed me, is not where I belong." Naomi came to the realization that she was not in the place where she was meant to flourish. So she packed up everything and hit the road that would take her back to where she belonged.

So we must not rush past this small but pivotal detail, notice that it was not guilt that moved Naomi. I am quite sure that no one around her in Moab thought there was anything wrong with her or any of her choices. She was living in the dark, who could notice? What inspired her to make a change? The thing that wooed her back to Bethlehem, was kindness, specifically God's kindness. She heard that God had visited His people and brought their famine to an end. This is what God reveals to us in Ruth 1:6. How did Naomi hear? We do not know but we can know what it meant to her, it meant that the things she wanted, everything she left home to find, was right there where she could have, should have stayed in that field of favor, that place where she was once close to God. In fact, I think one of the most beautiful verses in the Bible is Ruth 1:7

> *With her two daughter-in-laws she left the place where she had been living and set out on the road that would take them back to the land of Judah* (Ruth 1:7 NIV).

The name of her homeland, Judah, means, "celebration."[42] Those who stayed where God had placed them, stayed where God had promised to provide, stayed through the famine, bore up under the hunger, still believing even when believing got hard, they were celebrating and somehow word got all the way to Moab where Naomi had experienced little, if anything, that would be cause for celebration. That is when she realized she missed that, longed for that, needed that. That was when God stirred in her a desire to go home. You see, God did not have to remember Naomi, she never left His heart for one minute. It was now that Naomi remembered God, the sights, the smells, the barley fields ready for harvest, the feasts, the celebration, the friends who had stayed, and she simply said, "This is not where I belong. This place is not the place of my destiny, and it never will be."

I think Naomi knew that from the very beginning. Somewhere within her she knew that she should have stayed. Ruth 1:1 tells us that

Naomi and her family "sojourned there." That word means "to visit."[43] Their intention was for this to be just a temporary trip. Then in Ruth 1:4 in the King James Version it says they "dwelled" in Moab. This word translated "dwelled" is a different Hebrew word from the one that means just a short visit or temporary trip. This word means "to sit down."[44] You see, that is what happens when you leave where you should be and go somewhere else, try to get your needs met your own way, instead of waiting on God. You may think it will only be a temporary excursion, you are simply passing through for a moment, just stepping away for a second but, before you know it, you are still sitting there ten years later and, everything you have had to go through, you have had to go through all alone. Not only that but much of what you truly cherished has slipped away.

So it was in that context, with all of that history informing her, that Naomi speaks these incredible words to Ruth,

> *One day Naomi, her mother-in-law, said to her, "My daughter, should I not try to find a home for you, where you will be well provided for?"* (Ruth 3:1 NIV)

Not long before the moment when Naomi spoke these words, Ruth had come rushing in loaded down with all that grain and told her about this beautiful man she met in that field. That man had encouraged Ruth to stay with him, to come back there every day for more of what would fill her up to overflowing. When Naomi heard those words, when she saw all the evidence of the goodness of God coming through that door, and that look of joy and satisfaction on her daughter-in-law's face, I think Naomi started putting two and two together. I imagine it was not long after that, when everything was still, and Ruth had already gone to bed after a hard day's work in the field, that Naomi may have sat alone in the quiet, reflecting on the story that was unfolding before her eyes. There, amidst her silent musings, Naomi may have heard the voice of God, probably just a whisper in her heart, and it sounded something like this, "Welcome Home!"

You see, when I think of Naomi I think about that prodigal son Jesus talked about in the New Testament. You know, that guy who thought he would take everything his loving Father had provided for him and go do his own thing, get his needs met in some other place, until sitting all alone in a hog pen, like Naomi, that young man came to his senses. He expected that his father would be angry with him, just like Naomi said when she first came back into town. She came home thinking God was mad at her and that He would make her pay, was punishing her already. That prodigal son said "All I can expect my father to do is let me work for him, like one of his servants." That is probably all Naomi came home expecting, that God would feed them from the barley left behind by the reapers, that God would allow young Ruth to glean in his field, work for her supper, just like one of his servants. Yet even before that prodigal son got there, while he was still some distance away, his father came running, threw his arms around him, as if to say, "Welcome home!"

In much the same way, I can just imagine Naomi, as she sat there mulling over the events of the day, having one of those "Ah ha!" moments as she realized that God was running out to meet them, that quite to her surprise, He did not want to provide for them by simply allowing Ruth to work in that field, He had bigger plans than either of them had ever dreamed. If things fell into place the way Naomi suddenly realized that they could, God planned for them to own the field. Naomi's Heavenly Father was welcoming her home by running out to bestow upon her all the privileges of a daughter who never left. God was giving Naomi spiritual insight, revealing Himself through Boaz, to be her Kinsman Redeemer, the One uniquely positioned to buy back everything she had lost in the violence and competition of the field where she had gone outside of his beautiful protection.

I think this was that kind of moment for Naomi as she sat and reflected on what happened to Ruth in the field that day. She did not come home expecting this from her Father, would not have even asked for this, but, for the first time in a long time, she felt His arms around her, saw Him pouring out His love on them so freely, and she just could not help herself. Now that she was home, she started dreaming again, more accurately she began to recognize that God was dreaming dreams for both of them. Naomi could hardly overlook all the signs. She knew the fingerprints of God were all over these circumstances. Naomi knew how to interpret what was on God's heart for Ruth and speak that vision into existence. This is the same woman who returned to Bethlehem bitter, completely without hope. Naomi was not merely at the end of her rope, she actually proclaimed that she had no rope. What a transformation was taking place now in Naomi's heart that she could say with all confidence to her young protege, "As good as this is, as incredible as this seems, even this is not all God has for you, there is more to your story, God is not finished yet." What she was saying in that simple question, "Should I not seek a home for you?" was this: "It is not your destiny to merely walk with the servant girls and pick up the leftovers. That beautiful man, the owner of the field that you have just stumbled into, has not selected you for servitude, he has chosen you for love. You can live the rest of your life as the object of Boaz's affection, you are destined to be His bride."

In the third movie of *The Lord of the Rings trilogy, The Return of the King*, Princess Eowyn listens sorrowfully to what could be the final words of her beloved uncle, King Theodon, before he leaves the next morning for the battlefield:

"I have left instructions," her uncle reassures her. *"The people are to follow your rule in my stead. Take up my seat in the Golden Hall. Long may you defend Edoras if the battle goes ill."*

Eowyn asks soberly, *"What other duty would you have me do?"*

To which her uncle lovingly replies, *"Duty? No...I would have you smile again."*[45]

The actual Hebrew word translated "home" in this passage from the book of Ruth means, "a resting place, a settled spot, a place of security and quiet."[46] It points to the idea of a location where something or someone settles down and remains or stays. It is the same word translated, "still" in Psalm 23:2 where the Bible describes life lived in the protection and provision of our Good Shepherd saying, *"He makes me lie down in green pastures, He leads me beside still waters. He refreshes my soul"* (Psalm 23:2-3a NIV). Still waters are not running away all the time. They have found their destination and are content to stay. Can you imagine what it would feel like to be there? Home is a place where you no longer have to be uptight all the time, that place where you can breathe. You can kick off your shoes and just be who you are right where you are, without apology, at home. Being settled, being secure, putting down spiritual and emotional roots, always full, no other expectations than just to be who you were created to be and being fully assured that it is enough, this is what it means to be at home. Pretty hard to imagine? Oh, but wait, God can do more than we ask or imagine.

That is why Naomi's next statement is far more significant than her question,

> *Now Boaz, with whose women you have worked, is a relative of
> ours* (Ruth 3:2 NIV).

In the last chapter we examined the significance of this familial relationship within the Hebrew culture. A relative had a very specific and significant role that had already been ordained by God. The kinsman's rights and responsibilities were:

To buy back land sold by a relative to pay a debt

To buy back a relative sold into slavery because of indebtedness

To avenge the murder of a blood relative

To take the widow of a relative into his home to care for her and provide children that will continue the name of the dead

God's desire to position Himself to be our Kinsman Redeemer plays such a determinate role in so many significant decisions as God's story unfolds. A God with skin on is One that we can reach out and touch and even love, One with which we can actually have this intimate relationship we were made to experience. God knew we were impoverished. He knew we were enslaved. He knew our enemy was out to destroy us, to ruin our reputations and sully our names. He knew that our sin would make us destined for destruction. So God intervened in our story, positioning Himself to redeem us. As the Son of God became the Son of Man, our relative who could buy back every single thing that we have lost, all that has been stolen away, in this mortal struggle for our souls, He wrote us into His story, just as Ruth was about to take on a much more significant role in the story of Boaz. God knew that the only chance we would ever have of making it home would be for a kinsman to love us enough to come for us, to give His life to see us smile again.

So this is where I come undone! When God first showed me this, one night not too long ago, I had a full-on come apart. At that point in my journey I had been studying the book of Ruth consistently for over ten years, taught through it numerous times, spent two years of my daily quiet time meeting God in the book of Ruth every morning, but I never saw this quite this way until that moment. I realized that each time I came to this part of the story I had taught it all wrong. As I grasped its fuller meaning I found it to be absolutely exquisite!

This beautiful revelation God reveals to us in Naomi's words of home, begins in the book of Genesis chapter 2. We already know from Genesis 1 that God simply spoke the world, and everything in it, into existence. Almost everything, that is, except for that part of His creative process recorded in Genesis 2:7-8.

> *Then God formed a man from the dust of the ground and breathed into his nostrils the breath of life, and the man became a living being. Now the Lord God had planted a garden in the east, in Eden; and there he put the man he had formed* (Genesis 2:7-8 NIV).

Imagine with me that you are holding a piece out of a jigsaw puzzle in your hand. Your very life could be represented by that one piece of that puzzle in light of what this verse reveals. The puzzle, the mystery revealed as every piece falls into place, is God's story, with the beautiful part that each of us was created to tell, written in.

The word used in Genesis 2:7 translated "formed"[47] is not that same word that means that God brought into existence something that was never there before by simply saying it was so. No, this word means that God took into his hands the dust that He had previously spoken into existence in order to "shape" something new from it. It means He picked up the dirt, much as a potter would an unformed lump of clay, He pushed on it and pressed it into being just what He envisioned, just what He wanted it to become. He gave it this curve and a little dip right over there. He added a little sharp piece that sticks out on one side so that it would lock right into place, connected to those beside it, just like you might notice if you hold a piece of a puzzle in your hand. The exact shape He pressed into existence fit just the way He wanted. By His caress your story took on the shape for its place in His bigger story. This word in the Hebrew can also mean that God "predestined"[48] it. In the artistic heart of God, the Lord saw you. He saw the unique and beautiful shape that you would have before He formed you by His caress. He knew your destiny fully before it even started to unfold. He gave you just that shape, just those characteristics that would match His perfect, artistic vision. The whole process is so personal and intimate, unlike any other phase of creation. Then comes that moment when the puzzle piece finds its place.

When identity meets destiny we are home. Verse 8 of Genesis 2 tells us so. He had already created that beautiful garden where He would place Adam and Eve, where He would show up every day to walk with them and awaken their souls to all He dreamed for them. So, as He was shaping Adam, it was with that garden, that home, that precious intimacy, in mind. The same is true when it comes to Ruth. When God created Ruth within her mother's womb, as He shaped His unique vision for her life, planting the seeds of His vision in the soil of Ruth's heart, when He gave her a deep yearning to be a woman accepted among God's people, loved and even celebrated, God had already created a place for that vision to become her reality. He already knew precisely where Ruth would find the freedom to simply be who He created her to be, nothing more, nothing less.

Amazingly, what was true for Adam and Eve, what was equally true for Ruth, is true for you and me. It makes a lot of sense to me that there must be a huge connection between the vision of the woman God created you to be and the home that you long for in the deepest places of your heart. It is the character of God's creative process. He shapes each one of us to fit perfectly into the place where we will find our rest, the purpose of His design, the intimacy with Love Himself that we were made to crave. It is the pattern that we can see in His activity throughout history, written all across the pages of His Word. Before God formed the man He created the garden. Before He formed you inside of your mom, He created your home, a place containing all the elements of your destiny, predestined to empower you, optimized to give you freedom and rest. When we get there all He asks is that we stay.

Yet, watch this, Eve did not stay. Naomi did not stay. We do not stay! None of us stay, not when it looks like we might miss something we want, or when God does not answer as quickly as we expect. We run away from home, to all our Moabs. We run to get our own needs met just outside of where God has promised He will provide it, where He says we need only to be still. We do not stand still in our hunger, we do not stay, we run away and, just like Naomi and Elimelek we end up in the land of our enemy, missing home.

I do not think I could have seen this without a season of famine David and I endured over a recent four year period of time, a season that severely tested the depth our believing like few others. David was unemployed. After years of performing successfully in his career, He lost what he considered his dream job due to no fault of his own but simply because of a change in management. He remained without a job for twenty out of the next forty months. So we know a thing or two about famine. In fact, this was not our first season of dealing with job loss. As a salesman David had learned that the risk of losing your job due to corporate restructuring pretty much goes with the territory.

Yet I believe every day of that famine, that walk of faith was imbued with tremendous purpose. It was the intention of God to, among many other cherished lessons, get me ready to understand this part of what He wanted to teach me in Ruth's amazing story. You see, because we knew we were right where God had placed us, smack dab in the middle of our House of Bread, when our famine came, for the most part, we stayed. Oh sure, we had our moments of panic, but deep down we never wavered, we knew that God had us, that God had a new job for David that He could give any time He wanted. So when that job did not come, not right away, we believed it was for a bigger purpose and we stubbornly refused to leave God's field. What happened next was a truly extraordinary demonstration of God's extravagance, as He left extra handfuls everywhere we turned. He lavished His love on us, completely amazing us time and time again with His gracious supernatural provision. He made such a point of His miraculous provision that we began to think neither of us needed jobs in order to have all we needed, because we had everything we needed when we did not have jobs. A new job for David and a job for me, when those came, took on a completely new significance. They were not means of security. He had completely become our security. Jobs were just new assignments for us, new places for us to carry His grace. So it was in that context, with that powerful lesson still fresh on my heart, that I had this realization. It was never about the place, not Bethlehem, not the garden, any more than the provision of our need was about a job. It is not about the place, it is about what happens there. If what happens there, in that place of destiny, is carried with you, any location can be home.

The field Ruth walked in that day was different, felt like home to her, not because the soil or the barley were more exotic or unusual in that field than in any other Bethlehem barley field. Ruth was empowered to live out her destiny there, find the home of her longing heart, because in that field, unlike any other field, every day she was able to walk with Boaz, to eat at His table, listen to his dreams, and share her own. More and more, as days passed, his field would come to be home to her because of the relationship they developed there and the way it nurtured her soul.

What made the garden different than any other place on this planet was God's presence, His availability, His caring. Genesis tells us He walked with Adam and Eve there in the cool of each day. The agony of their choice not to stay was that it separated them from the One Who was their El Shaddai, their Everything. It is not for the place, the home, that you long. What you long for desperately is the beautiful intimacy that happens there.

In a marriage, the intimacy gets deeper, more profound, when you stay, over the long haul, through the hard stuff. It gets sweeter! I love the way Yoko Ono once described her relationship with John Lennon after his death. She said, "We were like two old soldiers who fought together in the war."49 David and I have embraced that description. We have looked across in the foxhole in the middle of a night of anguish, under fire, scared to death, and held on to each other. Within the span of any lasting relationship you go through stuff and it deepens your understanding of each other, it sort of braids you together. If we do not stay, in that spot, in that garden, we miss that. God gives us marriage so that we can understand our deeper longing to walk with Him, to stay with Him even when we do not understand our circumstances, because we know that He loves us like no one else ever will.

This is why we need a redeemer, someone who can buy back for us the home we have left again and again. Before God created the man He created the garden, the intimacy was waiting for the object of His affection. He did not create intimacy as an after thought. He created us for the intimacy, it is our destiny, it is what makes wherever we are, no matter what kind of famine we face, feel like our home. It is home because God is there. God did not create us so much for a purpose-driven life but for an intimacy-driven life, an intimacy we can only experience in the day in day out relationship that makes wherever we are close to Him our home. This is what we were made to crave. We were all made to hunger for home. So we feel the ache constantly until we stumble into Him, the One and Only One predisposed to love us like no one else can. He pays the price, He buys it all back, everything we threw away as we walked out the door. He stands waiting, runs to meet us, throws His arms out to redeem us, to give us back our home.

Your life, my life, are just like those pieces of a jigsaw puzzle, so unique, such mysteries, especially made for something, to fit somewhere, that place that is waiting for some reason, that will reveal my purpose, some destiny that will only happen when this piece comes to rest where it belongs, finds its home in a bigger story. I can not possibly understand what my piece of the puzzle means until I become aware of that bigger story. Come to think of it, what good is a puzzle piece if it is just left sitting anywhere, on a shelf, in a book, out in the heat of the sun, trampled under the uncaring sole of a stranger's shoe? That is not why a puzzle piece is created. That piece will never be all it was meant to be until it is finally at home in the vision of the One that created her, in intimate relationship with the One that bigger story is all about! That is why, at this moment, as God whispers His invitation to you, like Naomi, I am starting to dream again. I can see what He has been up to all along, I can wholeheartedly say that, like Boaz, God is asking you to believe, oh not just to believe, but to believe Him enough to stay. Even if all hell breaks out against you, stay. Only then, will you see Him fully and experience Him deeply and know that truly there is just no place like home.

Chapter 5

The truth you store up in silence comes back to you in the storm, and it lifts you away as on a life raft from the fears and disappointments that would otherwise pull you under. When you abide in his word, he abides in you.

— CHRISTINE CAINE, UNDAUNTED: DARING TO DO WHAT GOD CALLS YOU TO DO

GO DOWN TO THE THRESHING FLOOR

Since I was born and raised in the city of Knoxville and have now spent every one of my 59 years right here in the heart of Eastern Tennessee, I grew up waiting, dreaming, anticipating those five little words meant to elicit spontaneous outbursts of joy in the heart, "It's football time in Tennessee!" On September 6, 1980, as John Ward's iconic voice came across the loud speaker in Neyland Stadium to say just that, hearing those words seemed even more significant to me because I was holding the hand of my husband, David. Still in our first year of marriage, this was our first chance to attend a University of Tennessee football game together. It was a beautiful Saturday in early autumn which just happened to land in the middle of my husband's twenty-fifth birthday weekend. This was the opening game of the season as the University of Tennessee Vols were hosts to the University of Georgia Bulldogs, a long-standing intraconference rival. That fact alone could send tingles up the spine of a girl who grew up in Big Orange Country, but my excitement was also intensified by the fact that David had spent most of his first 20 years living in various cities within the state of Georgia. So having navigated through heavy traffic on our way to Neyland Stadium, we crowded into the stands and slid into our seats up in the nosebleed section, just in time to hear John Ward make his famous announcement as every one of the more than 95,000 fans jumped to their feet in anticipation of the ensuing kickoff.

At this memorable moment all I could see was orange. I do not mean that figuratively, as if to say I was delirious with excitement over my team. I mean it, quite literally. All I could see was orange. You see, I only stand five feet and one half of an inch when I exhibit excellent posture. So the minute every man, woman, boy and girl jumped to their feet, just as every pair of eyes, except mine and maybe those of a couple of school-aged girls who brought their cheerleader Barbies along, was focused on the field as we waited for the place kicker to make contact with the ball, I could see neither the field nor the kicker. All I could see was a sea of orange t-shirts and jerseys covering the backs of every diehard Volunteer fan who had been seated in front of me just a second prior. Suddenly the drums of the marching band began to rumble. Then the crowd joined in with a low hum which grew louder and louder as it crescendoed to a roar. Everyone stood poised, waiting for one extraordinary thing to happen and, at that very moment, it did, but not on the field. I have no idea what happened on the field because, at that precise moment, a plane flew right over the stadium to redirect my attention. It flew above the heads of each and every one of those orange clad people gathered to see the game that day. It carried for each of us an identical message expressed on a banner that was attached to the tail of that single-engine plane. It offered one idea for us to consider, one sentence for us to read and to take into our hearts, for each person who allowed themselves this momentary distraction, or anyone, like me, who had no chance of seeing what was taking place on the field anyway. Together we all heard the sound of the plane's engine inviting us to look up. Yet, though all of us shared in this significant moment if we chose to, I have to believe it was a totally different spectacle for one person in that crowd that day. You see, trailing behind that airplane was a banner that read, "Robin, will you marry me?"

If you are reading this now, then you probably already know that I am not Robin. As far as I could tell, none of the people standing near me were Robin, though she must have been amidst that huge crowd somewhere. So, though we all stood to our feet simultaneously and had the same opportunity to look up into that same sky to see that plane and the banner, there was only one woman who saw the details of her future attached to it. Even if Robins of all shapes and sizes were speckled through that enormous crowd, only one Robin heard her particular name spoken in that question and knew in her heart that it was meant for her alone. Somewhere in our midst there was one woman who had someone who loved her so extravagantly that he was willing to write it out unashamedly for every one of us to read. So I have to assume that there was one private, secret place in that stadium in which the unfolding of events had nothing whatsoever to do with that football game. I imagine there was no interest in the hot dogs, or the popcorn, or the sorority girls, or even me. It was just about Robin, and that one man who loved her enough to tell the world. Consequently, in the very next moment, the focus turned to Robin because it was Robin's turn to choose.

Now you may find this hard to believe but, after almost 39 years that have gone by since that happened, I still have no idea how she answered. I was in that stadium for this incredible moment. I saw the plane fly over head. I stood to my feet as the drama unfolded. Yet, somehow, it was possible, in the midst of all the noise and excitement, as all those people raised their voices together, one voice could be heard only by the one who loved her like crazy and chose this moment to proclaim it unashamedly. So I must admit that I did not see it. I did not hear her answer or watch the tears of joy stream down her cheeks to fall in droplets upon her smiling lips as she reached out for his embrace. I can only imagine what it must have been like when that one special man got down on his knee in perfect timing to speak her name in a gentle whisper and hold her destiny as he offered her his heart, saying, "Will you be my bride?"

This is where we have come in our journey, in Ruth's story, in your story and mine. As these two women first set out on their journey to Bethlehem, like me, Naomi was in the lead. She was the one who knew the way. She had been down this road before. Yet literally clinging to her was this courageous soul who was so desperate to be loved by God, at home with His people, and released to live out the life He first dreamed for her, that she refused to be denied. The intensity of her determination conveyed the fact that she would not be talked out of going unless someone killed her on the way. Perhaps you have come to just such a point of desperation. Maybe, like Ruth, you simply refuse, at his point in your journey, to let go or turn around. If so, like Ruth, I know you have had to push past your own brand of pain and literally fight for your destiny. I cannot help but hope that the eyes of some desperate women have fallen on this page because I am convinced that a truly desperate woman is just inches away from becoming dangerous. As I type these words for you to read I am believing God will anoint them to call out that beautiful warrior you were always meant to be. Ruth and you and I have believed to the point that we pushed through our pain and stayed on that road that would lead us closer to His heart.

God has put His crazy love on display for us in Ruth's story. He did not write it on a banner and fly it across the sky but He showed up and showed us Who He is in a self-portrait of a character introduced to us in Ruth chapter 2 named Boaz.

Boaz, her kinsman, this picture of God who strategically positioned himself in our skin, in our world, as one of us, showed us the incredibly extravagant love that God is holding out to us. Knowing every single thing that she thought should disqualify her for his love, Boaz came to her, spoke to her, left extra handfuls for her. He fed her, protected her, empowered her, gave her space, even to make mistakes without embarrassment, and before he sent her back home at the end of the day to a waiting Naomi, Boaz loaded her down with a bountiful portion of his harvest and topped it off with a to-go box from lunch. Then Boaz asked her to stay, to return to his field and stay close to him, day in and day out. There were all kinds of people in that field, the workers, the servant girls, but when Boaz issued that invitation he put Ruth's name on it. This was his banner pulled across the sky. Yet Ruth's destiny would not turn on that invitation, any more than Robin's turned on that banner pulled by a plane across the sky over Neyland stadium. Ruth's destiny, Robin's future, would be defined by each woman's response. Ruth began to understand the significance of her response that night as she talked with her mentor, Naomi, this woman God had brought into her life to disciple her, to teach her the ways of His people, to show her the way to His heart, her home.

So I must tell you, at this point in this story that has become so precious to me, more than ever before, I find myself feeling a lot like Naomi. You see, Naomi knew a little bit more about this story than Ruth did at this point. She had spent years in the middle of this place where Ruth had just recently arrived. She brought knowledge of God's ways and His Word that Ruth did not have, not yet. So when Ruth came home bubbling over about "the one" in whose field she had been gleaning that day, Naomi could see where this was going. She could see God's fingerprints all over every detail of what He had set in motion long before they had arrived. She knew Boaz, she knew the kindness that was his reputation. She knew his mother, a foreigner just like Ruth, who had courageously come to believe in the God of the Hebrew people and had been accepted as a part of their community. She could appreciate how that history predisposed Boaz to be kind to Ruth in the field that day. She also knew him as a part of the family, and being a relative meant Boaz had the right to redeem, if he chose to do so. He could rescue them from their poverty, free them from everything that had them caged. He could buy back everything that they thought they had lost forever, pick up the pieces of their broken dreams and give Ruth the fairytale ending that weaker women would have given up on before ever stepping foot on that road to Bethlehem. Naomi knew the cost and the danger of going anywhere else but the place God had made for her, anywhere outside of the intimacy He made them to crave. It is with all the knowledge of her backstory that Naomi said to Ruth, and I write these words to you, "Should I not seek a home for you?"

You see, I am convinced that you and I were made for the garden, made for the place right next to the One who has chosen us as the object of His affection. Each of us was made for intimacy, an intimate relationship with God, the One who made you just the way you are, Who loves you with an extravagance outside of anything you have experienced. That intimate relationship is the purpose of your life. It is what your heart cries out for, that gnawing hunger, that excruciating thirst that drives you, yet remains unsatisfied if you seek to get your needs met anywhere else. You were made to walk in His field, to stay in His field, to thrive in His field, to be at home next to Him, because you are not destined to work the field but to own it. He did not woo you here to the middle of this story to recruit you as His servant, He wooed you here to love you like crazy, to ask you to be His bride. Nothing will delight Him more than to see you smile again. So I feel a lot like Naomi because I recognize what God has set in motion, I see how He has positioned you to discover that you were made to be the object of His affection. I have to admit that before ever writing the words you are reading, I have spent some time dreaming again, dreams for me, dreams for you. As I have come to realize that I was made for, you were made for, this intimacy with God, I have to ask you with Naomi, "Should I not, wouldn't it be crazy if I didn't, seek a home, that garden, His field, this beautiful intimacy for you?" I know how to get you home, how to position you for the intimacy your heart craves, and that is truly the message between every word, every line in this next part of Ruth's story. God has put on display His extraordinary, extravagant affection for you, His beautiful character, the incredible lengths He has gone to in order to qualify Himself to redeem. He has put into one exquisite word His life changing invitation, as He whispers through Boaz to the heart of each desperate woman, "Stay!" What you do next, how you respond. will define your destiny from this moment on. I may never know your answer, I may stand and describe this moment years from now saying, "I don't really know if she said, 'yes' or she said 'no.'" Still I am convinced that there is a Robin reading these words right now. This is your time, your moment, God is whispering your name. He is choosing you. He has positioned Himself intentionally so that you can know that He is able, willing and has every right to buy back for you every single thing you have lost or that has been stolen away, ripped from your hands, in the violent struggle for your soul. He has wooed you with His unusual kindness and now He waits, in the quiet of this moment, for your answer. Can you hear His voice, do you feel His Spirit's nudging, the reaching out of His hand to take yours? I believe you do and, oh, how I hope you will respond with a resounding, "Yes!"

Before you were born, while this One Who saw every day of your life even then, and knew you would be here at this moment, while God Himself was shaping you into the one-of-a-kind beauty that He thought up, He knew exactly what you were made for. He knew that He would ask you, want you desperately, to love Him as He loves you, to find your destiny, your purpose, the song of your heart, your wildest dream, in your intimacy with Him. He knew that the intimacy you and He would share would so fill you that it would be impossible to hold it in or ever keep it a secret. He knew that just the overflow, the extra, of all He gives to you in your intimate moments, would spill out of you as, suddenly, you speak with His words, see with His eyes, love with His crazy extravagance, give out of His grace, be the woman He created you to be, carrying whatever part of Himself He would place inside of you, breathing it to life within you by His Spirit, so that it grows and flows through you to touch and change the world around you and offer this same beautiful invitation to every one you meet. That is His dream for you, to be set free to be you, no longer pretending, no longer ashamed. That is the destiny He has put your name on. Although it may seem much the same, that destiny, God is so complex and huge, limitless and creative, that it can look completely different for each woman in this world. Yet for each one, as was true in Ruth's story, there comes a time when you have to choose. There comes a moment, in the quiet, when it is just you and Him, that you must make up your mind. If we are to be free women, we must admit that we are desperate. If we are to be dangerous women in this world, if we are to be women who refuse to merely dream but really live lives of destiny, we must get there by way of the threshing floor. Without the threshing floor, all the planting, all the watering, all the Bible studies and the church services, come to nothing because they have all been pointing to this. Our hearts do not hunger for religion. We do not thirst for simply a set of rules and a fuller calendar. None of us need something else to do on Sunday mornings or any other mornings. We are desperate for a personal, intimate relationship, a perfect love that eliminates all reason to fear the truth. Without knowing that fact, and embracing that fact, we spend lifetimes searching for an unobtainable fix and settling for a series of emotional experiences that manufacture an unsustainable high. The harvest, your beautiful destiny, the life you were created to live, the woman first conceived in the heart of her God, all you have learned, all you have gone through, every take away, the entire harvest is totally lost, no matter how much is taken in, if we do not go to the threshing floor. So we will dig deeper to discover exactly what this entails by turning back to Ruth chapter 3.

> *One day Ruth's mother-in-law Naomi said to her, "My daughter, I must find a home for you, where you will be well provided for. Now Boaz, with whose women you have worked, is a relative of ours. Tonight he will be winnowing barley on the threshing floor. Wash, put on perfume, and get dressed in your best clothes. Then go down to the threshing floor, but don't let him know you are there until he has finished eating and drinking. When he lies down, note the place where he is lying. Then go and uncover his feet and lie down. He will tell you what to do"* (Ruth 3:1-4 NIV).

In chapter four we considered how each of our lives is like a piece of a puzzle. God formed us with His touch to fit His perfect design. Each puzzle piece only carries a part of a bigger story and will only find its true identity when it comes to rest at home within the context of a much bigger picture. In the same way, God has written you into His story. He made you to long for and only be satisfied with an intimate connection to Him as you find your home in a much greater narrative than your life alone could tell. Just in case you think I may be crazy - and I am, but not about this - let me show you something really cool that illustrates how your story fits within God's story through Ruth's story. Let me show you how Ruth's life, and remember she is a picture of you, was made to fit within a bigger story than she could have ever dreamed.

Ruth could not possibly grasp what God was up to, that her life story would one day be nestled between the books of Judges and 1 Samuel. None of the people we read about in the Bible saw themselves the way we see them now or had even a clue that we would know their names. So Ruth would have never dreamed that we would be dissecting her story thousands of years after it took place. Yet God was fully aware of the end from the beginning. He always knew what her story was meant to tell, why every detail was fashioned to fit just the way that it does into the bigger story of God. If you think God is unaware of what is going on in your world today or why, if it seems impossible to even imagine that He has a bigger plan for your life than what you can see from this present day's limited perspective, your God is far too small and as a result you may have greatly undervalued your own role in His amazing saga. You may not know that every detail of your life is packed with meaning, that you carry a beauty far more intricate than anything you have been able to dream simply because you carry the likeness of God. You have been placed just as you are right where you are to boldly put on display every single thing that you can glean from your personal, intimate relationship with the One Who thought you up before time began. As we examine Ruth's life, in the context of the greater story of God, we have a chance to try to wrap our minds around how much every detail of each of our stories matters to God and just how far He will go to be sure that what you walk away with, from whatever you have walked through, is not only protected but purified.

You see, at the time of Ruth's story, in the context of these moments, the heart of God was expressed in context of the history of the Hebrew people. Ruth did not grow up in that context. For the most part, neither did we. God has given His Word to tell us that story, the history that expresses His heart, that invites us to recognize that, for our redemption, all of history has set the stage. In the context of that history, in the midst of this intricate love story, God took a foreigner, this one woman who grew up outside of that history, and He placed her in the middle of that story intentionally, not just her, He placed you, He placed me, all the while whispering, "I know you" to each of us. Once we comprehend God's heart, expressed in this unveiling of the Kinsman Redeemer, we will know that not one thing about you, not one label that someone else has put on you, not one thing that you have gone through, not one dramatic event that broke you, nothing you have been left out of, not one place where you have gotten hung up along the way, is beyond what He can handle and even overcome. He can give you back the chance to be authentic. He can take you all the way to where you have always belonged. In His story, you were always meant to find your home.

God gave the Hebrew people some clues to help them understand the bigger picture they were designed to be a part of, some hints about it, foreshadowing of what their redemption, and yours and mine, would look like. He instituted feasts that the Israelites celebrated every year. These feasts were engrained in their culture. They were a part of their identity as His people.

Ruth's story is set in the midst of three of the most significant of those Jewish feasts, not by accident but by the deliberate providence of God. Just like that piece of a puzzle finds its meaning only in intimate relationship with a much bigger story, Ruth's story only finds its purpose, yours and mine as well, as a part of this bigger story God is telling, a story that now, in hindsight, we can see so much more clearly.

The feasts celebrated by the Hebrew people were given to them by God to be a witness, to remind them of where they had been, sort of like a photograph does for us. Everybody in my family knows I love to take pictures. Every holiday or family gathering finds a camera, or at least a cell phone with a camera app open, in my hand. Our oldest granddaughter, Morgan, did not always enjoy my passion to take her picture until one day I explained "I am having so much fun with you that I want to always remember this moment. So I want to take a picture, that I can look at later, to remind me of what we were doing and how happy we are right now." In a similar way, the feasts of the nation of Israel were sort of like snapshots of where they had been, to remind them of what they had experienced in the past and how God saw them through it.

However, the feasts were more than just pictures. Each feast was also a prophecy, an expression of what was on God's to-do list, a promise of what God was going to do for them in the future. Every time the Hebrew people celebrated a feast they were not only reminded of where they had been, they were looking ahead to where they were going, the Messiah they awaited, and all that God promised to do through Him.

Thirdly, each feast was given as a revelation, an opportunity to peer into the heart of God and recognize His character and passion. The feasts, these snapshots of the past, prophecies of the future and revelations of God's heart, were rich and precious elements of the Hebrew tradition. Yet even as they celebrated these each year, God's people failed to see how their story was part of a bigger story that they would only experience if they stayed in His field and pursued the intimacy He had wooed them to desire.

Three of those feasts create the context of Ruth's story. The first one is the feast of the Passover. This feast looked back at a time in their history when the people of God were living as slaves. They were not living their destiny, the essence of who God created them to be as a nation. They were not occupying the land God had set aside for them. They were servants in someone else's field, much like Ruth. They were out of place, no longer free to be who they were created to be, until God declared, "I will redeem them." So God came for them, much like He sent Naomi to call Ruth out of the ungodly culture of Moab. He fought for their freedom by sending a series of plagues, culminating in a plague that would strike down all the first born of their oppressors. As He did, He commanded the Israelites to put the blood of a single spotless lamb on their doorposts with the promise that, wherever He saw the blood of the lamb, He would pass over and not bring the punishment of death. So the feast of Passover was a picture of how God delivered His people from their slavery in Egypt and it revealed Him as their Redeemer, and ours as well, the One Who sets the captive free. It also pointed to, or prophesied, that one day the blood of the One and Only, the spotless Lamb of God, would set us free from our slavery to sin. This feast was taking place at the time that Naomi and Ruth prepared to leave Moab and head out on the road to Bethlehem. While God's people celebrated their freedom, Ruth and Naomi were taking their first steps toward their own. Their redemption story was at its beginning. Yet even then the story of Jesus was being foretold.

The Sunday after Passover (or the day after the first Sabbath, which is Saturday, after the Passover) the Hebrew people celebrate the Feast of First Fruits, the second feast that is a part of Ruth's story. When the nation of Israel came into the land God had promised, the first harvest they experienced was the barley harvest, just as it was as Ruth first came to her new home. Every year, as the barley ripened, the Hebrew people would take some of that first barley from different parts of the field as a representation of not only all that God had provided but all that He would provide in the days to come. Then they would wave the stalks of barley before God, signifying that this was only the beginning of all that they believed their God would give them. The people would wave the barley one way asking God for just the right amount of wind. Then they would wave it another direction, asking God for just the right amount of dew. They recognized that every piece of grain was a gift, a representation of the sweetness of God to provide for His chosen people. So this feast was like a photograph of the first harvest in the Promised Land, it revealed that God was their Provider, it promised Jesus, the Bread of Life, Who is the First Fruit of the Resurrection.

The third feast that completes the backdrop of Ruth's story was the Feast of Weeks, celebrated fifty days (seven weeks and a day) following the feast of the Passover. This feast, also known as Pentecost, was significant because it was a picture to remind the nation of Israel of the giving of the law after God brought them out of Egypt. The law was meant to reflect the characteristics that would set them apart from the unbelieving world as God's holy people. In a way, we might think of this feast as a marriage ceremony between the Hebrew people and their God because, with the law, He set them apart uniquely as His own, a nation chosen to carry His light to the rest of the nations of the world. Yet there would be another Pentecost, a day already on God's calendar even then, when He would set apart the people who had taken His name, by pouring out His Spirit on them to beautifully designate them as His bride, the chosen objects of His affection.

Below is a chart to summarize how each of these three feasts was a photograph, a prophecy, and a revelation:

FEAST	REMEMBRANCE	PROMISE	REVELATION
Passover	Deliverance from Egypt	The Lamb of God	God - Our Provider
First Fruits	First Harvest in the Promised Land	The Resurrection of Jesus	God - Our Provider
Weeks (Pentecost)	The Giving of the Law	The Giving of the Holy Spirit	God - Our Lover Our Bridegroom

The very setting of this beautiful story speaks of Jesus. Every intricate detail reveals that this Artist's rendering, this incredible self-portrait of God, is painted to perfectly unveil His heart to the objects of His crazy affection. The name of Jesus is whispered from beginning to end. The mystery of His majesty is unveiled little by little between the lines.

Ruth's story was written to fit into a story so much bigger than her own, a story that she could have never imagined. As she gave herself in intimate relationship with the one who had chosen her for love, she found her home, found her place in a bigger story, and stepped into her destiny. Could it simply be a strange coincidence that the unfolding of God's dramatic proposal for you to become His bride, begins at Passover, as Ruth makes her choice to leave Moab, to believe to the point that it changes her story, as God rescues her from the ungodly heritage that enslaved her? The God that brought His people out of bondage, initiated her journey to freedom at the time of the Hebrew feast of the Passover. Ruth could not know, yet we cannot ignore, the fact that years later, at this exact time on the 14th day of Nisan, your Kinsman Redeemer, God's Perfect Lamb, put His love for you on display for everyone to look up and see against the backdrop of the sky. Jesus said according to the gospel of John, *"And I, when I am lifted up from the earth, will draw all people to myself"* (John 12:12 NIV). Just as Naomi heard that God had visited His people and provided bread to feed their hunger, He has gotten word to you that He became that bread as He visited His people. He has wooed you to come to the cross and see the bread of His body broken to bring you home.

As Ruth and Naomi first set foot in Bethlehem, the place with a name that meant "House of Bread," the Hebrew nation prepared to wave their first fruits of the barley harvest to God, their Provider. God was watching them then, but always with His eye on the future when His Son, their Messiah that they had waited for, came out of His tomb alive, the first fruit of the resurrection of the dead! Can you grasp this? The Bread of Life broke through the ground, the First Fruit of God's resurrection harvest. Indeed there was a first fruits offering like never before that morning, signifying that the resurrection harvest of His chosen ones had only just begun. Jesus was the first of many who would come bursting forth, once dead but now gloriously alive. Offered as a sacrifice to God in the belief that there would be many more resurrections to come. Jesus explained it this way:

> *Very truly I tell you, unless a kernel of wheat falls to the ground and dies, it remains only a single seed. But if it dies, it produces many seeds* (John 12:24 NIV).

As Ruth's story asks us to believe to the point that we trust in his extravagant love, it is as if we too are walking into Bethlehem, not just any city but Bethlehem, the "House of Bread," seeing those fields bursting with exactly what we came in search of, the very thing we desire. He is your Bread of Life, He is everything you crave. Intimacy with Him is what you hunger for, and what you have tasted of Him so far is only the beginning, there is so much more waiting for you as you say "yes" to Him.

Then, on the very day that the Hebrew people commemorated how their God had set them apart to live differently, love differently, worship a very different God, to stand out starkly in contrast to the darkness of the nations around them, we see everything change in Ruth's story. Her deepest longings, her wildest dreams, begin to become her reality. Yet what is truly amazing is that at this same time many years later, as the Feast of Weeks was celebrated, everything changed with the giving of the Holy Spirit. The giving of the Holy Spirit takes the distinction of belonging to God to a whole new level. Believers are set apart in this world, not by the law written on stone tablets, but by the law written on their hearts, the transformative presence of the Holy Spirit. God has now come into us. That intimacy with the One Who made us, is something we can actually experience. The law, describing a holiness we could never conform to with our feeble attempts at outward perfection, was given to drive us to Jesus. So, on that day of Pentecost, the question that the law first stirred in our hearts was answered with His Spirit. His miraculous presence within us is the game changer, empowering us to live holy lives, set apart for God, with the living water of His intimate presence flowing into us, filling us, overflowing onto every other life we touch. Only the redeemed, those who have been bought out of our slavery because He just loved us too much to leave us there, know God so intimately, so passionately, that He places His very life within us.

It almost takes my breath away to gaze at the incredible forethought revealed in just the setting, the context, the perfect time and place of Ruth's story. It almost seems playful how God whispers Jesus in every word. He has written the name of our Kinsman Redeemer, as if in invisible ink, across every page so that only those who press in for the unseen things will take this magical mystery tour into the full and methodical telling of Love's story. Without a doubt Ruth's story is your story and Your Kinsman Redeemer is here! Now, as you see such intricate detail in His pursuit of your heart, as you know how long before you were ever born He made a way for you to be His, are you not almost compelled really, to say "yes" to a deeper intimacy with Him? As you see His love put on such bold display, will you go down to the threshing floor, lay yourself down, so that all that you are finds its meaning in His story?

RELEASED

Like a single puzzle piece, you are unique, unlike any other part of His beautiful bigger narrative. You were intentionally shaped just as you are, to long for, to crave, to thirst, to fit, to find your home only in Him. Without the relationship to that bigger story a single puzzle piece is useless. It may boast of interesting color and an unusual shape but really, who cares? The only way it fulfills its purpose is when it finds its place in a bigger picture. All our lives God has been wooing us, pursuing us, for the place we were made to belong. This is where our home is, finding ourselves in our relationship with Him. This is what He envisioned, knew about in detail, as He made you exactly as you are. He did not merely speak you into existence. Unlike any other part of creation, He shaped you, touched you, formed you with His caress. That feels right to us, even if we have never realized that until now. Just as a newborn is only at home in its mother's arms, we long for His touch, to be close to Him, to stay in His field. It is the home of our deepest longing.

Yet, because of our frailty, because of our sin, our stubborn insistence to experience what we might otherwise miss, we taste things that can never satisfy us. Eve did not stay within the boundaries God set before her because she thought she might not experience something, but the something she would have missed had she not taken that matter into her own hands, was the death and destruction that came with her sin. We are so much like her. We stick our toe over the line from the time we can crawl. We touch what says, "Do not touch." We leave when we should stay, when anyone with a right mind would certainly stay in a field of such favor and perfection. We do not stay in the garden, did not stay in the field, did not stay in perfect fellowship with God. Then, like Naomi, we went through stuff. We got hurt. In fact, I think we picked up stuffed and carried it with us from that moment on. Remember what happened with Eve. One day she was naked and unashamed and the next moment she was hiding when He came, covering up who she was. Naomi only meant to make a little visit, take a side trip into another field, and ten years later she was still there and she had lost almost everything, including her pleasant personality. She completely lost who she was while she was gone.

I do not think it is unintentional that God spoke these words to Moses, *"There is a place near me where you may stand on a rock"* (Exodus 33:21 NIV). No wonder we are insecure and isolated. No wonder we are wounded and confused. No wonder we are bitter and worn out from carrying emotional baggage. It seems impossible to think we can get back to the garden, that we really do have any hope of finding

126

home, when we have spent so much time so far away. Our wandering has changed us. Our sin has distorted who we once were. We carry back so much more baggage than we had when we left home. That is why we desperately need to go down to the threshing floor. We can never experience our destiny, never be the women we were dreamed of in the heart of our crazy lovin' God, unless we do. God says of us, like He did of the children of Israel when they cried out to Him as slaves in Egypt, "*I will redeem you*" (Exodus 6:6 NIV). In other words, I will buy every single thing back that they have lost, that has been stolen, that they sold in desperation, every beautiful part that has been marred and distorted and abused.

Ruth had not come to Bethlehem unscathed, you can bank on that. Ruth grew up in the land of Moab where mothers, overcome with their own fear and insecurity, sacrificed the well-being of their children. She came from a place where fathers, rather than fight for their families, opted for peace at any price and sold out their children in the process. She lived within a culture where parents were so caught up in the fear that comes from worshipping lesser gods that they abandoned those they were supposed to love on the altar of self-preservation and greed. It was not pretty in Moab. It was a place of darkness, and violence, and an every man for himself way of living. It was a place of selfishness, and helplessness, and godlessness, and cowardice. Ruth could not grow up in a place like that, in a culture so depraved, in an atmosphere so empty, without picking up a few things along the way, carrying some baggage to Bethlehem. Her puzzle piece was distorted, bore the marks of injury. Could it still match the dream of the God who first touched her and shaped her and made her to be free? Even if we grasp this idea, that who she was born to be, who you are and who I am was first envisioned in the very heart of God, we must face reality. We have to live in this imperfect world where abuse, criticism, ridicule, rejection, sin, betrayal and more causes for brokenness than we have time to name are a big part of life. We desperately need to know what it means to have a Redeemer for the vision of the women you and I were meant to be, for each name, every identity, that has been all but snuffed out or stolen away. When we meet Him, in each of our come to Jesus moments, we are not as we once were, we carry the wounds, the labels, the weight of our experiences while we were away from home.

Though he knew going in, before he ever approached her, before he ever spoke the first word, Boaz, the picture God gave us of Who He is in this story, knew every single thing she brought with her into that field that day. She is first described to him as "the Moabite from

Moab." This is like being referred to as "the jerk from Jerkville." Though Ruth thought she left Moab when she clung to her mother-in-law on that dirt road out of town, Moab came along. It followed her into her future. She carried that place, and its effects on her, into that field. She was not only from Moab, she had been disfigured by her godless upbringing, she carried some stuff out of that place in her and on her and with her that day.

Do you? I do. I hear the tape playing, see it when I look into the mirror, it has created the insecurities I wrestle, the fears that I fight, the pain that weighs me down, every unforgiven offense hangs on me and keeps me off balance. In a way it changes me, distorts the one I was created to be, or at least it seems to do so. Knowing who she was and from where, every single thing about her that disqualified her for love if love depended on such things, Boaz, this portrait God paints of Himself, chooses to love Ruth and invites her and, each of us with her, to say "yes" to Love, to become His bride, to understand that we are the much desired object of our own Redeemer's affection. He can handle the whole package, the good, the bad and the ugly. He invites us to believe that He can set even girls like us free and buy back everything we have lost or that has been stolen away.

Your redemption unfolds in your intimate moments with Him, as He says what only He knows to say, as He gives you back your destiny, your identity, the life you were made to live, the truth of why it matters so much to Him. You may have said "yes" to His proposal in a crowded room, even a packed stadium, but you will never fully discover just how much you are loved, nor live out your destiny in the fullness of what it means to be His bride, unless you taste true intimacy with God, until you can say, "I am my Beloved's and He is mine!" with every ounce of your being.

Naomi could see what God was up to, she understood the heart of God as revealed and expressed through the feasts she had celebrated throughout her life as a part of His chosen people. Every word God was speaking through Naomi now was calling that vision out, speaking Ruth's destiny into existence. That is precisely what is unfolding as Naomi says, *"Should I not find a home for you?"* and *"Is not Boaz a kinsman of ours?"* She is coming to the realization that Ruth is going to get her "happily ever after." With all that in mind, Naomi speaks these next few words, *"Go down to the threshing floor"* (Ruth 3:3 NIV).

Just like Naomi, I can see where this is going for each of us. I have lived long enough to know that God did not merely bring you here to these pages to inform you of the details of Ruth's story, or even mine.

God has invited you to something more exciting, more passionate, more beautiful than any chick flick or Disney princess movie you have ever seen, because this story, this very true story that comes to us as Ruth's saga unfolds, ends up being your story, and it is a falling in love story, a story of finding the One your heart was made for, stepping into the home you always dreamed of, coming into a season in your relationship with God in which you find yourself relaxing completely in who He uniquely created you to be, released to live that destiny you were made for, empowered by His fervent affection.

Naomi knew that in order to get all the way to the end of this happily ever after story, Ruth was going to have to take the next step. She was going to have to be vulnerable, yet bold. Ruth was going to have to go to the threshing floor, which, I have to tell you, at first glance did not mean much to me at all. Not having grown up on a farm, not having spent any time really in an agrarian culture, I had no idea what happened on a threshing floor nor why Ruth, or I, for that matter, or you, might need to go there. Only after I spent some time in this verse, and did some in-depth study about threshing, have I come to realize just how essential the threshing floor is in cultivating an intimacy with God that is deeper and richer than ever before. What you have tasted of God so far in your relationship with Him is merely the first fruits of what He has in store, no matter how long it has been since you said your "yes" to Him. This is where you find the more of God. God is after the consummation of this exclusive oneness that He created you to share with Him.

David and I have been married for almost 40 years. I will never forget that crisp night in November as I walked around to the back door of our church's sanctuary, under the light of a full moon, and readied myself to take the hand of this beautiful man who had inexplicably chosen to love me. Our sizable church sanctuary was filled with family and friends who came to witness our vows, to celebrate our promise to live the rest of our lives as man and wife. Our wedding took place in public, in front of hundreds of people who gathered in that sanctuary that night, but the marriage itself, for the most part, has been quite the opposite. Much of what is involved in a marriage is a private matter, it is a day to day union, a level of intimacy that I share with no one but my very own bridegroom. My wedding may have been public, but my marriage, the real nitty gritty stuff, the extraordinarily sweet stuff, the essence of what makes us man and wife, happens in the quiet, when it is just David and me. I like it that way, don't you? That is the complexity, the fullness, the beauty of marriage. If being married to David meant nothing more than walking into church, hearing the music, listening to the preacher's words and saying "I do," then our relationship would be neither deep nor truly meaningful. The public part, what took place between David and me in that church sanctuary, is only a taste of what has come to comprise our love story. Without the intimate, private moments we have shared, I am afraid it would not be much more than a casual infatuation.

Do you want to merely be infatuated with Jesus or do you want to fall truly, madly, deeply in love with this One Who has both the power and the passion to redeem every single thing you have lost along the way? He is that Lover of your soul Who will speak the words that can counteract every false accusation, embarrassing imperfection, or rebellious offense that has left its mark of shame upon your heart. If the woman you were intended to be now stands marred and masked by what you have done or all you have been through, He is wooing you to an intimacy that will become your everything, where His gentle whispers call out the beauty that Love already sees.

What Naomi was explaining to Ruth in these verses is that Ruth would have to put forth some effort, that she would have to be intentional about wanting to go deeper in her relationship with this beautiful man. Why not go find him, take advantage of a chance to be alone with him, after all the ways he has demonstrated how kind and protective, strong and affirming he is? Who would refuse to take that chance? Would any excuse be worth missing this encounter with this one who had shown her such unusual thoughtfulness, extravagant benevolence, extraordinary attentiveness, and incredible selflessness?

So if you begin to see in Boaz the dazzling brilliance and beauty of the One Who is waiting for you there, once you realize that this is the kind of God Who is willing to lavish you with words that will strip away the shame and the guilt, the insecurity and emotional baggage that bears no resemblance to who you really are, then you will hardly mind saying "Alright, I will wash. Okay, I will put on some perfume. I will put on my best dress and I will go to where He is. I am going to get down to that threshing floor so that I can be alone with the One who loves me like no one else ever can." In other words, I will be intentional about it, carve out some time, make it a priority, do whatever I have to do to pursue an intimate relationship with this One Who is proficient in redemption.

We need to know what happens on the threshing floor, what is involved in the processes of threshing and winnowing, because, while probably few, if any, of us have harvested a lot of barley, you may find threshing a little more familiar than you might guess. Each of us does our own version of threshing, with or without much insight into how to properly go about it, on a regular basis. We take the details of a given situation, lay them out on the table, and furiously try to figure out what is really going on, sort out the truth from the misunderstanding, separate what is valuable from what we should simply let fall to the floor. A comical example of how we try to sort truth from fiction is found in a scene from one of my favorite movies, *You've Got Mail,* in which the character of Kathleen Kelly tries to make sense of a disappointing experience of waiting all evening for a friend who promised to meet her at a coffee shop but, as far as she knew, never came.

Christina: So? What happened?

Kathleen Kelly: He never came.

Christina: He stood you up.

Kathleen Kelly: I wouldn't characterize it that way. I think something happened. Something unexpected that made it impossible for him to. What if he showed up, took one look at me and left?

Christina: Not possible.

Kathleen Kelly: Maybe there was a subway accident.

Christina: Absolutely!

Kathleen Kelly: A train got trapped underground with him inside.

Christina: And no phone.

Kathleen Kelly: And you know how those express trains create suction.

Christina: He got sucked onto the tracks.

Kathleen Kelly: The third rail.

Christina: He's toast!

(George enters the room)

George: What happened?

Kathleen Kelly: He was unable to make it.

George: He stood you up?

Kathleen Kelly: Maybe he had a car accident. Those cab drivers are maniacs.

Christina: They hit something and you slam into that plastic partition.

Kathleen Kelly: Or his elbows could be in splints, so he couldn't dial.

Christina: Or he could be unconscious.

Kathleen Kelly: In a coma.

Christina: Stuck in intensive care.

Kathleen Kelly: With a heart monitor beeping.

Christina: And like...

Kathleen Kelly and **Christina:** No phone.

(George hands them a copy of the New York Post with a headline that reads, COPS NAB ROOFTOP KILLER)

Kathleen Kelly: COPS NAB ROOFTOP KILLER? What? What are you saying?

George: It could be. He was arrested two blocks from the cafe.

Christina: Is there a picture?

(They see the picture of a man with his jacket pulled over his head.)

Christina: That explains it.

George: He was in jail.

Christina: And there was a phone.

George: He only got one call, so he called his lawyer.

Christina: You are so lucky!

George: You could be dead.

Kathleen Kelly: He couldn't possibly be the rooftop killer.

Christina: Remember when you thought Frank might be the Unabomber?

Kathleen Kelly: That was different.[50]

Do you recognize yourself in that conversation? Perhaps you now realize that you have done some threshing, some hashing out, sorting between what is true and what is imaginary. I know I have, sometimes with little more accuracy than Kathleen Kelly and her crew. Just as you could hang all kinds of tags and labels on a puzzle piece that could cover up and distort its original appearance, we pick up lots of things throughout each day that we hardly know what to do with. The takeaways we carry are almost always a mixture of the good and the bad, the stuff we really want to hang on to and the things we would really rather forget, some truth and some lies. These are the scariest sort of lies too, you know, the ones that have just enough truth in them to take hold and refuse to budge. We carry all kinds of information with us, like labels and lies hung from a puzzle piece that, left unopposed, can keep that piece from ever finding its place. Threshing can be a healthy exercise of analyzing what we should hold on to and learn from any given experience, or, it can be a complete disaster, depending on what kind of filter we use and who we invite into the process.

This is the significance of Naomi informing Ruth that Boaz would be at the threshing floor. She was sending Ruth, not to do this all alone, but to intentionally meet Boaz there. You see, Ruth had never done this, but Boaz was an expert. Which piques my interest, given that Boaz owned the field. He was a man of standing in Bethlehem. He had servants. It would seem that he should feel no obligation to do the threshing himself. Yet Boaz did not delegate the task to someone under his authority. Boaz chose to go. He understood the purpose of the process and he would not miss it for the world. Threshing is the most essential aspect of bringing in the harvest.

The threshing floor was a level circular area. It was about 25 to 40 feet in diameter, prepared in advance for a specific purpose. During that preparation, the workers would take the ground and stamp it down, wet it and press on it in all different kinds of ways. Then they would sweep it and remove any stones found within that circle of ground until it was not only level but perfectly smooth. This circle would probably be located on a hill, somewhere out in the open, to take full advantage of the wind, an essential element once the winnowing began. A border of large stones was carefully placed around the circle to contain every speck of the precious grain. All of this was made ready in advance so that, when the time was right, when the wind was at its peak, usually around 4 or 5 o'clock in the late afternoon, the threshing process could begin without delay.

As the threshing began, the sheaves of grain, containing everything the reapers had picked up in the field, were laid out on the open floor. Oxen or donkeys were yoked to a piece of wood studded with stones that would drag behind them. The grain to be threshed would be piled up in the center of the circle and pulled down into the path of the animals. The wooden drag would then be pulled over the grain so that the stones embedded in the wood would gradually break the grain from its stalk and separate it from the hard, inedible coating. Sometimes the thresher, along with members of his family, would even stand on the drag to add extra weight. The key to the process was in applying just the right amount of pressure to separate the grain without crushing it. The partially threshed grain would then be turned by the thresher over and over so that every side was exposed to the weight of the drag. Though separated from the grain, the worthless, inedible elements of the stalk and the coating, called the chaff, remained in the mixture, along with any dirt that the reapers picked up inadvertently with the grain in the field.

When this mixture was totally broken apart, it was picked up and tossed into the air. This part of the process is called winnowing. The thresher did this so that the worthless chaff would be exposed. This chaff, which weighs less than the grain, would be blown away by that wind, allowing only the precious grain to fall back to the floor. Every sheaf of grain had to go through this arduous process. Every bit of it had to be broken open to separate the good from the bad, the valuable from the worthless. It all had to be exposed to the wind in order for the elements, that would otherwise spoil the harvest, to be blown away. At the end of this process all that remained was the pure and useful harvest of grain that God had provided for the nourishment of His people. The work would then be followed by a jubilant time of celebration.

Why do you think Boaz did this himself? When he could have delegated this process to a servant, why did he refuse? One reason could be that it was crucial that this process be done correctly. Carelessness would render the entire harvest lost. There could not be any short cuts. Only the owner of the field might care enough to see this all important labor all the way through to its end. This was ultimately his responsibility.

Another possible consideration was that these were dangerous times. The book of Judges, which takes place at the same time as Ruth's story, describes a harvester named Gideon, who was so scared that he was threshing his grain down in a hole, in an old dried up well, where it must have been nearly impossible to catch even the slightest breeze. (paraphrased from Judges 6:1-11 NIV) Boaz, in contrast with Gideon, displayed courage and confidence in personally participating, and even sleeping on the threshing floor, to protect all he had worked to accomplish.

A man like Boaz also would never want to miss such a rich experience. He must have enjoyed being there among the people who worked beside him, felt invigorated by a hard day's labor, enjoyed stepping back to survey how far they had come. Surely such a kind and generous soul looked forward to the unrestrained celebration that naturally erupted when their labor came to an end. Boaz was there because he cherished the harvest, it was his treasure, it was his joy. He relished how those kernels of barley felt in His hand as he breathed in their faintly sweet aroma. Boaz oversaw each part of this process from start to finish, from out in the field in the heat of the day, as the reapers picked up the grain and tied it up in bundles, to the threshing floor where that grain was pressed on and purified, because he valued the fruit that this painstaking process would yield in the end. He refused to stand uninvolved or watch from a distance. He was fully engaged because that harvest mattered so much and so did the ones who brought it there from the fields.

Can you grasp the significance of the fact that God chooses to portray Himself as this fully accessible field owner who intentionally places Himself in the middle of the action? As we picture this gracious man right there among his people in the thick of all the activity, giving himself fully to the labor as well as the celebration, we see the true essence of God's heart exposed. In the middle of your crisis He is there. In the midst of your chaos He is that unexplainable peace that holds you tightly through it. In the thick of your battle He leads armies of angels to fight for your heart. In the middle of your family, as you gather around your table, He sits among you, relishing in the laughter and the love. Even when it feels like you have lost your way completely, as you wonder where God is anymore, you can be sure that He has not forgotten you and has never left your side. God, the owner of the field, the One who has chosen you for love, will be waiting for you, anxious to gently brush away the dirt and break off the hardness of what you have walked through on your way to your time alone with Him. Your Kinsman Redeemer will personally supervise that separating of the lies from the truth, the worthless trash from the treasure that nurtures and defines your beauty. Can you see why He would never entrust this to anyone else? Somewhere in all of this stuff we carry, His pure harvest, the true identity of this woman of His dreams, the beautiful one-of-a-kind creation that is you, is in the mix. Though your splendor may be hidden beneath a protective shell, it may be covered up by scars, distorted, mislabeled, even marred, God sees His masterpiece ready for the unveiling. Only His words, His touch, can gently break off the shell that for a season was given to protect you, to truly restore your soul. God embraces this process because without it the entire harvest - the nourishment, the growth, the character and convictions that were to be gleaned from your life's experiences - is totally lost.

Why should each of us carve time out of every day to spend alone with our Kinsman Redeemer? Why should you open His Word and wait to hear Him say your name? It is the miracle that releases the magic. In the quiet, alone with the One who loves you extravagantly and holds nothing back, the lies and hurts begin to fall away and who you were always meant to be is set free to emerge. God will meet you there, if you will go to find Him on the threshing floor. Your relationship with Him was never meant to be merely a public spectacle. He is inviting you into a beautiful intimacy, an extravagance of grace and passion, that protects what is beautiful about you and gently removes every worthless thing that you were never meant to carry.

So, in response to Naomi's prompting, Ruth goes to the threshing floor.

"I will do whatever you say," Ruth answered. So she went down to the threshing floor and did everything her mother-in-law told her to do (Ruth 3:5-6 NIV).

As soon as Ruth heard that this was her chance to say "yes" to this kind and generous soul who had captured her attention, this man that Naomi spoke of with such trust and admiration, someone who was not only positioned, but also most likely willing, to buy back every thing she had lost in Moab, she said, "I will!" without hesitation. In fact, she not only said she would, she did.

Just think of the inherent risks Ruth took in going to that threshing floor. It was dark. It was night. The enemy was near. Those already working there might see her. Her intentions might be misconstrued. She could be exposing herself to danger, to gossip, to the chance that she and Naomi had misinterpreted Boaz's acts of kindness. The outcome of her actions was completely beyond her control. She could be taken advantage of, falsely accused, ridiculed, even assaulted, possibly abused or openly rejected. She certainly risked embarrassment, the chance of getting it all wrong, saying it all wrong, looking stupid in the eyes of the very people among whom she so hoped to, at last, belong. Ruth's knees most likely trembled all the way there, but she kept walking. That is what mattered for Ruth, what matters most for us as well. These are the very same risks we take as we go running after God, if we sell out, full out, to an intimate relationship with Jesus. The threshing floor is no place for sissies. It is for those who, though trembling, find the courage to abandon our futile attempts at self-protection to grab hold of the chance to finally become fully free.

After all, not every risk resulted from taking Naomi's advise and heading down to the threshing floor. Just consider what Ruth stood to lose if she gave into her fear and opted not to go. What if she played it safe and just put off making a decision either way? It can be so tempting to hide who we are, thinking that is what playing it safe really looks like. Yet we could easily end up, like Gideon, doing the silliest things, things that make no sense at all, have no chance of setting us free to fulfill our glorious destiny, because we are so afraid of this garbage that other people say about us, perhaps directly to us, or the labels and the reputations that may stick to us, if they disagree. In the face of risking verbal abuse and manipulation, anger and physical attacks, rejection and ridicule we may decide to wall off our hearts to keep all the bad things out. Yet we soon realize that we are the only ones we imprison by giving into our fears. If we do not go, we lose everything, we abandon the lives we were meant to live, give away our power and give up on our dreams. The harvest is completely lost, everything we have been through has been for nothing, unless we take the risk to go to the threshing floor.

I just love how this beautiful relationship between Ruth and Naomi has developed and deepened into such a rich friendship by chapter 3. Ruth continues to open her heart to share with her mother-in-law all the details of her unfolding love. Naomi teaches Ruth how to respond to this invitation to intimacy. She counsels Ruth about how to position herself to move closer to love's opportunity. Then Naomi assures her, if she will believe to the point that she will go alone to be with him and wait to hear His voice, he will come, he will say the words that only he can say. What a powerful and freeing truth to apply to our relationships with one another. Every woman can hear from God for herself. You do not need any go-between. God is inviting you to intimacy. In the context of His unusual love He wants to speak to you Himself. A wise and loving friend will take you to the door of intimacy, she will show you how to position yourself at His feet, and then she will say "You'd better go in alone."

There are things that I cannot tell you, because I do not know what God longs to say. I can tell you how to hear from God. I can tell you about what I have experienced in my intimate encounters with Him. I can tell you what it looks like so that your expectations will be increased. Yet if you are longing to know His heart, if you want to know how He feels about you, if you want the more of God, to go deeper still, you have to go in alone. Only He can speak those words you need to hear that are relevant and personal, particularly suited to lead you to your destiny.

When our oldest daughter, Brittany, was about six years old she told me that she wanted to ask Jesus to come into her heart. We snuggled up on the couch together as I explained all about how she could do that and shared what that meant to me. Then she turned and asked me if I would just do it for her. I guess it seemed like I knew the way, I understood just how to go about it so much better than she could. Still I had to love her boldly and say "No, honey, I can't. This is something you have to do for yourself." I could tell her what to say but this was her prayer, her decision. I had to leave space for God to meet her there. The hard thing was that she did not pray right then, or even make her decision that night. I had to watch and wait and pray. I could do no more than that. My role was to simply offer her a sample of what I had experienced, believing that it would increase her appetite and bring her to the table for more. Not too long after that conversation, Brittany did approach God in the solitude of her heart. She made her own decision to enter into a beautiful, eternal love relationship with her Kinsman Redeemer when it came out of her own heart's desire, when it was right for her, when it was real to her. She grabbed hold of a relationship that I told her about and it became her own. She could not ride my coattails and still truly know His love, truly know how He feels about her, truly understand the value that He sees in her. Her intimacy had to be her own or it would never be intimacy at all.

Without a trip to the threshing floor the whole harvest is lost, it all becomes tainted by those worthless things that get picked up wherever we go. That is why God invites us, woos us, urges us, waits for us to come, and personally meets us there. With Him there is the safety we only long for behind our walls. With Him there is nothing to fear. He knows the authentic you. He is delighted with you already. He understands the need for this threshing process and knows just how to go about it. He knows how much pressure to apply to break open your heart, exposing the worthless things you have buried there, to discard them and leave only what is pure. His gentle touch will heal your wounds, as He listens as long as it takes to leave it all on the floor at His feet. He will whisper the words your soul longs to hear. You just have to go meet Him. No one else can have those conversations. You must be vulnerable and bold.

Naomi gave Ruth invaluable advise, offered her the benefit of her many years immersed in the Hebrew culture. She had so many experiences that Ruth had never had in Moab and she freely shared those with her young protege. Then Naomi said "I can take you this far, but God will have to take you the rest of the way." That is a beautiful gift that we can offer each other as friends. It is why, as I write these words, I feel a lot like Naomi. The question God asks us at this point in Ruth's beautiful story is "Will you believe, not just believe, but will you believe to the point that you will go alone to be with Him and wait to hear His voice?" I do not think Ruth knew exactly what to do when she got there. Naomi knew, but she could not go. So she told Ruth what to do, how to position herself. Then she told Ruth to simply rest in His presence and wait to hear his voice.

WILL YOU **BELIEVE** TO THE POINT THAT YOU WILL **GO ALONE** TO BE WITH HIM AND **WAIT** TO HEAR HIS VOICE?

God speaks to those who are His. You have been invited to know this One Who already knows everything about you and has chosen you for His love. Now this sacred romance that God has written you into can begin to be the truth of your experience. As you come to Him alone, in the quiet, and lay your life at His feet, He is yours and you are

His. No one can ever come between you and His grace when you have fallen in love with the sound of His voice and embraced every single thing He says about you as the only truth of your story.

You should know this about your Maker, Who is your Husband, as the prophet Isaiah describes Him in Isaiah 54, from the very beginning God has been a talker. Genesis 1 tells us that the world was empty and without form. Then God spoke and everything changed. In John 1 Jesus is called the Word. He not only spoke the world into existence but the pages of the Bible are filled with stories of those who have heard Him speak to them. God walked and talked with Adam and Eve in the garden. It was Jesus who leaned over to look down into an old dusty well where Gideon was trying to winnow his harvest in hiding. His Word echoed down into that hole in the ground, to call out the "mighty warrior" this fearful farmer was meant to be. Jesus went out of His way to sit by a well and talk to a woman, who was accustomed to being shunned and, as a result, was desperately thirsty. He spoke to her about things no one but God could have known and gave her a drink of a living water that no one else could have offered. Jesus taught in the temple, in homes, on a hillside, as he walked with His disciples. He spoke to Mary Magdalene in the garden right outside of His own tomb. The Holy Spirit spoke in many languages through the mouths of his disciples at Pentecost. When He speaks, you will recognize that it is Him. That is Jesus's promise as He described Himself as our Good Shepherd, He assured us, *"His sheep follow Him because they know His voice"* (John 10:4 NIV).

So let me ask you this, have you ever picked up the phone to hear a friend's voice, or sat down at a table to talk with someone you feel close to over a cup of coffee, or met your husband for dinner, at a time when you were anxious or hurting or confused or trying to sort something out, so much so, that you could hardly wait to get there to talk about it? What if, when you arrived, you were not the first to speak? Perhaps your husband started telling you about his day or your friend had a story about her kids. Was it difficult to really hear them with your mind was so full, so frantic, so preoccupied? Is it really hard sometimes to listen when your soul is jumbled with so much turmoil? This reveals part of the value of the threshing floor. The first thing a harvester would do upon arriving at the threshing floor is simply pour everything out that they brought from the field, dump the entire load of what they picked up throughout the day. There was no need for them to know how much of it was garbage. The very first step in the threshing process was to bring it all and lay it down at this place that was prepared to handle it. What a beautiful aspect of our intimate encounters with God? We can just come and empty ourselves. We have such freedom to purge in our prayers because our Father already knows what we carry in our hearts. We cannot shock or overwhelm Him. He is prepared to handle it with care.

The problem is that, for many of us, this is not just how our time of prayer begins, this is all that we experience when we pray. Can you imagine a harvester coming in from the field, with his crazy mixture of barley and waste, and just pouring it out, dumping everything there and walking away empty-handed? What would be the point? Why harvest the barley at all? If you simply pour the whole mess out and go home, you leave just as hungry as when you came. You walk away with nothing to nourish your soul. You simply display a complete misappropriation of the purpose of the process. When you come to God in prayer, when you meet Him on the threshing floor, you empty yourself, that is true, but is it not craziness to stop there when you can leave with so much more? To simply use this incredible opportunity to vomit up all we are worried about is not truly prayer at all! We come to prayer to have a conversation, to be known and to know, to experience the intimacy of relationship. We pour out ourselves and all that we have picked up along the way, only so that we can take Him in, hear His voice, let Him tell us what to do with what we have just walked through.

When you come to your threshing floor throw down everything you carried in, say it, write it (That is what I usually do because it slows me down), lay it out in the one place that is completely safe, safe because He is there. Yet never let that be all that you do. He cries out to his beauties, *"Call to me and I will answer you. I'll tell you marvelous and wondrous things that you could never figure out on your own"* (Jeremiah 33:2-3 MSG). It pains me to think of all the words God might have spoken but no one was listening, answers He so wanted to give but we were on our way out the door without giving Him the chance. No, we want answers that chase us down on the run in one hundred and forty characters or less. That, love, is not intimacy! Intimacy takes time. Intimacy can not be hurried. Intimacy lays her body down in the quiet to hear what her Lover has to say, because when He speaks, she is changed. We gain perspective, understanding, wisdom, all the things we could never figure out on our own. Ask Him to take you through the process of separating truth from lies, understanding what is real and what is garbage. After you have said what you have come to say, open His Word, ask Him to speak and He will.

So when you come to the threshing floor to find your Redeemer the first thing I suggest is that you take whatever you picked up in the field and dump it on the floor, get it all out in the open. Write it down. Speak it aloud. Whisper it in your heart. Then take a breath. Ask Him to speak to you as you open His Word. Expect to find Him, hear Him there, because John tells us plainly, *"In the beginning was the Word, and the Word was with God, and the Word was God"* (John 1:1 NIV). When you open His Word He is there. To read it is to go to where You know you will find Him. Something in the Word of God will speak to your situation or prepare you for one. Look for truth that addresses your heart's question, jumps off the page as if it were living and breathing, because it is. It will separate for you what is fiction and what is true, what is pure emotion running rampant in your soul and what is rock solid and sure, though it must be accepted by faith. This experience will change everything, set you free in ways you cannot imagine. When you open up the very Word of God you have stepped out of the shadows to lay down at His feet, waiting with expectation to hear His voice. You have come to the threshing floor.

As you read the Word of God be sensitive to the Spirit, pay attention to whatever stands out to you and identify why. Does it answer a question you have asked or does it raise one? Does it provide direction, comfort, understanding, courage? If it seems like God has attached your name to something in the passage that you read, He probably has. Sit with Him there. Do not rush this chance to be alone with Him. Dive in and become immersed in the truth that you have found. Look up the definition of a word in the Hebrew or Greek text. You can do this using a search engine or a Word Study Bible. Read a further explanation in a commentary or turn to a cross reference to see what more God may reveal. You can use a search engine to find a commentary or other Bible study tools online. Keep a journal and write what God is revealing to you, put into words how it moves you, what questions or thoughts this passage stirs. You may only read a verse or read a couple of chapters before something stands out to you. When He speaks, you will know it is Him. Do not hurry this moment, this chance to look into the eyes and listen to the whisper of this unusual, beautiful One Who has chosen to speak words of life and love to your seeking soul. In other words, be vulnerable and intentional.

Ruth would never end up at the threshing floor by accident, and neither will you. Be purposeful and be open. Be real with Him. Be attentive to how God may whisper His love, speak something only He could know. Hearing each beautiful expression of His love, spoken with your name attached, will forever change you. This is intimacy, not merely talking at Him, but talking with Him. His every expression of love, over time, will give you the courage to stand, to raise up your hand, even in the midst of a huge crowd of people, shouting unashamedly, "Yes! That's me! I'm Robin! And I will!"

You know I have been thinking quite a bit about Robin as I have poured over these words God gave me for you. After all these years I was just wondering, do you think she thought for one second, "What if there is another Robin in this crowd? What if that message is meant for somebody else, but not me?" Do you think she might have doubted for a second that this question written in the sky was directed at her? I think she knew exactly who sent that message because he held her hand in his, she felt his closeness and she knew his heart. She had been walking with him long enough to recognize such a genuine expression of his devotion and, maybe not to expect it, but to happily embrace it when it came. I would not be at all surprised if he gave her hand a sudden squeeze, or used his elbow to give her a gentle nudge that would grab her attention. Perhaps he even placed his hand beneath her chin to raise her eyes to see His affection so boldly exposed far above everything else that was happening around her.

Robin was with that one who loved her with a crazy passion, and so are you. Even at this moment you can take the chance, you can choose to believe that your eyes have fallen on this page for a reason, that God is waiting for you to come to where you know you can find Him. A God big enough to perfectly place Ruth's story in the middle of His bigger story, Who gave everything to intentionally position Himself to give you back who you are, has brought you to this story to woo you into His chambers. You can meet Him all alone, in the quiet, in the dark, in a whisper, in a prayer, in His Word, one on one, and let Him tell you who you really are, separate the dirt and the lies from the precious harvest of everything you have gone through. Such an encounter can quickly become your secret garden, the place you were made for, where you can fully give yourself to intimacy with Him. Do not wait. Seek Him. Pour it all out where He can be found. Go down to the threshing floor.

In Ruth we read these words,

When Boaz had finished eating and drinking and was in good spirits, he went over to lie down at the far end of the grain pile. Ruth approached quietly, uncovered his feet and lay down. In the middle of the night something startled the man; he turned—and there was a woman lying at his feet! "Who are you?" he asked. "I am your servant Ruth," she said. "Spread the corner of your garment over me, since you are a guardian-redeemer of our family" (Ruth 3:7-9 NIV).

When she uncovered his feet and laid down, when Boaz discovered her curled up in the shadows, she was saying "yes" to her redeemer, she was believing that this was her game changer. This Moabite girl was going all in, putting every speck of her hope in this one who had the power to change her life.

To ask someone to "spread the corner of their garment" over you or to ask that they "cover you under their wings," is to use two alternative translations of the same Hebrew phrase. This was not as strange a choice of wording as it might seem to us today. Ruth was saying "yes" to his protection and provision for her, to an intimacy that would define her as this man's bride. So in taking her place at his feet she was answering her own version of the question, "Robin, will marry me?" Or, in this case, "Ruth." She had decided to let him tell her who He saw her to be and call out the woman she was destined to become, no longer a foreigner, no longer a woman far from God, no longer an outsider, no longer a beggar in someone else's field. She laid all that stuff down, left it all on the threshing floor, to take hold of the words that only this man was in a position to say to her and make them true.

So how did Boaz respond when he found her there, alone, in the dark, in the quiet, in a whisper, saying, "yes" to his unspoken question?

"The Lord bless you, my daughter," he replied. "This kindness is greater than that which you showed earlier: You have not run after the younger men, whether rich or poor. And now, my daughter, don't be afraid. I will do for you all you ask. All the people of my town know that you are a woman of noble character" (Ruth 3:10-11 NIV).

John Ortberg uses a great illustration of how it feels to reach out to God in this way in his book, *Get Out Of The Boat*.[51] He writes that renowned French priest, Henri Nouwen, once wrote of the lessons he learned from some friends who happened to be circus performers, trapeze artists, to be specific. They were part of a performing troupe known as the Flying Roudellas. Nouwen learned from these friends that there are two kinds of performers in a trapeze act: the flyer and the catcher. Nouwen's friend explained, "People think the flyers are the stars, because we're doing somersaults in the air and it looks really cool but the real star is the catcher."[52] You see, the flyer swings high above the crowd on that trapeze, but, in every performance, the moment comes when he must let go. So he arcs out into the air, lets go of that bar, then he must remain as still as possible while he simply waits...not to fall, not to fail, not for some disaster to end it all. The flyer waits, expecting the strong, reliable hands of the catcher to reach out in perfect timing to pluck the flyer from the air. Nouwen's friend goes on to explain, "The flyer must never try to catch the catcher."[53] The flyer has no other part to play than to wait in absolute trust. The catcher will catch him, but he must wait, believing that to be true.

This is what it means to go to the threshing floor, you place yourself at the feet of your Redeemer, and wait. You leave it all on the floor at his feet, and you wait. You say "yes," flinging yourself out there, daring to believe in the impossible, and you wait. You pour out your soul, all that you have picked up along the way, and you wait. You become perfectly still, and you wait. You wait expecting to meet Him there. You open His Word that promises to never come back empty, expecting to hear His voice, expecting to know when He speaks your name, identifying what is true and pure and beautiful about you and discarding the rest. You let go, refusing to thrash about in anguish, expecting to feel His grasp catch you mid-flight, expecting to uncover the true harvest of the life you were made to experience, expecting, by faith, knowing, that you will be safe in the arms of His passion.

Where have you found yourself in this story? Perhaps, like Ruth, you are grabbing hold with both hands, reaching out to embrace this intimacy you have only tasted. Maybe, like Naomi, there was a time when you were full and you long to go back to that place and be able to share, once again, out of the overflow of your intimate connection with God. It may be that, like Orpah, you have walked away from this incredible invitation and tried desperately to get your needs met on your own. Could this be your time to turn around and set out on that journey toward God? Could this be your moment to open your heart and let someone walk that road beside you? What really matters most is a clarity in knowing that the purpose of our relationships with each other, even as I share my own life with you through the words on this page, is to offer an invitation to the intimacy that is available right now for you to enjoy with God yourself. The relationship that He invites you to experience is one in which you may not get it right all the time or always achieve perfection. He is willing to meet you in the middle of the process, in the midst of the mess, because He already loves you like crazy. He wants to tell you Himself just how He feels about you. He sees such beauty in the woman you are right now, right where you are. You were created by His tender touch according to His brilliant and intricate design and now, this invitation to know Him intimately, is offered so that, through that intimate relationship with your passionate Creator, He will release in you all of the beauty that has been tucked away since before you were ever born. What I share with you from my experience is only a taste of what God has in store. So this is the door. You are standing at the threshold. Can you smell the aroma of what is waiting just inside? This is the place to hear His voice, to take the chance to know His heart. These pages are as far as I can go on your journey into intimacy. You have to take the next steps alone as you take your place at His feet. Then Love, more unusual and extravagant than anything you have ever experienced, will meet you there. Take some time here. Go down to the threshing floor.

Chapter 6

Nothing on earth compares to the strength God is willing to
interject into lives caught in the act of believing.

— BETH MOORE, *BELIEVING GOD*

FEARLESS

It was like a scene out of my worst nightmare, something off
American Horror Story or The Walking Dead. There had been several
break-ins in our neighborhood. I had even witnessed a couple. So I
was aware that the possibility of discovering that an uninvited guest
had invaded your home was a real one. Still, somehow, I never thought
it would happen to me. David was out of town on business. The girls
were tucked safely into their beds. On this quiet evening, I was
relatively at ease spending the late night hours alone, quite unaware
that I was not alone after all.

It was about midnight when I turned off the television, deciding
to go to bed. On my way past the couch I ran into the exercise bike
that I had dragged in from another room earlier in the day, thinking
I could ride while I was watching television. Of course, this was a total
delusion. I never rode that bike. So it is no wonder that I forgot all
about it being there. Just as I collided with the bike I saw, out of the
corner of my eye, some sort of movement in the kitchen. As I quickly
reached to turn on the kitchen light, I could hardly believe my eyes.
There, in my own kitchen, I came face to face with the unwelcome
intruder.

Looking down on me with a sneer as if to say "I dare you to make
one move, Lady!" was this absolutely humongous, "pukey-green"
grasshopper-like creature. Seriously, this was the biggest bug I had ever
seen. This winged antagonist was at least two and a half inches long.
He was wiggling his legs in an eerie sort of way, taunting me, daring me
to make the first move.

Immediately, I knew that I was in desperate need of a weapon. My
eyes quickly scanned the room, stopping to focus on the coffee table as
I decided to arm myself with a magazine. I backed toward the stack of

magazines I found there, keeping my eyes frozen on my adversary as I reached for my latest issue of Today's Christian Woman. Yet somehow, just imagining slimy green bug guts smashed across the face of someone like Anne Graham Lotts or Amy Grant, was kind of unsettling. Besides, my nemesis was now on the ceiling. There was no way I could reach him assisted only by a magazine. This job would require a weapon that provided a bit more vertical assistance.

Thinking on my feet, I quickly decided to abandon the magazines and head for the pantry to grab the broom. Adding a degree of difficulty to this maneuver was the fact that this bug was perched directly in the line between me and the pantry door. Still I made a run for it, but just as I was passing directly beneath him, as bugs are known to do, this guy decided to take flight, sending me into a panicked zig zag pattern reminiscent of one of those television police dramas in which the brave officers, in the middle of a shoot out, move from behind one car to another, dodging bullets as they hit the ground on every side. When that bug took off, I was head down, zig zaggin' my way across the kitchen, then through the pantry door. I grabbed that broom and was back at my original position at the edge of the kitchen in no time. Heart pounding, I stood panting for breath as I plotted my next move.

In all fairness, I must reveal that this was not the first such grasshopper to maliciously invade my home that evening. No, just a few hours earlier, his equally evil twin brother had promptly met his demise at the hands of a friend who just happened to be paying me a visit at that inopportune moment. I have to admit her courage in the face of danger was inspiring. I watched in amazement as, without flinching, my friend killed that rascal with her bare hands, assisted only by a paper towel. So I was a little embarrassed, as you can imagine, as I stood there armed with a broom, frozen by my fear. I was embarrassed, mind you, but not stupid. Maybe she did not mind the risk of having bug guts oozing between her fingers, not to mention the possibility of a bug that will not die, but not me. I would take a decidedly more conservative approach.

With the thoughts of my friend's courage as my inspiration, I attempted to muster up more than my usual amount of bravery. Taking a position of faith, I stopped to pray that, even if I missed, God would strike that grasshopper dead right before my eyes. I rushed across the kitchen, screaming in my mind, "The battle is the Lord's!" Then with one sudden swoop I landed my broom squarely on top of that bug, who had made his home on the cabinets right above my refrigerator.

With a tremendous amount of pride and a faint smile upon my lips, I watched as that bug fell dramatically, almost as if in slow motion, to the top of the refrigerator.

Despite the lateness of the hour I took a moment to celebrate my unlikely victory with my version of an end zone dance. Then I reached to turn out the light and headed for bed, leaving my adversary to be disposed of in the daylight. As I headed down the hall, suddenly a terrifying thought crossed my mind, stopping me in my tracks, "What if somehow he survived the assault? What if he's only stunned and will soon regain consciousness with revenge on his mind?" Once that thought entered my mind I knew it would be impossible to walk down that hall to my bedroom until I checked his pulse or something.

I stood up on my tiptoes to try to get a better look but that was hopeless. I took a few steps back and perched myself up on the arm of the couch. Then I watched in shock and horror as that big, ugly, green grasshopper, who now appeared to be at least five inches long, was starting to move. In fact, in a matter of seconds, he had made it back up on his feet and was stumbling around, half dazed, on the top of my refrigerator. No more than a moment passed until this alien monster from the insect world had his second wind and seemed ready to try his wings. To my horror, I watched as he flew again, landing back on my kitchen ceiling.

I think this entomological terrorist actually enjoyed it as I, with all the attitude of a two year old's tantrum, began dragging a chair in from the dining room, muttering defamatory statements about this bug all the way. Strategically positioning myself directly beneath him, I stepped up onto that chair, and began practicing my upward motion with the broom, so as to be sure that I would strike a more solid blow. Then, just as I completed my sixth or seventh, okay, maybe twelfth, practice swing, he flew again, this time landing on the wall right above the stove in my direct line of sight.

This was the fatal flaw in his strategy to elude me. I had reached the end of my patience, being that it was now nearly one in the morning. I made up my mind that there would be no more fooling around. I climbed back down off of the chair, firmly planted my feet on the floor, practiced my swing just a couple of times, and said another prayer. Then I resolved in my heart that on the count of three, without hesitation, I was going to swing that broom with every ounce of strength I had to rid myself of this pest, once and for all.

I began the count...one...two...three. Then with a rare amount of ferocity I began my brutal attack. However, by some freak accident, as

I circled that broom around, somehow the end of the handle got caught in the crook of my arm. So with every bit of strength I had, instead of smashing that grasshopper to smithereens, that broom ricocheted back and hit me squarely in the forehead, knocking me three or four feet into the living room where I landed right in front of that bike, banging the back of my head against one of the pedals. I sat there dazed, wondering if a person could give themselves a concussion with a broom, picturing my children finding me the next morning, unconscious, with a zombie bug standing on my chest, arms raised, tiny little fists in the air, swaying to the sound of Queen's "We Are The Champions."

Well, believe it or not, I did eventually kill that grasshopper. The details of my victory are neither pretty nor quite as interesting as the parts of this story I have already shared. So I will leave those to your imagination.

All of this is more than just a funny story. It is a treatise on how fear is able to so distort our perspectives that we willingly give our power away. A quiet evening at home became an hysterical flurry of frenetic energy with hardly a moment's notice because of fear. If I am honest, I must admit that this sudden radical climate change had virtually nothing to do with that grasshopper, or any particularly powerful characteristics I ascribed to him. The fear, that formed the catalyst for my crazy, was inextricably rooted in how I viewed myself, a false perception that rendered me helpless in the face of this tiny opponent. No matter how small that grasshopper was, I obviously saw myself smaller. My low self-estimation was fueled by how I had let the experiences of my past, and the voices in my head that echo the words of my every critic, drain my confidence. I gave away my power to an adversary who should have trembled at the thought of challenging me, and, the sad truth is, this was hardly an isolated incident. I have given my power away far too many times in my life, before that night and since.

When was the last time you trembled in the face of a grasshopper? Grasshoppers come in all shapes and sizes, you know, and they are hardly ever bright green. In fact, often they wear the camouflage that blends right in with the fabric of life. They simply possess a tremendous resilience, put forth a relentless effort in their attempts to take control of what we do. Before we know it these illusionists will pull off an outrageous role reversal that casts us in the roles of the victims that they were meant to play. They are the face of our fears. Your grasshopper could be anything or anyone you allow to to get in your head, planting seeds of insecurity, convincing you that you are not enough and you do not deserve your God-given destiny.

For many of us, our giant grasshopper is a past failure we can never undo or a present flaw we have yet to conquer. The memories of heinous acts of abuse can intrude into a woman's life experience and imprint their influence on her thinking, convincing her that those acts will always define her. Mean girls, haters, bullies and critics can leave you diminished or defeated, as you have repeated their harsh and thoughtless critiques over and over again, until you might as well have their words tattooed on the insides of your eyelids, because they are in front of you every minute of the day.

A classic example of this can be found in the Old Testament book of Exodus. Just consider the words God spoke to the people He had chosen as His own:

See, I am sending an angel ahead of you to guard you along the way and to bring you to the place I have prepared. Pay attention to him and listen to what he says. Do not rebel against him; he will not forgive your rebellion, since my Name is in him. If you listen carefully to what he says and do all that I say, I will be an enemy to your enemies and will oppose those who oppose you. My angel will go ahead of you and bring you into the land of the Amorites, Hittites, Perizzites, Canaanites, Hivites and Jebusites, and I will wipe them out...I will send my terror ahead of you and throw into confusion every nation you encounter. I will make all your enemies turn their backs and run. I will send the hornet ahead of you to drive the Hivites, Canaanites and Hittites out of your way. But I will not drive them out in a single year, because the land would become desolate and the wild animals too numerous for you. Little by little I will drive them out before you, until you have increased enough to take possession of the land (Exodus 23:20-23, 27-30 NIV).

Could God have provided a more vivid description of what He was promising to do for His people? As they finally arrive at the edge of this beautiful, lush, fruitful land, we want the story to continue with, "They ran in, with an angel of God ahead of them, riding shotgun to a whole swarm of hornets, and experienced fully the destiny that God had promised." That is nothing like what actually happened. Instead, God's chosen people stood trembling at the edge of this territory that God promised would most certainly be theirs. They sent in spies who came back to tell them that this land was every single thing God had said it would be and more, yet consider how they received this news:

> *Then Caleb silenced the people before Moses and said, "We should go up and take possession of the land, for we can certainly do it." But the men who had gone up with him said, "We can't attack those people; they are stronger than we are." And they spread among the Israelites a bad report about the land they had explored. They said, "The land we explored devours those living in it. All the people we saw there are of great size. We saw the Nephilim there (the descendants of Anak come from the Nephilim). We seemed like grasshoppers in our own eyes, and we looked the same to them"* (Numbers 13:30-33 NIV).

What a role reversal the people of God let their fear perpetrate on their collective believing! Even the tiniest challenge looms large if we shrink ourselves down to the size of a grasshopper. If these freedom fighters chose to adopt the persona of an indefensible insect, in contrast with the incomparable identity God had spoken over them, no wonder they trembled at the thought that these enemies would most likely squash them like bugs.

Likewise our self-perceptions drastically alter the level of confidence we bring to the pursuit of our dreams. Whatever thoughts we allow to deviate from the truth of what God has said about us will give root to our most debilitating fears. We may stand right on the edge of the life God destined for us, poised to get back every single thing we have lost in this battle for our souls, and wave a white flag of surrender to our fear. Until we are relaxed in our true identities, nourished by who God says that we are, we will continually find ourselves running away from the very situations God says we should own. Sheer panic will drive us to construct false identities, lived out in untrue realities, in hopes that no one will peer behind the curtain to find out this is all just a sham. Perfectionists, overachievers, people pleasers, mean girls, mind gamers, material girls, perpetual victims, as well as the bullies that terrorize them, are every one pretenders, all bit players on stages built by insecurity.

How drastically different our daily existences would be if we were fearless! As Ruth's story continues, we will discover that we can be. Once we find our way to the threshing floor, what happens next in those intimate moments will move us beyond our desperation and release us to run with abandon toward everything God has in store.

So let me ask you a question, "Where did you lose your confidence? Who stole away your power? When did you begin to feel afraid?" Sometimes it happens all at once, with some traumatic event, but often it is in the little by little that our confidence erodes, that we become afraid that we will never really be beautiful, or lovable, or wanted, or truly good at being who we were meant to be. God tells us in Ruth's story that He is unwilling to settle for that, unwilling to leave you believing that you may never be enough. So He wooed you to this moment to release you from fear's stranglehold. In Boaz we see that this God, Who created you just the way you are for His own enjoyment, has intentionally positioned Himself in the human family so that He could give you back your power, your courage, the confidence that you really can get back to the garden and bask in the intimacy that Adam and Eve once let slip through their fingers. God is not only inviting you to believe to the point that it changes your story, but to believe to the point that it makes you fearless!

You see, God's Word tells us that perfect love casts out fear. Yet you will never know perfect love, you will never experience that kind of freedom, apart from this beautiful intimacy with Jesus that He has wooed you to discover. So if, like me, someone's words have ever crushed your spirit; if, like me, you have ever endured an abuse or offense so painful that it left you afraid to ever let yourself get into a situation like that again; if your head keeps repeating words that leave you paralyzed and trembling, or furiously building bigger, thicker walls to hide behind, here is the thing, that is not freedom. That will never feel like home. It will feel like a cage because it is a cage, and you, daughter of the King, were never meant for a cage.

By now, I hope this beautiful Old Testament story of Jesus, this love story that God has written you into on purpose, is soaking into the very fabric of your being so that, before we are through, it will flow easily over your lips and take up generous real estate within your heart. I hope life finds you thinking of these intricate details and even retelling them again and again. I hope you never forget this journey, this study of a girl, so much like you, whose story began in a place where God was completely left out. I hope you can picture the two of us walking side by side on the same road that these two women traveled, arriving just in time to see fields ripe and ready for harvest. I hope you find yourself gleaning precious truths as you read, identifying with Ruth as she picked up leftover grain in one of the nearby fields of Bethlehem. She thought that field was chosen randomly, much like you may have picked up this book without thinking it could contain a love story that can unlock the cage of your fear. Yet Ruth's arrival in that field had been designated by God, long before she arrived there, because it was the field of someone who was predisposed to love her by His design. Hunger drove her to that field that day, but favor met her there. So as she walked through the door with a boatload of grain at the end of her time in that field, even poor, bitter, tired, old Naomi could see what was going on, and, though it had been a long time since she had even had anything to hope for, she began to recognize the fingerprints of God. So much so that Naomi began to call that vision out as she told Ruth what to do. Naomi had walked with Ruth in Moab, she had walked right beside her on the three day trip to Bethlehem, they walked into town side by side, shared the first loaf of bread from that abundance of barley. Yet the time had now come when the next steps had to be taken by Ruth alone. Naomi understood that. If Ruth wanted the destiny she dreamed of, she would have to step out from among all the other servant girls, and let go of her fear to grasp the life she was made to experience. Naomi could not go with her. She could not do this for her. However, she could tell her how to get there because she had been there and she knew the way.

I often find myself identifying with Ruth as I reflect upon this story. I have gone trembling, in the quiet, in the dark, to position myself at the feet of my Redeemer, waiting, needing desperately to hear His voice say my name and change my story. Yet right now, I identify with Naomi. I can just picture this seasoned soul, leaning against the door facing, watching Ruth until she disappeared into the shadows, whispering a prayer that this intimate encounter would be everything she hoped and prayed it would be. Naomi was unable to control the outcome, so she held her breath as she waited to see what God would do. Both of these women had to make a faith decision, one to let go and another to grab hold. Somewhat like the decision of one to write what another will pick up and read. So in the quiet, in the dark, Naomi waited and Ruth made her way to the threshing floor, where she would make herself vulnerable, make herself available, believing in the words of her mentor that her Redeemer would not let her down.

That is why I have been dying to know what has happened in your life since you read the last chapter. Did you go? Did you sneak away to the threshing floor, in the quiet, to position yourself to hear the voice of your Redeemer? Did you open God's Word expecting to hear His voice? I hope you did. That is where we left Ruth, headed to the threshing floor, on her way to meet this beautiful man whom she had met, quite by accident she thought, when her hunger drove her to where he was. She went out craving kindness, graciousness, yes, even magic, just like you and I do all the time, and the moment she looked into his eyes she saw that it was there. It was Naomi who first realized that this kindness was an invitation. She understood that the time had come for Ruth to make her choice, to go to the threshing floor, so that she could encounter him in a more intimate setting.

Do you think Ruth was afraid? I do. Fear is one of the toughest battles any woman faces. So if Ruth is a picture of you and me, she was probably scared out of her mind and she had good reason to be. She was taking a huge risk to go down to the threshing floor all alone, not knowing who might be lurking in the shadows, with a terrorizing enemy living right there in the middle of the land where the people of God lived. So as she walked, I imagine she did so with some trepidation, not fully knowing who or what she might encounter, along the way or when she arrived. Then add to any circumstantial anxiety the words Naomi had used to describe what went on in other fields. Fields with owners not nearly as kind as Boaz were characterized by vicious competition. A mean girl mentality reigned in the other fields. As Ruth walked through the dark perhaps images of the potential violence and abuses that Naomi's warnings described began to manifest in Ruth's imagination. Every crackle of the underbrush must have made Ruth jump.

All the ordinary fears, based on real and imagined threats, were probably only magnified by Ruth's unfamiliarity with the places and the people that surrounded her. This was all so new. She was, after all, a stranger. In fact, every time anyone even mentioned her name they called her, "Ruth, the Moabite." No one seemed to ever lose sight of the fact that she was not one of them.

Do you walk through your world wearing a label someone attached to your name? Feeling different? Maybe even ashamed of where you are from or where you have been or what you have gone through? Then this story is your story because Ruth was that girl. She probably did not know another soul who had a story like hers. She could have let shame hold her back from her dreams. She could have let embarrassment keep her in hiding. Yet she came, despite her fear, because, if she let fear stop her, she would always be who they said she was, her story would never be changed. So, in spite of shaking knees and trembling hands, she refused to be denied this chance to experience her destiny.

Ruth's mind must have been racing, imagining the worst, bombarded with questions. "What will people think?" "What if I am doing this all wrong?" "What if I end up looking foolish?" "What if I misunderstood his words, his acts of kindness toward me?"

There was plenty to fear and yet I have failed to even touch on the one element in this part of the story that may have been the scariest aspect of all. Once Ruth got to the threshing floor, she had to wait. Are you kidding me? After pressing past the pain and the fear and those crazy things that she imagined, she makes it to where she knew he would be and she had to just sit there and wait to see how this would all turn out. Do you hate to wait? I do, because while I wait, sometimes I lose my nerve. Sometimes I begin to run through all the endless and ever growing list of "what if" scenarios in my waiting. I might be bold at the beginning, but, if I have to wait, all bets are off.

Ruth quite possibly had to wait for quite a while. Do you remember Naomi's instructions? Naomi told Ruth to go early and then wait until Boaz had finished eating and drinking and celebrating the harvest. She told her to wait as he came to lie down and, then, to move into position and wait until some subconscious awareness of her presence awoke him from that sound sleep that comes quickly after a hard day's work and a good meal. This passage will reveal that Boaz did not see her the first minute she got to the threshing floor. Remember they threshed the barley at about 5 in the afternoon and yet these next verses will reveal that by the time Boaz noticed her it was in the middle of the night. Ruth must have been terrified by the middle of the night. She had probably talked herself in and out of staying more than once, and she probably heard that all too familiar screaming in her head telling her this was nothing short of crazy, that she was stupid for going through with this plan. She may have been looking for an escape route at the very minute that Boaz began to stir, because there was something Naomi failed to tell her. She failed to tell her how this whole thing would end because, I suppose, she did not know, not for sure. All Naomi could say was, "Trust him. He will tell you what to do." Naomi could offer no guarantees to Ruth that this would all come out the way they wanted. She only knew that the outcome was out of their hands, that the outcome rested in the hands of the one who had shown himself to be safe and kind and generous and protective. If Ruth failed to go they would never know how Boaz felt about her but, if she took the chance, if she walked this out, they would have to wait to see what he would say.

Is there anything you are waiting for, a risk you have taken, yet you still cannot know where it will lead? Is there anything hanging in the balance right now in your life? Is there an outcome you cannot control?

If so, I can almost guarantee that fear is rising. We find ourselves in the shadows with Ruth so easily. You and I are fragile, and often fearful. Much of what we hope for is beyond our control, perhaps even outside of our understanding, but it is within our reach.

So I do not know if your fear talked you out of positioning yourself to hear God's voice after reading the last chapter. I hope you took the chance. Oh, how I hope He met you there and you heard His voice speak a word that has changed you forever. I still hope, if you did not go to meet Him on the threshing floor, that you will. You see, what was true for Ruth is true for each one of us. We have to take the chance. We must believe before we see. We must tune our ears to hear Him, even in the face of our fears. You will never reach your destiny walking by fear, letting your doubts lead the way. We must determine to seek Him in His Word where He will be found, even if we come trembling. Then, as He speaks, as we find our names on His lips, we must choose to believe what God says about us. Otherwise we will forever cower in the shadows of how people, who have no idea of who we are destined to become, define us. There is no in-between.

We know where He will be. Each of us knows how to get there. You may now be reading these words right along with fellow travelers, sisters, other daughters of this beautiful King, other women who have been chosen for love, and men too, yet each of us, in a real sense, sits in this moment alone. Each of us must own our own choice, whether or not we will pursue our own intimate relationship with a God who held nothing back but came offering Himself completely, unreservedly for us. You can come to these pages and walk away unchanged, maybe entertained, but still not believing to the point that it changes your story, to the point that you will push past the pain to trust in this extravagant love. You or I might come, yet not stay, never sell out, full out, never make up our minds not to stray ever again into some other field to feed our hunger. Or we can make our home forever with Him, realizing the very thing we were made for was intimacy with This One Who loved us first and loves us like no other. We must decide if we will believe enough to go it alone, in the dark, when no one is watching, to take the risk to tear down our walls of self-protection, to lay down at his feet and be still until His voice pierces the silence. As Ruth lay down at Boaz's feet she was going all in, letting go without a net, waiting perfectly still, expecting that he would be her catcher.

We are at that same crossroad. We could live the rest of our lives carrying all the dirt and the garbage that other people have plastered across our lives, or put all our hope in this One Who knows who we really are, knew us completely before we were born, and has the wisdom to separate the truth from the garbage. He alone has the power to wash the dirt away and give us back all that is  true and has always been true about us. It is in that moment that courage replaces fear, confidence replaces paralysis. That is when freedom breaks the chains of all that has held us fast and held us back for far too long. So God is asking each of us another question, His Spirit is stirring, waiting for your answer, "Will you believe to the point that it makes you fearless?"

WILL YOU **BELIEVE** TO THE POINT THAT IT MAKES YOU **FEARLESS?**

Ruth answers that question in the third chapter of this book that bears her name. Ruth has gone alone to position herself to hear the voice of her redeemer and when we left her she was waiting and we were waiting too. Now the drama continues to unfold.

> *When Boaz had finished eating and drinking and was in good spirits, he went over to lie down at the far end of the grain pile. Ruth approached quietly, uncovered his feet and lay down. In the middle of the night something startled the man; he turned—and there was a woman lying at his feet! "Who are you?" he asked. "I am your servant, Ruth," she said. "Spread the corner of your garment over me, since you are a guardian-redeemer of our family."* (Ruth 3:7-9 NIV)

When Boaz realized that someone had positioned themselves intentionally to be able to hear him, so close she could reach out and touch him, he turned in her direction. Do you get that? What does this say about you? It means you have gotten God's attention. The very One Who breathed the stars into place, Who holds the earth on its axis, has stopped to turn His focus to you. He sees you, He knows the faith that brought you here, caused your eyes to focus on the words on this page. Like Boaz, He wanted you to come, and now that you are here, you hold His attention.

In the dark, far from the view of everyone else who was sleeping there on the threshing floor, Ruth had taken the chance, she had made herself vulnerable. I think you could say she was putting her faith in that man, believing that he would notice her and speak to her and hear her heart's cry for love, knowing the desperation that must have brought her to this point at this moment. I love the Hebrew wording used here because where the translation puts it simply, "he turned," the original language says so much more. This word means "to bend, to clasp."[54] So I can just see Boaz, not just turning but, reaching out to her, just as God is reaching out to you at this very moment. His hand is extended, He is reaching out to take hold of you, to pull you even closer to His heart. It reminds me of one of my favorite verses found in Psalm 18, which says, *"You stoop down to make me great."* (Psalm 18:35 NIV, 1984). What a picture those words paint for us to envision. This God who created everything is bending down to see you, to lift your head, to cause your eyes to look straight into His, and, as your eyes meet His, it is passionate, extraordinary, incredible love that you find there. That same favor you first discovered in His field, is on display for you as He reaches out to meet you right here, right now. A revelation like that changes you forever! Boaz, in his response, takes this girl from Moab and moves her far beyond her experience as just a beggar picking up leftover grain in a rich man's field. As he reaches out he sweeps her up into His dreams for her, into this story so much bigger than anything she could ever imagine. As he turns, as he bends and reaches out, Ruth is most certainly holding her breath, waiting to see if she was right to come, right about his intentions, waiting to see if this beautiful man's hope for her is that she will be His bride. Does that just blow your mind? As Jennifer Lopez would say "it gives me goosies!"

I envision Boaz lying on some sort of bed roll or mat that lifts him just a bit off the hard ground. I picture Ruth positioned at his feet, slightly lower, on the ground. Suddenly he stirs, becoming aware that someone is there, Ruth gets his attention. So he sits up and bends down, leaning forward, reaching out, until he touches her, he holds her in his grasp, pulling her toward him. Perhaps he even takes a hand to raise her chin, so that her eyes meet his. He pierces the darkness and breaks the silence with his voice, the voice she has waited to hear. It just gives me chills to think about it, this beautiful man of extraordinary wealth, influence and graciousness and this girl from Moab hand in hand, looking into each other's eyes, as, at last, he asks the question she has been waiting to answer, and as Boaz asks Ruth, God asks you, "Who are you?"

This is your chance to give an answer to that question that will make the difference between a woman gripped with fear and a woman unbound by her fearlessness. If you answer the way Ruth answered, there is a new freedom waiting, freedom that will give you back that confidence that your enemy has stolen away. I just love how Ruth identifies herself here. Her beautiful answer reflects such boldness, such strength and vulnerability. It expresses a confidence in Boaz that was real and raw and rare.

Reread her response.

> *"I am your servant, Ruth," she said. "Spread the corner of your garment over me, since you are a guardian-redeemer of our family."* (Ruth 3:9 NIV)

Her answer was instantaneous, she knew just what she wanted to say. Naomi, her mother in the faith, had explained to her everything this man's kindness had set in motion, how her kinsman redeemer had set the stage for her happily ever after. So Ruth came alone, in the dark, in the quiet, to find him. She laid herself down and watched for him, waited for this moment when he would find her lying there at his feet. She had at last gotten his attention, roused him from his sleep. He leaned in, pulled her close. "Who are you?" he asked. "I am your servant, Ruth," she replied, without hesitation.

Notice Boaz asked her, "Who are you?" Yet her answer tells us more than that. She could not just tell him who she was without, more significantly, revealing whose she was. That was the first part, the most significant part, of what she came to say. She said, "I am yours." Do you see that? She said not just "I am yours" but "I am your hand maiden." The Hebrew word is "amah" and it means, "a bond servant."[55] According to *Merriam-Webster's Collegiate Dictionary,* a bond servant is "a person bound in service without wages."[56] So it is not just someone hired to do certain tasks and paid for their efforts, it means a slave, it means you own me.

Now watch this, think about it. If you characterize yourself as someone's slave what does that say about who you are? On the most obvious level, if you are someone's slave, you do whatever that person says to do, right? If I am your slave and you ask me to prepare a meal, what will I do? I will cook your food. If you ask me to wash your clothes, as your slave, I will do the laundry. So, in essence, if you identify yourself as someone's slave, by implication you are whoever that person says that you are in any given moment.

In giving that answer, Ruth was willingly submitting herself to Boaz's leadership. Submission is not for sissies, despite what people say. Submission requires a strength of trust and a depth of discipline, sometimes setting aside your wants for the needs or desires of another.

To say, "I am your servant," identifies a singular purpose that a weaker woman would never choose. Ruth had seen the kind of man Boaz was. She had not simply heard about his kindness, she had experienced it, as he welcomed her into his field, and fed her at his table. Boaz had empowered her and protected her. As she heard his words of blessing and affirmation, she had come to know the heart of this man. Now she had come to put herself intentionally at his feet, and, as she speaks those words, "I am your servant, Ruth," she is saying, in essence, "I am whoever you say I am." She would be defined by the willingness of her kinsman redeemer to choose her as his own.

In light of the fact that Boaz is a picture of God to us, imagine yourself coming to that place. What would change if in boldness you fling yourself at God's feet, choosing to go all in, believing in His passion for you which was willingly, openly put on display? When you are strong enough to decide to submit to His design, to be known only by the name He chooses to call you, that is the stuff dreams are made of, that is when your destiny really, brilliantly comes into view. Will you say to Jesus, the One who has chosen you for His extraordinary love, Who calls you His bride, your Kinsman Redeemer, "From this moment on, I am whoever you say that I am?" When you say that, when you truly embrace that as your identity, nobody else gets to tell you who you are ever again!

Life gives us a sweet taste of such single-hearted devotion by showing us what our relationship with God is meant to look like in the imperfect, yet beautiful, picture of marriage. I married my husband, David, almost 40 years ago. Before I met David, however, I dated some other guys. I dated Bill, and Greg, and a guy named Tommy. I dated an Eddie and another guy named Peter. I liked them all and I wanted all of them to like me. Sometimes I waited for the phone to ring, hoping to hear one of their voices speak my name. Sometimes I was afraid of how I would feel about myself, of what it would mean about me, if they chose to never call again. So here is the weird thing. For the past 40 years, I have not once stared at the phone wishing one of those guys would call even one more time. I am no longer waiting to hear any of their voices say my name. Not even a minute's sleep has been lost worrying about whether they were thinking of me or what they were thinking about me. Once I said "yes" to David, once I gave him my heart, deciding I was his and his alone, the opinions of those other guys completely lost their power. Not one of them ever got to tell me who I am or determine how I felt about myself again.

Have you internalized an identity that was once given to you by someone else? Have you given away your power to stand in your truth by letting the choices or the words of someone in your life, or even someone who used to be in your life, define you, limit you, or make you afraid? Or is it only me? Where did you lose your freedom? Where did you lay down your right to be who you are right where you are, and to know that you are good enough, worthy of love, without changing a thing?

Stop to consider the words of Jesus from the gospel of Luke, "*No one can serve two masters. Either you will hate the one and love the other, or you will be devoted to one and despise the other*" (Luke 16:13 NIV). When you let someone else tell you who you are, stick their label on you and expect you to carry it away, you might as well lay down at their feet, wave the white flag of surrender and say, "I am your slave," because, in essence, you are saying to them, "I am whoever you say that I am." In giving away this right to define you, you have begun to worship, give a greater weight or importance to, a lesser god.

Yet this realization contains the makings of a glory day, not a guilt trip. You see, if you are living under the banner of someone else's opinion, criticism, ridicule, or influence, you are living in a cage. You are allowing someone who should never own you, to own you, to control you, to keep you tied up in knots as you seek to win their approval through each new performance. God wants to give you back your freedom to do you. He alone can redeem every single speck of our self-respect and courage, and empower each of us to be the desperately dangerous, fearless person He first conceived and longs to release.

David put it this way,

> *Truly I am your servant, Lord; I serve you just as my mother did; you have freed me from my chains* (Psalm 116:16 NIV).

Are you ready to let those chains fall away? Would you choose to break out of this cage? In the quiet of this moment you can come lay down at the feet of the One Who knows your name. He has chosen you to be the object of His extravagant affection. You can choose Him back by saying, once and for all, to your Kinsman Redeemer, "I am whoever You say that I am."

Here is the cool thing, Boaz never asked Ruth to stop being who she was. He knew everything about her that would disqualify her for the love of such a beautiful man and yet that man loved her like crazy.

The same is true for you. God already knows exactly who you are, every single part, every mess you have made, every moment when you might have rejected Him and walked away, and He opened up His arms and opened up His heart, gave His everything to buy back everything you have ever lost or that has been stolen away, including your freedom. Living in slavery to the haters, or even those who love you imperfectly, will load you down with other people's baggage. Being a slave to The Only One who can love you perfectly and does so extravagantly, will set you free! It will set you free! What if the next time somebody's words of criticism get stuck in your heart you run to Jesus? What if the next time someone's decision about you threatens to mischaracterize or belittle you, you come running to where He is, fling yourself down at His feet and refuse to leave until you have heard His voice tell you who you really are? What if the next time you forget that you are His favorite, that you are His beautiful daughter, the one He has chosen for love, you go find Him in the quiet and ask Him to remind you of how He sees you, of how He feels about you? Would that conversation calm your panicking heart and break the chains of somebody else's forced enslavement? How would it change you if you made your way to the threshing floor, where you know He will be waiting, and found your home, your refuge only in His presence and in the words He speaks to you there?

I read something many years ago that really stuck with me, that every single thing that goes into your mind stays there, on some level of consciousness, forever. This is a concept pictured brilliantly by walls of colored marble memories, stacked as high as they could go, in the animated feature film, *Inside Out.*[57] Every cruel word, every false accusation, every word of ridicule, every criticism, or smirk of disapproval, gets in our heads and stays. How do any of us get around that? It seems so impossible to overcome. If God gave us minds with such enormous capacities for retention, how can He possibly expect us to break out of this prison that our memories form around our hearts? Oh, He does not wait for us to somehow strategize our own jail break. God breaks in. Little by little He runs our enemy out of the land to bring us home. He deposits truth to cancel out the lies, whispers beautiful words to silence every ugly accusation. Rather than brain wash us instantaneously He renews our minds one conversation at a time. Every accusation, false label and mistaken identity is overpowered in His presence as He speaks His truth about who we are again and again. We are radically changed into who we were always meant to be only in the context of intimate relationship with the One Who knows us, Who speaks our true names into existence.

So many of us carry in our souls the harsh, critical, hateful words that have been spoken over us by an abusive or needy parent, an intimidating competitor, a past rejector, maybe even a domineering pastor or boss or so-called friend. Broken, each one of them, putting their brokenness on us, thinking we could carry it away from them. Even though their bitterness stayed with them, it also transferred to us, that one bitter root, as the writer of Hebrews called it, carried a poison that stayed in our system, tainting every thought it comes in contact with, playing on like a broken record or a repetitive meme.

Paul explained the process in his letter to the believers in Rome,

> *Do not conform to the pattern of this world,* (don't let this world's opinions shape you, define you) *but be transformed* (you may start out as a worm but you can come out a beautiful butterfly) *by the renewing* (part of this word means piece by piece) *of your mind. Then you will be able to test and approve* (or agree with) *what God's will is* (God's intention, His direction for your life, what God has already determined to be true, the dreams He dreams for you)—*his good, pleasing and perfect will* (Romans 12:1-2 NIV with parenthetical comments added).

God is waiting on the threshing floor. You can bring everything, the pure grain as well as the trash that you picked up along the way, to be separated under His watchful eye, preserving the harvest that will feed your soul and nourish the truth of who you were created to be.

Ruth's answer to Boaz was huge because she was saying, "Nobody else gets to tell me ever again. I am sold out, full out. I have laid myself down at your feet. If you decide you want to love me, I am loved, no matter what anybody else ever thinks about me. If you decide that you want me, I belong, no matter who else tries to exclude me. You own me. I am asking you to determine my destiny. I am your slave, forever captured by your love! I am whoever you say that I am!" Ruth said, "I am your servant, Ruth."

Remember that story of the girl whose life was forever changed by this question that was put on display over Neyland Stadium, "Robin, will you marry me?" I have no way of knowing if Robin glanced up and saw that on her own or if her would-be bridegroom lifted her head so that her eyes could see his love, extravagantly put on display. It could even be that a friend, or some friend of that bridegroom, got her attention and pointed to this demonstrative declaration of his passion. The Bible actually speaks of such a friend in the context of your story as well, in words spoken by John the Baptist, recorded in John 3...

> *You yourselves can testify that I said, 'I am not the Messiah but am sent ahead of him.' The bride belongs to the bridegroom. The friend who attends the bridegroom waits and listens for him, and is full of joy when he hears the bridegroom's voice. That joy is mine, and it is now complete* (John 3:28-29 NIV).

Naomi was just a friend of the bridegroom. She pointed Ruth in his direction and explained to her that this unusual kindness that Boaz had extended in the field was more than just a generous act of a generous man. It was an invitation, a proposal of sorts. Boaz was making it known that as a kinsman he could and was willing to redeem her, if she so desired. So now, in coming to find him alone, in the night, with no one else around, Ruth's answer to this invitation to be written into his beautiful story, was, "yes!"

> *Ruth said, "I am your servant, Ruth," then she continued, "Spread the corner of your garment over me, since you are a guardian-redeemer of our family"* (Ruth 3:9 NIV).

That seems like a strange thing to say, *"spread the corner of your garment over me."* This phrase is actually translated in other places in the Bible as *"hide me beneath the shadow of your wings."* I once systematically studied each verse in the Bible that held this phrase with either of those translations. The bigger picture created as those verses are analyzed collectively evokes images of protection, provision, deliverance, affection, healing, marriage and covenant. Imagine a husband putting his coat around his wife to shield her from the cold. He would be protecting her, providing for her need. He would be showing affection, demonstrating his intimate relationship to her, even living out his covenant promise to have and to hold, to love and to cherish.

Though Ruth said, "I am your servant" she had now come to realize that his dream for her was bigger than her own. He did not want her to be his servant, he wanted her to be his bride. He was not inviting her to merely pick up leftovers in his field, he desired for her to own that field with him. Ruth had come to the threshing floor hoping that Naomi was right, that this dream, for the two of them together, was bigger than her own dream would ever be without him.

Again, this is true about your Redeemer as well. His dream that He longs for the two of you to share is bigger than anything you can ask or imagine. Ruth, was saying, "If you are asking me, if what Naomi has told me about you is true, that you are inviting me to be your bride, to be in intimate relationship with you and only you from this moment on, then, my answer is definitely, 'yes.'"

Ruth said, "Yes," to the invitation of her redeemer. Have you? Each one of us is just like Ruth, we too are impoverished. Each of us has experienced tremendous loss. Every one of us needs a Redeemer, someone who will love us enough to change our story, to take us from a place where God is left out to a deeply transformative relationship with Him. We are broken, flawed. Like Eve, every one of us has tried to get our needs met in our own way. We have left the garden, left the house of bread, maybe thought we could be good enough, even hyper-religious, but we have failed, messed up again and again, fallen far short of perfection. The Bible calls these flaws, our acts of defiance, our imperfect choices, "sin." If you can identify with that, if you agree with me that you are one of the messed up ones like I am, that you are not perfect, that you have not always made the right choices, then you must know that those choices have put this huge divide between God, who is perfect, and each of us who is not. The separation is so vast that, though we all long for home, for the garden, to be in an intimate relationship with Him, we cannot get ourselves back there, no matter how hard we try. We can never undo all we have done. To be separated from a perfect God is just the natural result of our imperfection. In light of all our bad choices, it is the death that we deserve. Yet God loved us so much that He could not bare that separation. So, when we could never get ourselves back to Him, He came to us. The Son of God became a man on purpose, so that as a relative, like Boaz, he could give us back all we have lost in this war for our souls. Just like Boaz came to Ruth, knowing everything that disqualified her from his love yet loving her anyway, Jesus came to you. Knowing all the ways you are broken, He still chooses to give you His heart. He loves you and is reaching out to you in this moment. He may have used a friend, a sister, a daughter, a stranger to position you so that you could hear His voice and feel his hand reaching out to pull you close. Yet He has not chosen you to be His servant, He wants you to be his bride. So before we move forward I have to ask you, not have you been in church, because just like a wedding is nothing compared to a marriage, church attendance does not substitute for an intimate, transformative relationship with Jesus. I am asking, "Have you ever said 'yes' to his invitation to know Him intimately, to have an authentic, personal relationship with the One Who made you who you are and has the power to set you free to live that destiny out?" If you have never truly said "yes" to that beautiful love relationship and you now want to accept his invitation, He longs to give you back all you lost the minute you left the garden. So if your answer now is "yes," would you pray this prayer with me?

Lord, no matter how hard I may have tried, I know I am not perfect. I am broken and flawed and have spent much of my life in a place where You were completely left out. Now I know that, despite everything I am that should disqualify me, You have chosen to love me. You put on skin on purpose and came to find me. You paid by dying in my place, for my sin, to buy back my life out of slavery, to set me free to live my destiny. Your death bought back my life and my name. Now, in return, You are simply asking me to find my home in Your inexplicable love and be your bride forever. So, Lord, if that is what You are asking, my answer, is "Yes!" I want to live the rest of my life knowing I am the object of your affection. Thank you for receiving me just as I am. I am believing to the point that this changes my story forever and coming to You, God, in the name of my Kinsman Redeemer, Jesus. Amen.

If you said, "Yes" to Him just now or sometime in the past, you have opened the door to the intimacy you were made to crave, a oneness that will tell you who you are and set you free for eternity. Like with any intimate relationship, you have opened a door to unique privileges that you do not have with anyone else.

Marriage in the Bible, as well as today - though it is often forgotten in our modern culture - is a covenant between two people, a relationship that rests in a promise and is sustained by faith in that promise. Covenant was a very significant concept in the culture of the Old Testament. It signified a promise between two parties, an agreement that was literally carved into stone and symbolized by cutting an offering of sacrificial animals and shedding their blood. It was a permanent agreement through which two people or groups of people pledged to stand together, so much so, that the enemies of one became the enemies of the other. In fact, two people who entered into a covenant would exchange robes so that, if you saw one of them coming, you would not be sure which one of these covenant partners it actually was. They were that closely identified, the two had become like one. Each party promised everything they had, all their strength, all their resources, to be given to protect and provide for their covenant partner. Those of us who have experienced marriage, even with all its imperfections, can probably understand this concept of covenant, at least somewhat. Even if you are not married, you certainly know people who are married, have seen people make those promises and then spend the rest of their lives living them out.

When Ruth said "yes," to Boaz, when you said, "yes" to Jesus, whether just moments ago or sometime in the past, you may not have fully realized it but He gave you His robe. He took the dirty rags that were the best you had and exchanged them, giving you His spotless robe of righteousness to be your covering, so that you would be so identified with Him, that this world could hardly tell you apart. Your Redeemer shed His own blood to cut this covenant, and, when your enemy attacks, everything Jesus has and all that He is, He will use to defend you because you are His bride. He will say the words that will tell you who you are to overpower every attack, every word of ridicule, every criticism that has been hurled as a weapon in your direction.

For Ruth that began as soon as she came to that threshing floor to say, "yes" to Boaz. Just listen to Boaz's response,

> *"The Lord bless you, my daughter," he replied. "This kindness is greater than that which you showed earlier: You have not run after the younger men, whether rich or poor"* (Ruth 3:10 NIV).

The first words out of Boaz's mouth addressed that fact that she had been wearing the label of an outsider, a Moabite from Moab. Boaz gave her a new name. Now He called her, "my daughter." The same is true for you. No matter where you came from, what you have endured, how you got here or where you lived along the way, from the moment you say "yes" to God, He calls you His daughter and that will never change.

There was a time in my life, after 16 years spent with friends all around me, I ended up pretty much alone. Our family had come to a new church and, because of wounds inflicted in our former church, we pretty much did our best to remain invisible. That satisfied for a while until finally I dipped my toe into the water by becoming involved in a small group women's Bible study. Unfortunately, a couple of women there got a little territorial, misconstrued my desire to get involved and jumped on me with false accusations. As a result I was heartbroken and terrified. I felt like such an outsider, so different and unknown in this new place. I was just about to turn and go back into hiding, when another women said just the words I needed to hear. This woman, inviting me to a different small group, said, "I want you with me." In reaching out to me, she gave me a place to belong, a circle of friends, and eventually a place to teach, to do what I was made to do, to be who I am and live in that freedom. That is what Boaz gave to Ruth. He called her, "my daughter," and, in so doing, proclaimed, "No matter what anybody else has to say, or whether anyone else wants you or rejects you, you can belong to me. We are in this thing together."

Imagine how it felt for Ruth to hear His voice speaking out of the darkness, telling her that she belonged. Imagine how it felt for her to hear this man of such amazing character, who was kind, attentive, protective, and generous, this man everyone in Bethlehem admired, say those words, call her family, invite her to belong. She knew him as a man who was true to his word. At that moment he had taken her in, putting a protective arm around her, covering her with the corner of his garment, and he would bring everything he was to seeing her destiny unfold. It had to ease her fears for Ruth to hear this man of such grace, gently, affectionately refer to her as his "daughter."

The word Boaz uses to describe the motivation for Ruth to make such a bold request is the Hebrew word, "chesed" or "hesed "which is translated here as "kindness."[58] This is one of the most significant words in the Old Testament. It is used almost always to describe an attribute of God. Yet, on a rare occasion such as this, it is attributed to a person, namely Ruth. I believe Boaz chose that word intentionally, because he attributed the unfailing kindness he had seen in Ruth's character as a reflection of the unmissable fingerprint of God on this unfolding story, echoing Naomi's recognition.

The Hebrew word, "chesed," is very difficult to translate accurately into the English language because it says so much more than any one English word can express. It means kindness, love, goodness, mercy, loyalty all wrapped up together but it also carries with it the idea that such feelings motivate a person's actions, and do not come and go, but are lasting, even eternal. It is probably best described as an inclination to do good to someone based on an inherent compassion or essential love that motivates one to a lasting loyalty, like that which is usually found only in the context of a family. It is a word that describes action, deeper than emotion, a decided kindness. "Chesed" is not necessarily an ooey-gooey emotional love. This is a steadfast willingness to protect, to be kind, to provide, to fight for, if necessary, to be loyal to, to do what needs to be done because of being in relationship within a family.

The Old Testament often speaks of God as being motivated by "chesed" to act on behalf of His people. This word is used 26 times in Psalm 136 where it says over and over again, *"His love endures forever."* That is the most profound mark of "chesed," it endures, it transcends. That is why, most often, it is used to describe God's enduring love and loyalty to us simply because we are His children. "Chesed" prompted Him to create everything we see around us. It prompts Him to make sure we have food to eat. Such a depth of kindness motivates Him to work miracles on our behalf. Because of "chesed" God came with mighty plagues to free His people from their slavery in Egypt. He brought them out by parting the Red Sea and defeated their enemies by drowning them in the same waters that He parted to lead them to freedom. These are acts of kindness and goodness that flow from His intrinsic, unending compassion toward those who are His. "Chesed" caused God to lead and provide for the Hebrew people during their extended stay in the wilderness. Despite their unbelief, He fought for them against every enemy they encountered, until they reached the home He prepared for them in the land that He first promised to Abraham. "Chesed" motivates God's refusal to abandon us in our sin. This unusual capacity for kindness provided a spotless Lamb, a once and for all sacrifice, to free us, a Kinsman Redeemer to buy back everything we have lost on the battlefield of a war that we could never win without Him. You see, this is so much more than simply the story of Boaz and Ruth. This is the story of Jesus, our Kinsman Who came to redeem us. This bigger story, God's dream, our destiny, is brilliantly foretold in Boaz's love story for Ruth. God's love, His kindness, His mercy, His goodness has always been there and His love endures forever.

In the story of Ruth, this word, "chesed," is specifically used three separate times to describe the beauty of the permanent, enduring kindness and loyalty exhibited by the characters in this story. In Ruth 1:8 Naomi uses the word, "chesed," to describe her hope that the Lord would look after and provide mercifully for her two daughter-in-laws, even as they stayed behind in Moab. She even said that they had exhibited that same sort of enduring kindness toward her. Although the word is not specifically used it was surely an expression of "chesed" that prompted Ruth to cling to Naomi and refuse to let anything but death part them. Then Naomi uses "chesed" again in Ruth 2:20 to describe the unending love that must have prompted God to position and prepare Boaz, to predispose him to be attracted to Ruth, and give him the capacity to love and accept her because of his own relationship to His mother who had once been a foreigner. Naomi recognized that such kindness caused God to strategically place not just anyone, but this particular man, Boaz, as a near kinsman that could bring about Ruth's redemption. Now, in Ruth 3:20, Boaz uses this same word to describe the loyalty and beauty of Ruth's decision to choose him over the younger, and maybe even more attractive, men that she could have wooed and most certainly won there in Bethlehem. We see this rare capacity for loyalty in the overarching kindness of this magnanimous man of standing who had, with his unusual favor, wooed Ruth to this moment. It is "chesed," this unfailing, enduring, unshakable commitment of loyalty and kindness, that is at the heart of the concept of covenant in the Bible.

So at this moment in this beautiful love story God is illustrating for us that the bond between Ruth and Boaz, the promise they were making at this moment, was not something that would change like the wind or fade away over time. God made that same promise to you when He shed His blood, cutting a brand new covenant on the cross. God knew you fully at that moment, though you had yet to be born. He saw your destiny and was making a promise to bring everything He had and pour it out, so that you might live your story.

When you say, "yes" to Him, when you bring all you are and lay it at His feet, just like Ruth laid herself at Boaz's feet, God attributes that same characteristic to you. Do you see that? Boaz said to Ruth that this kindness, this "chesed," was greater than she had shown earlier. Boaz was blown away by this gesture on Ruth's part. So you can know that when you come to God, alone, in the quiet, when you lay yourself down at His feet, asking Him to sort out the truth from the trash, trusting Him to tell you who you are, God is undone over you. He is as undone over you as you are undone by His sacrifice. How incredible! He sees that unusual, enduring kindness and beauty that drove Him to the cross in what drives you to approach Him in the quiet and lay everything down at His feet.

When Boaz recognized that Ruth had come to him, that she was laying at his feet, that she was asking him to make a covenant with her, that she wanted him to become her kinsman redeemer, he was greatly moved by her kindness. To see her respond to what he could give her, blew him away. Of course, he would meet her there. Of course, he would do what she asked. Of course, he would bring everything he had to fight against any enemy who threatened her. Of course, he would redeem her, this one who had expressed such beauty, and kindness, and loyalty, "chesed." In using that word, Boaz elevated her, he lifted her head, he valued this expression of trust.

Boaz accepted her as his own, elevated her, and then he spoke to her greatest need at that moment.

And now, my daughter, don't be afraid (Ruth 3:11 NIV).

Why do you think he said that? I think it was because he knew she was afraid. He knew she was bombarded with all kinds of reasons to fear. Yet He knew that his words, his act, would have the unique capacity to eradicate her fears. He was saying that he would be her safe place, her refuge, her protection from every onslaught and every storm. As the object of his affection, she could be fearless.

God is whispering that same message to you, at this very scary moment, when everyone has an opinion about who you should be and what you should do. He is saying "You no longer have to be controlled by fear! I am here, now, to tell you who you are. Nobody else ever has to hold that kind of power over you again. They cannot own you, because you are mine."

In the movie *One Fine Day*,[59] Michelle Pfeiffer's character has to take her little boy with her to the office on a day that she must make a presentation to her boss. Just having her son there was complication enough, but to make matters worse the boss is terrified of children. Actually he claims to be afraid of children, yet as the scene unfolds, the viewer realizes that this man is actually afraid of the illnesses children might have and, in turn, transfer to him. So are we. We are not nearly as afraid of the opinions of others, as we are of the thought that we might become infected by their beliefs about us, we might let them distort how we see ourselves. We might start believing that what they say is true. This is what makes my moments alone on the threshing floor with my Kinsman Redeemer so powerfully significant. This is where the truth sets us free. Truth immunizes us to false accusations. If I hear the voice of God in the morning, telling me how He feels about me, telling me who I am, revealing how He defines my destiny, I may get stung by the words of the haters and bullies, but His Words will have inoculated me from infection.

Without God, how do we attempt to silence our fears? What do we tend to try to do with all these labels and opinions that we pick up along the way? We set out to prove that anything hurtful that is said does not ring true. If I might fear that I am unlovable I may try to adapt my behavior in a way to change opinions. I might bend over backwards to please everyone around me, or attempt to make myself indispensable. If I might possibly be stupid, then I will work harder than everyone to affect results that will prove me to be the smartest person in the room. I will not only want, but need, to have all the answers all the time. If I am afraid of being wrong, then I have to set out to be perfect. For fear of being an outcast, I will push too hard in relationships. The very things we are afraid of, hold us hostage while we try to disprove them. In the end, the very thing we focused on is made more powerful by our efforts, and our constant attempt to silence the opinions we most fear can result in a self-fulfilling prophecy. The woman who is afraid of rejection pushes people away with her constant efforts to please them. The woman who tries so hard to be perfect in the eyes of those around her ends up isolated behind her spotless walls. No matter how hard we try to get rid of these labels, the ones we most fear will determine our destinies, those words we run from end up becoming an inextricable part of who we are, by dictating so many of our decisions. Those efforts to avoid the labels can result in those very labels becoming embedded in the hard drives of our souls, operating in the background to drive our behaviors, making us slaves to the very words we are desperately trying to disprove.

Not only do my fears begin to dictate my behaviors, they will lead me to attempt to control the behaviors and decisions of others as well. If someone does anything that might add evidence to one of the labels I am trying desperately to overcome, they stand in the way of my efforts to disprove it. So I am forced to try to control that person's responses, behaviors, and opinions. I may go overboard to avoid their rejection, disapproval or criticism as my fear not only holds me captive, but establishes them unknowingly as the warden of my self-imposed prison. I become enslaved by the decisions and reactions of that person, in a failing effort to control what another says, how that person feels, and how they behave.

Such a strategy is doomed to fail because whatever someone says to me, thinks of me, does to me, even how someone responds to me with nonverbal cues, comes out of their heart, not mine, reveals who they are but cannot truly speak to who I am.

Jesus explained,

> *A good man brings good things out of the good stored up in his heart, and an evil man brings evil things out of the evil stored up in his heart. For the mouth speaks what the heart is full of* (Luke 6:45 NIV).

Someone else's words or actions reveal only what is going on in that person's heart. Their words say nothing about me. You see, there are actually people who have the capacity to love even those that society deems as the most unlovable creatures. Such a capacity flows out of the compassion and kindness of God, deposited within them, empowering them to give their hearts away. No one could motivate such generosity of spirit by any amount of persuasion. Likewise there are people in this world who are impossible to please, no matter how hard you or I might try to make them love us and keep them happy. The factors that determine the outcome are internal matters, within the soul of another, that we cannot possibly control. Believe me, I have tried.

Thus, we are powerless to buy our true selves out of this slavery to what other people think of us and how they respond. Without an intervention that breaks the hold of our enslavement we are locked into a perpetual cycle of self-abuse. We desperately need a redeemer. We must go meet Him on the threshing floor and let Him tell us who we are again and again. We will never have the capacity to outrun everyone's opinions, or outperform all the lies, fulfilling the mandates of our coping mechanisms. Apart from the redemption of our identities we are doomed to be men and women of fear. Yet fear will never release the dreams God has for you. A love so perfect that it can overcome all our fears has left heaven on a rescue mission to restore our souls, empowering us to live fearlessly.

In the night, in the dark, in the face of her fears, Ruth strategically put herself next to the one whose words had the power to release her to run with abandon in the truth of who she was created to be. She positioned herself where she knew he would be and waited. She waited for him to say he was willing to redeem her and, with that, speak her destiny into existence.

You and I come to the threshing floor afraid of all the same things that Ruth must have feared. We are every bit as vulnerable and fragile as this young woman from Moab, just as loaded down with the baggage of shame and insecurities offered to us in hard moments by hurtful words and the unreasonable expectations of flawed people. What she did might be as strange to us as it must have seemed to her upon hearing Naomi's instructions. Yet if we will follow in her footsteps, if we will put ourselves right next to our Kinsman Redeemer and wait for Him to speak, when He speaks words that only He knows to say, it will free us from the fear of opinions that can never define, or even begin to describe, who He has created us to be. Boaz's words to this young girl from Moab had the power to change the course of her life from that moment on. Our fears must drive us to the threshing floor, where our Redeemer will separate the trash from the true harvest and we can walk away changed.

These words can become our mantra,

> *I sought the Lord, and he answered me; He delivered me from all my fears. Those who look to him are radiant; their faces are never covered with shame* (Psalm 34:4-5 NIV).

Yet the freedom God offers us on the threshing floor goes beyond words. Boaz promised to take action as well.

> *And now, my daughter, don't be afraid. I will do for you all you ask...*(Ruth 3:11a NIV).

This is covenant. These words that were spoken by Boaz are emblematic of all God is promising you. You are not alone in this. Boaz met Ruth's "yes" with his own. Everything God is, when you say, "yes" to Him, will come against everything and everyone that comes against you. No more reason to tremble at the threat of someone else's rejection when you have been chosen for love by the One Who is Love personified. God's love goes far beyond mere words, it is Who He is, what He does, how He will meet you at the point of every doubt, every heartbreak, every need.

Not only will God say what only He would know to say, God can do what no one else could ever do. Boaz could do things that would change otherwise unalterable factors in Ruth's life. She was an outsider. Boaz had the capacity to bring her into a family. She was impoverished. Boaz was in the position to buy her field. She was childless. Boaz was willing to marry her and give her a son to carry on the name of Elimelek's family. She was alone and Boaz said "Stay in my field. Cling to me." Boaz was the one person that could speak away all those things that were not meant to be a part of her destiny and follow up with actions that would bring his words to life. Once he said those words, "I will do" every single matter was as good as done. She would belong, she would be accepted, she would be welcomed, she would be provided for, she would be loved, she would be married, she would have a family, she would have a home. With just a word, a single promise, Boaz changed everything. Boaz had the unique capacity to refine her circumstances with a permanence that would define her from that moment on.

Yet there is more.

All the people of my town know that you are a woman of noble character (Ruth 3:11b).

How did this man of standing know just what Ruth needed to hear, all the words that would hold the power to answer every unspoken question? Think about the internal conflict that must have taken place within Ruth's soul as she approached this conversation so integral to her story. She surely imagined what others might be thinking of her, the kinds of things that might be said if anyone discovered her there in the shadows. Ruth must have wrestled with intense spiritual opposition because our own spiritual paths are so marked by hostility against our souls. We can imagine her struggle as we walk in Ruth's shoes in the dark, all alone, in pursuit of this dream only God could make true. We shadow box our way to Him all the time. We wrestle spiritual forces, raucous and intimidating, on our way to beautiful believing. We struggle to silence the internal name calling, our own versions of "the Moabite from Moab." We replay the tapes of past criticism and rejection, projecting on present moments every unhealed wound. Ruth must have endured that same sort of mental anguish, fearing the future, doubting her destiny. Perhaps her steps slowed, almost came to a complete stop a time or two, as she talked herself into and out of turning back. All forward progress toward the dream was sustained upon shaking legs. Tears must have welled up in her eyes as she waited to be discovered. She carried all her emotional baggage with her to this place where Boaz lay. She wrestled demons, real and imagined. Rendered helpless to control the outcome, she fought through her fear in the waiting, until his eyes met her glance, until his hand reached out to welcome her, until his voice, only a whisper, said all she needed to hear to overcome all she came through to get there. Could anyone else's words define her, deny her this destiny now? Not a chance. Only Boaz's words mattered in this moment. His words of acceptance and affirmation would silence all the rest. His response to her pursuit had the power to open the cage of her circumstances, releasing her to run toward this delightfully incredible, seemingly impossible dream.

Boaz begins by telling Ruth he knew what other people were saying about her. He had heard the whispers, been in on some of the conversations. You see, Boaz refused to watch from a distance. He had made himself accessible. He had chosen to walk among his people. He came to the threshing floor to personally protect the harvest which gave him opportunity to eat with his servants and celebrate the abundant provision of God as one of them. Boaz knew what people were saying about her. His nature made him approachable, he walked among his servants with an open heart, willing to listen, to know and be known. Unwilling to solely speak through an overseer, he opted to lead relationally, as accessible to anyone who stumbled into his field as he had been to Ruth on that very first day. So, as he revealed his secrets to Ruth, as he offered to tell her what other people were saying about her, his words carried the authority of authenticity. What he would say would be truth spoken to counter every real mischaracterization and imaginary assumption that fueled her fear on her way to finding him.

Right off the bat Boaz gave Ruth a new reputation. "The Moabite from Moab" tag that had followed her to Bethlehem was replaced by a new description. Boaz said everyone has become convinced that you are "a woman of noble character." Say what? Ruth probably turned to glance behind her, making sure his beautiful words were not meant for someone else. Turning back she likely pointed to herself as if to ask the question, "Who me?" How sweet the sound of such extravagant words, far beyond anything she asked for or imagined. Sure, she longed to be accepted among God's people, but to be admired, so well spoken of, had to be beyond her wildest dreams! I wonder who first spoke those words in reference to Ruth. Could it be that Boaz had been planting seeds of this new reputation with his own words of affirmation? Perhaps his people were beginning to see this "Moabite from Moab" through the eyes of their master. Maybe the favor shown to Ruth by their master had become contagious among those who served him.

The Hebrew word translated "noble" is the word "chayil"[60] which means "a force." This word describes a person of unusual courage, strength, wealth and power. It is the same exact word that Naomi chose in describing Boaz as, "a man of standing." Could it be that Boaz was sharing his "glory" with the one that he loved? We have no way of knowing exactly how much time transpired between the events of chapter two and Naomi's recognition of Boaz's many expressions of favor as an invitation to redemptive relationship in chapter three. As Ruth walked each day with Boaz among his people in the safety of his field, as they talked happily over lunch, as she basked in his protection, provision and passion, his powerful presence brought out the best in her, released the beauty that was waiting for love to give it wings. No wonder onlookers began to notice how much alike they had become, how right they seemed together. It was only natural that she would come to be described in similar terms, recognized as "a force" just as he was. There is an undeniable power in the presence of a woman who knows who she is, who has been set free from fear by a perfect love. She walks with dignity, head held high, at home in her skin, released to run with abandon in pursuit of her dreams. In contrast, such power, such incredible freedom, is absent from the life of a woman who is frantically running here and there, trying to please or appease everyone and control all her outcomes. So in the quiet, in the dark, Ruth came to where she knew she could find her redeemer and waited to hear His voice. She brought everything and laid it down, trusting this man to tell her what was true. Just imagine how her heart must have sank as his words continued in verse 12.

> *Although it is true that I am a guardian-redeemer of our family, there is another who is more closely related than I* (Ruth 3:12 NIV).

Say what? There is another? Noooooo! You see, when Boaz said, "I will do all you ask" he knew something about Ruth's situation of which she was unaware. Yet Boaz was not disheartened nor deterred. This other kinsman was no surprise to Boaz. The knowledge of his existence did not cause Boaz to protect his own heart. Before he even revealed to Ruth the presence of a nearer kinsman, he had assured her that he could handle this. Boaz would look out for Ruth and make sure she was well provided for, even if those gifts would have to come at his expense. Boaz was confident and unyielding in his commitment to seek whatever was best for this young woman who was the apple of his eye, the object of his affection.

So just as Ruth left her fear on the threshing floor, God allowed that decision, her new freedom, to be challenged and strengthened in the testing, because this God refuses to play nice with a cage. He will not leave it intact for us to run back to at the first sign of trouble. He lets us get pushed back in, chased back in, thrown back in, until we refuse to leave that cage without dismantling it. With this complication in her circumstances God was showing us that He is so confident in His ability to make us free indeed, that He will let a victory get questioned, pressed against, and threatened. He will make us decide to lay our fear down again and again until we are done with it. This revelation that there was a nearer kinsman must have felt like a punch in the gut to Ruth. Surely a fear of this unknown outcome, must have reared up within Ruth's soul. Undoubtedly that rising fear showed up on her face pretty quickly. Yet Boaz spoke again to put those fears to rest. His words separated the truth from all the panic-inducing lies. His tone was soothing yet protective, wrapping her heart in another layer of conviction, letting her know that he could be trusted, even with this.

> *"Stay here for the night, and in the morning if he wants to do his duty as your guardian-redeemer, good; let him redeem you. But if he is not willing, as surely as the Lord lives I will do it. Lie here until morning." So she lay at his feet until morning...*(Ruth 3:13-14a NIV).

So Ruth lay at his feet until morning. In his presence she could lay her fears down and rest, refusing to let them dominate her thoughts and keep her awake. Boaz's confidence, his wisdom, his integrity overcame her fear like a warm blanket that becomes a comforting barrier between us and the cold. The cold is still there but we are not so affected by it.

So you would think that would be enough. Boaz had already given her quite a story to take home to Naomi, some kind of dream to watch for and wait on. He had given her his word. Yet he had even more to give, more to reveal about his generous heart. We see the more of God in Boaz's tender provision.

> *So she lay at his feet until morning, but got up before anyone could be recognized; and he said, "No one must know that a woman came to the threshing floor." He also said, "Bring me the shawl you are wearing and hold it out." When she did so, he poured into it six measures of barley and placed the bundle on her. Then he went back to town* (Ruth 3:14-15 NIV).

With tender words Boaz had separated all the lies from the truth about Ruth, even this potentially life-altering truth. He assured her that he could handle it. Even before she picked up anything extra, faced any false accusation or rumor or judgement or gossip, he looked after her reputation and protected her from hurt.

There are times when God will step between you and your accuser. You might have never seen them coming because He was standing up for you before they arrived. That is the protection you find under the corner of His garment. Isaiah described it this way, *"Whether you turn to the right or to the left, your ears will hear a voice behind you, saying, 'This is the way; walk in it'"* (Isaiah 30:21 NIV). God may close a door, turn a corner, change your direction and you may not understand why. That is when you can choose to trust that, perhaps, He knows there is something right up ahead that you cannot see, that you cannot know, and He is simply handling it.

As Ruth went home to tell Naomi about her time alone with this beautiful man and all that he revealed in their conversation, Boaz was already heading to town to go to work on her behalf. You see, God never throws up his hands. He never paces the floor. He never gets overwhelmed. He just gets busy. He just does whatever it takes, pays whatever it costs, to get you to your destiny. He never gets tired of being God for you. Just as Boaz wasted no time in heading out to meet this challenge, God has gone ahead of you, boldly facing whatever stands in the way of you living the life He dreams for you. While you lay down and rest, He acts. While you bask in the thoughts of the last time you heard His voice, He is moving all of His resources into position to bring about everything He has promised. Our fears are always rooted in what we believe about ourselves. Our freedom always rests in Who He is and His extraordinary capacity to speak our dreams into existence. He is your Boaz, your Bridegroom, the One Who has chosen you for His love, your Kinsman Redeemer. When you lay yourself down, when you say, "I am whoever You say that I am," to your Redeemer, you step across the threshold to freedom. No one else gets to define you ever again. As you find your way to the threshing floor again and again, you become fearless!

Chapter 7

The One who lives outside of time invites you into a reality that is informed by His perfect plans to give you hope and a future. God speaks in the past tense about battles you're currently fighting. And He buries the shame of yesterday in order to resurrect the moment you are in and sustain you in the season He is calling you to embrace.

— *STEVEN FURTICK, CRASH THE CHATTERBOX: HEARING GOD'S VOICE ABOVE ALL OTHERS*

SAVIN' YOUR SPIT

If there was ever a moment when making a great first impression was paramount for me it came during a summer that was filled with more first impressions than any other in my storied life. Between my junior and senior years in high school, this was the summer of 1977. I had attended a week of activities in the late spring of that year known as Volunteer Girls' State. Girls who were ascending seniors in high school from all over the state of Tennessee were selected by the teaching staffs of their schools to gather on the campus of Middle Tennessee State University to receive hands-on experience in leadership while operating a mock state government. Our activities included everything from speech writing and political campaigns to elections and enacting legislation.

While participating in this prestigious event, I was elected the mayor of the fictional city of Robertson, whose residents occupied the expanse of exactly one floor of a college dormitory. I was then nominated by my party as their candidate for the office of governor of the Volunteer Girls' State. The opposing party nominated a formidable candidate, Melody Mosley, whose alliterated name was only the first clue to her razor-sharp focus and precision in all things political. She was born for just such a moment. She was poised, articulate, always immaculate in her appearance with a demeanor that oozed confidence as well as competence, and, from my perspective, even superiority by comparison. In contrast, I stumbled through my week with such a deer-in-the-headlights expression on my face that anyone who might actually notice me, in the shadow of my towering opponent, probably guessed that I never dreamed of waking up there. Needless to say, Melody wiped the floor with me in our one and only debate and, in turn, handily won the gubernatorial election. However, I put in a good enough showing, with my impassioned dissertation on the path to world peace, that I was selected, along with Melody, to represent the state of Tennessee as a senator to Girls' Nation.

Just a few weeks later I found myself seated next to Melody, forced to endure my very first airplane flight under the watchful eye of my nemesis. Naturally, Melody was completely at ease, having probably jetted around the globe and back in her sixteen brilliant years on this planet. In contrast, I sat, with a white-knuckled, death-defying grip on the arm rest, waiting for my heart to take a second beat. As the airplane engines accelerated for take off, I took one giant leap out of my comfort zone, never to return to the wide-eyed innocence of that moment again.

This entire week spent at American University was filled with all kinds of anxiety-inducing experiences. Following my maiden airplane voyage, I discovered I would be sharing a tiny dorm room with Melody for the entire week. Before the week was through I would endure a wild solo ride in a DC taxi cab and even a one-on-one conversation with an actual member of the president's cabinet, the real life counterpart to my role in, yes, you guessed it, President Mosley's administration.

Arguably at the top of any list of the many memorable moments President Mosley and I shared was a trip to the office of the then Senate Minority Leader, Howard Baker, for a private meeting with him. Not only had Howard Baker been a Senator from my home state of Tennessee since I was 7 years old, he was also the Republican who ironically seemed to influence the trajectory of the Watergate hearings, when he ushered in the toppling of the Nixon presidency with his one penetrating question, "What did the President know and when did he know it?" So, suffice it to say, Senator Howard Baker was a man of standing and one of my heroes. After serving 18 years in the Senate, including 4 years as majority leader, Senator Baker went on to serve as the chief of staff in the Reagan White House and this country's ambassador to Japan under President George H. W. Bush. If ever a 17-year-old girl would want to have her act together it certainly would have been on that day as I walked into the Senate office building, which bore the name of Senator Baker's father-in-law, former Senate minority leader, Everett Dirksen.

Senator Baker was a man who was accustomed to walking among the powerful and influential, those with rare polish and poise, who would gasp at the slightest hint of ever being caught with their proverbial pants down. So, even in my early morning grogginess, I felt the pressure of the prominence of this privileged encounter. Of course, I could never seem to escape the added, though quickly becoming more familiar, pressure of always standing in these special moments next to Melody, whose one comment earlier in the week, about how shockingly different I look without makeup, has haunted me and caused me to go to great lengths to spare anyone else that horror to this very day. Perhaps the only small comfort I have now, as I reflect back on the event I am about to describe, is that, more than likely, I was disappearing a little more each minute in the ever-increasing glow of Melody's glistening glory.

So I might as well cut to the chase to let you know that this encounter with this prominent figure in American history did not really go quite as smoothly as I would have liked. By now I suspect that somehow this fact might not surprise you. Let me begin by explaining that one of the requirements of Girls' Nation was that whenever we left campus, for any of our numerous excursions in the nation's capital, we were required to "dress up." When I say "dress up," I really mean worse than what you might be thinking, because we had to wear panty hose, we had to wear what were often referred to at the time, at least in the South, as "Sunday dresses," and we had to wear high heels, I think, or maybe that was just me trying to land myself somewhere in the stratosphere of Melody Mosley's aura. Believe it or not, we even had to wear white gloves.

It was miserably hot in DC that summer as we rode on a bus all around that historic city. The demands of our rigorous daily schedule required that we wake up quite early each morning, rush through a jam-packed slate of activities throughout the day, and then, stay up late working on political campaign materials, skits and songs that were presented by various groups throughout the week, speeches, and legislation. Add to all of these responsibilities the fact that I was seventeen years old. I was probably going to stay up way too late even if my work was completed at a decent hour. So, for this girl who has never been very much of a morning person, as this hectic week progressed, mornings, along with their demands, were becoming increasingly difficult to manage.

By the time the day of our meeting with Senator Baker came, I got up later than I should and stood in the shower longer than I had time to. As a result, I was just pulling up my panty hose when I was supposed to be running down the stairs and heading to the bus. I hurriedly ripped open the brand new package and did the control top wiggle that was handed down from generation to generation as the only effective way to pull something that starts out that small over something that has probably never been anywhere close to that size since diaper wearing days. I was still stumbling into my second shoe as I went running out the door and down several flights of stairs to catch a nearly packed and ready bus. I was in such a hurry that I hardly gave it a thought that something was amiss. Okay, maybe sometime during the bus ride, I may have had the slightest inkling that my wiggle may have wobbled, but, in reality, I had no idea. It was only when we stepped off the bus in front of the Dirksen Senate Office Building that I began to realize that something was seriously wrong. Although my bottom most assuredly went up as I stepped up onto the curb, my panty hose were definitely going down.

Understand, I did not see him anywhere in the vicinity. I have no information to indicate how he could have possibly heard about it, or whether or not he has had his own painful panty hose mishap somewhere in his past, but I will never believe it was mere coincidence that Paul Simon wrote and released a song later that same year with the lyrics, "You know the nearer your destination the more you're slip sliding away!"[61] The only thing worse than a control top catastrophe in the middle of the hallowed halls of Congress was the fact that I now had to turn and tell Melody Mosley what was going on. In fact, I had no choice but to inform her that my precarious situation strongly demanded, even at the risk of keeping Senator Baker waiting, that we duck into the nearest ladies room to take some sort of evasive action!

Despite my first, second and third impression of Melody I have to say that she did her best to provide aid in my time of tremendous distress by quickly reaching into her unsurprisingly well-stocked purse to pull out two sizable safety pins. "Perfect," I thought. She even waited patiently while I stepped into a stall and quickly fastened one to each side of my grossly missized and/or misshapen out-of-control top hose, attaching each to what I believed to be the much more reliable elastic band of my underwear. Then, without even a second thought, we made a mad dash down the hall and were standing in the very presence of one of the most powerful men in the United States government before I realized that my well worn and oft washed underwear waistband was no match for the gravitational pull. The only shred of dignity I had left was now hanging in the balance between tightness of my gluteus muscles and the intensity of my silent prayers. To top it off, just in case you think I made this up, this agonizing moment was preserved on film. By courtesy of the office of Senator Howard Baker I actually have photographic evidence, unsightly bulge and all, and I suppose Melody does too.

Well, believe it or not, this is where we have arrived as Ruth's saga continues to unfold. Although she will never have the pleasure of experiencing control top panty hose, nor safety pins for that matter, as we pick up her story she has had a private encounter with one of the most powerful men in her society and it did not go as well as she planned. When we left Ruth in the last chapter she had intentionally positioned herself to hear her redeemer's voice. She had come to the threshing floor, so that this beautiful man, who was predisposed to love her, could show her how to separate truth from the lies. In the still of the night the fact that she had intentionally positioned herself so near to him got this man's attention. He reached out and took hold of her, pulling her close to look into her eyes and discover who was there. What he found in this woman who was waiting in the shadows was a tenderness, a sweet surrender, expressed as she identified herself only as his servant. In other words, she was saying, "I am whoever you say that I am," recognizing that the fulfillment of her destiny was completely in his hands. She was giving her life to him, laying her will down for his, as she made an incredible request, asking this man to spread the corner of his garment over her. What she was saying to this man of standing, this force, was in essence, "If you are asking, if you are really willing to take me as your bride, my answer is, 'yes.'" This was all well and good until Boaz blew the doors off her dream with the revelation that, although he was willing to take her as his bride, there was a nearer kinsman who had first dibs.

Those words must have hung in the air between them like an anvil. Scripture provides no evidence that Ruth had any prior knowledge of the existence of a nearer kinsman. So I imagine this news felt just like a punch in the gut that knocked the wind completely out of her sails. Surely some sort of instant panic attack threatened to sweep over Ruth's soul, powerful enough to carry her away in its grasp, until Boaz broke the silence once again in a soothing tone meant to urge her to hold anxiety at bay a little longer, saying,

> *Stay here for the night, and in the morning if he wants to do his duty as your guardian-redeemer, good; let him redeem you. But if he is not willing, as surely as the Lord lives I will do it. Lie here until morning* (Ruth 3:13 NIV).

This bomb drops from out of nowhere and now Ruth is suppose to just lie down and sleep. Never mind that her destiny hangs in the balance, that someone she knows nothing about has the power to undo her happy ending. Have you ever stood in her shoes? Imagine having every detail in place for your dreams to be fulfilled, until just as you, with shaking hands and breath held, seem to have perfectly placed that last card on the tall tip of a precarious tower, you feel a sneeze coming on. When tomorrow is the day that everything hinges on, who can sleep? Instead we spend hours staring at the ceiling or, in Ruth's case, the stars. Tossing and turning, we replay every moment of that conversation and plan out every conceivable scenario, as if we had any control over the outcome. How could Ruth lay down and sleep with such an ominous decision hanging in the air? Defying logic, somehow she did, according to our passage,

> *So she lay at his feet until morning, but got up before anyone could be recognized; and he said, "No one must know that a woman came to the threshing floor." He also said, "Bring me the shawl you are wearing and hold it out." When she did so, he poured into it six measures of barley and placed the bundle on her. Then he went back to town* (Ruth 3:14-15 NIV).

Notice it only says she lay there. There is no mention of sleep. Maybe she did, or maybe she tossed and turned, like I would have, until she could lay there no longer. So Ruth got up and headed home. What a goodbye that must have been! If I were making a movie of this story I know precisely how I would direct this scene. I would begin with the camera tightly focused on Ruth's face, her brow furrowed with the weariness of a sleepless night and an unpredictable outcome, tears welling up in her eyes, arms filled once again with that bounty of barley. Then slowly I would zoom out to include Boaz in the distance, watching as she walked away, desperately wishing she never had to go. Narrowing the focus then to the face of Boaz, I would turn the viewer's full attention to his own pained expression, the outward manifestation of the internal agony of not knowing how the events of the next few hours would unfold. All the while I would fade in with the chorus of the Rascal Flatts song, "What Hurts The Most."[62] As each viewer begins to empathize with the trepidation of Ruth and the turmoil of Boaz, lead vocalist, Gary LeVox, would be heard plaintively belting out the lyrics, words that could have been written for them, describing the heartache of being "so close" to your happily ever after, yet completely at risk of seeing everything you dream of come to a gut-wrenching end.

What a mixed bag of emotions must have propelled Ruth down that path. Hopeful, anxious, confused, yet feeling known and affirmed, burdened by dread, yet buoyed by desire, her mind must have raced her home. She was piecing it all together, parsing every word, processing every bit of information, attempting to predict how this was all going to end. Now she was going to tell Naomi. Surely Naomi would know some way out of this craziness or, at least, the two of them could wring their hands and cry this out together.

Perhaps Naomi already knew about this wrinkle. God leaves that detail out of the text. At the very least Naomi may have suspected there would be others vying for Ruth's heart, other men who could possibly want Ruth, or might be in a closer position to redeem Ruth, if they had the desire and/or the means. She must have met the nearer kinsman at the last family reunion before she and Elimelek left for Moab. It is entirely possible that Naomi knew this when she said "*he* (speaking of Boaz) *will tell you what to do*" (Ruth 3:4b NIV). Naomi knew Boaz was different, in a class by himself. She knew that no one would love Ruth the way Boaz could, and surely would, if given the chance. With full knowledge of the nearer kinsman, perhaps Naomi was urging Boaz to fight for Ruth's heart and their futures.

In this moment in Ruth's story we again see such a picture of God's story that He has written each of us into, for in that story, we have a Kinsman Redeemer, One of unusual means, who has intentionally positioned Himself as a relative, Who has the right and the desire and the wealth with which to buy us out of our spiritual poverty. Yet He is not the only one vying for our hearts either. There are closer kinsmen who would love to steal us away from His love.

Naomi may very well have known about the nearer kinsman. We cannot be sure, but we know she knew Boaz. So, if Naomi knew of the existence of the nearer kinsman, she was undeterred by his presence in their world. She remained convinced that Boaz was the only redeemer who could release Ruth to live the life of her dreams. His extravagant generosity and grace of spirit, his tremendous standing, his moral character, his strength, his purity, his passion singled him out as unique, unusual, completely different from all the others. This man was a force, such a picture of our Redeemer. Our God is not the only one competing to win our hearts, but He is most definitely the Only One Who will love us perfectly. Knowing Boaz, Naomi sent Ruth to seek him, to ask him, so that he could tell them what to do.

In so doing, Naomi models how we can empower those we love. What more can we do, when the destinies of the people that matter most to us are at risk, than send them running to Jesus? Faced with disappointment or rejection, misrepresentation or devastation, when our own husbands, sisters, daughters and sons, when our closest friends face the hard stuff that heartbreak is made of, we must send them to our Boaz. He stands ready to redeem every single thing they have lost or stand to lose in this war for their souls.

When our destiny hangs in the balance, we must run to Him for our battle plan. However, brace yourself, because the Commander of the Lord's Army has been known to adopt unconventional battle strategies. Think about what was on the line for Ruth at this moment. What was at risk? Ruth's future hung in the balance. Her status in Bethlehem society, the way others looked at her and responded, might be greatly affected by the way this all played out. Because she had no prior relationship with this nearer kinsman, as far as we know, she must have had no knowledge of what sort of man he was or how he might treat her. Her future safety and happiness hinged on this man's decision. The character of the one who chose to fulfill the obligation of redemption would greatly dictate what happened at the gate. Would his words of rejection humiliate her, reenforcing her reputation as an outsider among God's people? Would his acceptance of her rip her away from the kindness of Boaz? Either way, his decision was fodder for potential loss and embarrassment. If this kinsman accepted his role in her redemption, then his character would control the details of Ruth's life from that point on, both those that were highly significant and many more trivial aspects of her daily existence. It just seemed like this man, someone she knew nothing about until Boaz unveiled his part in her story, had the power to wreck Ruth's destiny.

So, if you loved her, if you desperately wanted things to work out for her good, if you wanted to make sure that she got her happily ever after, and, perhaps most importantly, if your own future would be affected as well, what would you tell her to do? As she walks through the door with this news that her future, as well as yours, would be decided at the town gate later that very morning, what words would come tumbling out of your mouth in response?

"Get down there and get involved!" Is that close? Perhaps you might even say, "On second thought, maybe both of us should go!" as you rush out of the room to get dressed and grab your purse. Most of us, I suspect, would want to say, in one form or another "Don't just stand there, do something! Fix it, or get out of my way and let me fix it! Let me call somebody who knows a guy. At the very least, we must hide in the bushes, get a glimpse of this guy and, if he does not measure up to Boaz, we will trip up this nearer kinsman before he ever gets to that gate!"

You see, the truth is that Naomi would be greatly affected by the outcome of this. Ruth and Naomi were family, a packaged deal. Whoever redeemed Ruth would take responsibility for her mother-in-law as well. Naomi was just too old to bear children. That fact made Ruth the one eligible for redemption but she would never abandon Naomi or be asked to do so. Naomi's future happiness hinged on this deal, almost as much as Ruth's. It seems quite natural for both of them to want to control the outcome, maybe even to cook up a plan to manipulate the decision. It would come as no surprise to read that they headed out the door to go down to where this discussion would take place, to, at the very least, put in their two cents worth, or, better yet, try to set some wheels in motion behind the scenes to fix this the way they wanted. What you may not know is they actually had a legal right to do just that. A Hebrew widow did not have to stand idly by while she was publicly rejected.

We find this explained in Deuteronomy 25. In these verses we actually see the potential bride, the one who waits to be redeemed, is on the scene, there at the gate where the transaction takes place.

> However, if a man does not want to marry his brother's wife, she shall go to the elders at the town gate and say, "My husband's brother refuses to carry on his brother's name in Israel. He will not fulfill the duty of a brother-in-law to me." Then the elders of his town shall summon him and talk to him. If he persists in saying, "I do not want to marry her," his brother's widow shall go up to him in the presence of the elders, take off one of his sandals, spit in his face and say, "This is what is done to the man who will not build up his brother's family line." That man's line shall be known in Israel as The Family of the Unsandaled (Deuteronomy 25:7-10 NIV).

Wow! That widow described in Deuteronomy was bold. Even though these words would not be the first ones that spring to my mind, were I to find myself in such a situation, to call a man who dared to refuse her "The Unsandaled" seems like fighting words to me. I have never said that to anybody...but I have wanted to say it, spit and all.

After reading these verses, what is your take away? How do you think it would be viewed within the Hebrew culture if this nearer kinsman said "No, thanks!" rejecting Ruth unapologetically for everyone there to see? It sounds like such a rejection would be considered a major insult and a cause for tremendous shame. The embarrassment of such a public humiliation would be a horrible disgrace for Ruth to bear. Even though she was attracted to the kindness and depth of character she had found in Boaz, if the one who has the right to redeem, who was possibly younger, perhaps even more popular, would come to the city gate in front of the city elders and say, "I don't want her," that could easily hang another negative label around her neck. Now the phrase she had come to be known by could evolve into, "the unwanted Moabite from Moab." She could walk away feeling ugly and unlovable. Such a rejection might possibly make her less desirable to others. She could come off looking like a loser, a reject, a misfit, a charity case. All the towns people would know that she was not chosen by this man who was first in line, and just imagine what they would say and think and believe about her. You can almost hear the whispers, "You know, she is a Moabite from Moab, no wonder he didn't want her."

So again, if you loved her, and you had an interest in this as well, what would you tell her to do concerning this possible public humiliation? Consider what Naomi told Ruth to do...

Then Naomi said, "Wait..." (Ruth 3:18a NIV)

Say what? That is not what I would have said. That word would not even make the list of my top twenty-five probable responses.

Naomi said, "Wait?" In the Hebrew she used the word, "yashab" which means, "sit down."[63] The King James Version translates it, "sit still." Given that definition, "yashab" seems more difficult than merely waiting. Does this mean I cannot pace the floor as I wait to hear the news? I cannot call my friends and spin this around and around while we wait? Naomi not only said "Wait," she took it to the next level if she was instructing Ruth to sit down, sit still, and do nothing at all to influence what happens. Such a response called for a deeper discipline, a whole new kind of trust.

Ruth could choose between two completely different responses at this dramatically significant turning point in her life. With option one, the Deuteronomy option, the way of the law, she had every right to march right down to that gate and stand up for herself. She could tell that nearer kinsman he had no right to reject her. She could demand respect, try to convince him that he was making a terrible mistake. She could defend her reputation. She could take control of this situation and even turn it on her rejector. In other words, she could pitch one crazy fit, calling him names and literally spitting in his face, if he dared to insult her by refusing to redeem. Whereas, with option two, the option that rested in placing complete trust in Boaz, she could sit down, sit still and simply wait.

Shakespeare might have put it this way, "To spit or not to spit. That is the question." Pondering our position, deciding what we think Ruth should choose to do, can become a little murky because it may not feel, at this moment, that this is only about Ruth. As we think about what Ruth should do, what we would do, we have history through which we filter the options. We bear on our hearts memories of other moments, other kinsmen even, memories of just how quickly things can go south at the proverbial gate. Have you ever felt the sting of someone's rejecting words? Has there ever been a time when you held out your heart to someone who should have held it carefully but instead, whether by carelessness or viciousness, that person let it fall to the ground? Has there ever been a time when you were misrepresented before others, when your character was questioned? Can you think of a time when someone, maybe even in front of people who wielded powerful influence, had the chance to stand up for you and failed to do so? Has anyone ever embarrassed you, belittled you, taken advantage of your naivety or an innocent mistake you made in order to get a great laugh at your expense? Has anyone ever tried to control you with shame, or, in anger, given you a slap, either physically, or emotionally, or verbally, or spiritually? Has the harshness of someone's criticism stuck like a dagger in your chest? Did you walk away feeling diminished by hurtful words hurled as weapons? Whether it was intentional or not, has someone ever let you down, even broken your heart, or failed to be who you needed them to be at a crucial moment? Has someone you loved ever walked away? Perhaps just the thought of Ruth passing up a chance to spit in this guy's face, triggers the memories of every spit-worthy moment you or I have had to endure. Maybe the whole jumble of emotions that accompany those experiences, now come flooding back as, suddenly, this is not just Ruth standing there at the gate, we are back in those painful moments and the option "not to spit" does not even enter the picture.

It intrigues me that this moment takes place at the gate. If you think about it, throughout Ruth's saga, the setting is almost like another character in this story. Every time Ruth moves to a new location, even the backdrop against which her story unfolds reveals details that cannot be ignored. Ruth's story begins in Moab, a place not that far from the people of God or their promised land, but a place, nonetheless, where God is completely left out. In the culture of her homeland, a relationship with this One True God embraced by Naomi was, both physically and spiritually, a foreign concept. Yet this was the only setting Ruth had ever known. Moab probably felt not only familiar but safe to Ruth, even though in terms of empowering her to reach her destiny, it was not safe at all. The setting of Moab tells us from the start that Ruth was far from home because she was far from God.

Each of us has a Moab of our own. We all have those places we came from, with people and past experiences that were never going to get us where we are going. Yet they have this pull, this tie, almost a voice impossible to silence. We too are Moabites from Moab, just like Ruth. We had to leave some things behind to get here. At the same time, what we have been through comes with us, it has a hand in shaping us, in getting us ready, creating a craving that can no longer be denied.

Driven by that hunger, Ruth's story, and ours, moves to the road, the journey from Moab to Bethlehem. This was a path that would lead to Ruth's destiny but only if she had the courage to hold on, to desperately cling to it. It was a place of transition, of moving, of change, a place where Ruth had to make up her mind. In fact, another woman in that same spot, facing an almost identical set of circumstances, chose differently on that road. Every person who has picked up this book, who has examined the truth this story holds, has had to decide whether or not she will push past the obstacles to stay with it. As you are reading the words on this page, in the middle of chapter seven, you have distinguished yourself as one who has pressed on, and pushed through, so that you are still here. Driven by hunger for bread and so much more, you have proven your determination to believe to the point that it changes your story, even if it means you have to push past whatever stands in your way.

That road led Ruth and Naomi to Bethlehem, the House of Bread, and immediately they saw the fields ripe and ready to harvest. Ruth soon stumbled into a certain field where her physical appetites were more than satisfied, where her soul was fed by the extravagance of this one who was predisposed to love her. Just as I hope God has fed you here. Ruth spent her days gathering up everything she could put her hands on. Once she came home with a boatload of barley, even Naomi began dreaming again.

This led Ruth to the threshing floor where she learned to separate what was valuable from what was worthless. It was a place where the harvest was purified and protected. It was a place where Ruth was intentional about being alone with Boaz so that she could learn to hear his voice, come to know his heart. She came to him seeking redemption, believing that this relationship could actually buy back all she had lost along the way, pieces of herself that had been stripped away in a land where God was left out. The threshing floor was a place of intimacy. Yet it was also a placed vulnerability, where the enemy was always lurking. Ruth had to trust Boaz in a deeper way to seek him there. That setting offered an invitation for us as well, to seek out a chance to spend time alone with our Kinsman Redeemer, to say "yes" to His incredible invitation to know and be known by Him. The threshing floor comes to symbolize the freedom to lay everything down at His feet, so that He can separate all that is true, the pure harvest of all we have endured, and cast aside all the garbage we have picked up along the way that weighs us down and holds us back.

Where are you in your story? Are you still living far from God? Are you moving toward him but constantly being tempted and challenged to turn back? Are you getting your first taste of His extravagant love, just beginning to discover how crazy He is about you? Or are you sitting at His table before an all-you-can-eat buffet? Are you drinking in all that He has prepared in advance to quench your thirst? Are you feeding others out of your overflow? Is He the One you are most anxious to talk about when people ask you how things are going? Are you now consumed by your passion for Him? Are you sneaking away, just to sit at His feet and wait for Him to open His heart to you? Are you now defined only by what He says and how He feels about you and whatever He tells you to do? Can you imagine that your relationship with God could go deeper still, that finding the life you were meant to live might require you to be willing to lose it? Can you imagine doing the unimaginable for love?

Now the setting shifts again, the story takes us to the town gate. Cities in Bible times were surrounded by walls. The Old Testament tells the familiar story of how God's people simply surrounded the city of Jericho and shouted as God miraculously toppled that city's wall, a wall so thick, so strong, that Rahab's home was built on it. How about you? How thick are your walls? Have you insulated yourself against pain? Perhaps once, after getting deeply hurt or disappointed, you started building, determined to never give anyone a chance to hurt you that way again. Have your walls become so strong that whole families of memories live there? I know all about walls.

The cities described in the Bible had walls but, because the citizens could hardly live in total isolation from the outside world, every wall had at least one gate. The gate or gates provided a way for the people of that city to come and go. So our new setting, the gate, has a personality too, it has a role to play in Ruth's story, as well as in yours and mine. You see, a town's gate was the one breach in a village's wall of protection. Therefore, it was the most vulnerable place in the city. If an enemy mounted an attack on your city, their number one objective would be to take the gate. If you take the gate, you take the city. To occupy a city's gate would enable an enemy to control who or what goes in and who or what comes out. So to be at the gate was to be at a place of extreme vulnerability. The gate was the place where decisions were made and business was transacted. Destinies rise or fall on such decisions, creating places where the villagers were most susceptible to the hurt, misunderstanding, and the rejection that those decisions might bring. How fitting such a setting is for this moment when Ruth's destiny hangs in the balance.

The gate is symbolic of where Ruth has come in her story. Suddenly she comes to the most vulnerable moment she has yet to face. On the threshing floor she put her heart on the line with Boaz but she had already seen the favor in his eyes. Now her destiny would rest in the hands of a stranger. The mere shifting of the setting to the Bethlehem gate gives us the tip off that this is a moment of tremendous vulnerability in Ruth's life, a moment that most of us would fear.

What images spring to mind when you hear the word, "vulnerable?" What sort of emotions do those images elicit? What types of situations are most likely to trigger those feelings to come to the surface? Perhaps you feel most vulnerable when your truth, your weaknesses — failures and all, are exposed or when the outcome of a given situation is out of your control, as it was for Ruth. More than anything I think of vulnerability as what it means to be open to getting hurt, my walls have been breached, someone has taken the gate and I have opened my soul to another to the extent that I can no longer fully protect myself from potential heartbreak. Love creates vulnerability, as does change. Also, trust me, if your panty hose are headed to your ankles you have entered the land of the vulnerable, perhaps never to return with your dignity intact.

Webster's New Collegiate Dictionary defines "vulnerability" as "the capacity to be wounded."[64] In light of that definition, do you think of vulnerability as a strength or a weakness? You see, the answer to that question is most clearly identified by how you respond when you find yourself in a situation that has the capacity to break your heart. What are you doing right now in the places where you feel the most vulnerable? Are you building walls, closing the gate, posting a guard, or are you waiting, sitting, trusting? Are you strategizing a way to manipulate the outcome in your favor, or are you trusting Someone of greater authority and influence to protect and provide whatever you need because you know how He feels about you? When your destiny hangs in the balance do you set your heart on your Kinsman Redeemer or does your fear send you running away from home?

Come to think of it, home is perhaps that place, unlike any other, that exposes us to the greatest vulnerability. Yet we were made for home. Our hearts were made to fearlessly rest in vulnerability. Our souls crave the freedom of a gate, to experience intimate relationship that is safe and secure, that invites us to be just who we are, right where we are. Our earthly homes were created to picture that sort of safety, offering relationships without walls, whetting our appetites for the relationship we can only fully experience when we make our home with our Kinsman Redeemer. Is it any wonder that our enemy would set us up to be wounded again and again in that place, in order to prevent us from finding our strength? Many of us come from a history of abuse in places that should have been safe, secure and nurturing. So we isolate, and insulate against all would-be attackers, every situation that makes us feel vulnerable. In light of what we have walked through to get to where we are, how strong must a person truly be to embrace vulnerability, to stare the potential to get hurt right in the face and refuse to flinch? Yet if God, through Boaz and Naomi, was urging Ruth to stand in her vulnerability, could it be that you or I might be barricading our hearts from the very thing that was meant to provide our freedom? Could our Redeemer be calling us out, from behind our walls, to find our true strength not in what we can do for ourselves but in all He will do as we wait?

> *Then Naomi said, "Wait, my daughter, until you find out what happens. For the man will not rest until the matter is settled today"* (Ruth 3:18 NIV).

In this moment at the gate Ruth could gain everything her heart desired or she could lose it all. Yet Ruth chose to sit still and hold on to her spit. To choose as Ruth did, in such a destiny-defining moment, is to believe what I heard Steven Furtick say in a recent sermon, "While we wait, God works." You see, Ruth could be still only because she was convinced that Boaz would not be still. Boaz was headed to the gate. That is how our saga continues,

> *Meanwhile Boaz went up to the town gate...*(Ruth 4:1 NIV)

While Ruth sat down, sat still, and waited, Boaz sprang into action. He knew just how things operated at the gate, how to navigate through the dangerous waters of vulnerability. Ruth was deferring to his judgement. She was believing that Boaz would look after her destiny even better than she could.

> *Meanwhile Boaz went up to the town gate and sat down there just as the guardian-redeemer he had mentioned came along. Boaz said, "Come over here, my friend, and sit down." So he went over and sat down. Boaz took ten of the elders of the town and said, "Sit here," and they did so. Then he said to the guardian-redeemer, "Naomi, who has come back from Moab, is selling the piece of land that belonged to our relative Elimelek. I thought I should bring the matter to your attention and suggest that you buy it in the presence of these seated here and in the presence of the elders of my people. If you will redeem it, do so. But if you will not, tell me, so I will know. For no one has the right to do it except you, and I am next in line"* (Ruth 4:1-4a NIV).

Stop and think about that for a minute before we complete our reading of verse 4. What did we just learn about this guy that came to meet Boaz at the gate? He was not only a nearer kinsman, he was the nearest one, their closest relative. Can you connect with that at all? Who are the people who are close enough to deeply hurt you, who are those positioned to affect you the most with their inadequacies, or their struggles, or their sins, or their poverty, or their rejection or their need? In all probability, the ones who came to your mind are the people who are the closest to you.

The wording in verse 4 explains the unique position of this kinsman saying, "no one has the right to do it except you..." That word, translated "except," in the Hebrew means "to scatter."[65] In other words, "Everybody else is scattered compared to you." This nearer kinsman was truly set apart in a crowd of those connected to Ruth in various ways. He was uniquely positioned to meet her needs and love her well or prove to be inadequate, disappointing, and perhaps, even rejecting. Though you have probably never been up for levirate marriage, you must have someone who stands that close to you, close enough to break your heart. Who is the person or the people who are close enough to really do some damage? Is it a mom, a dad, a husband, a sibling, a child, a precious friend, a church leader, or an employer? Most of us have more than one "nearer kinsman," vying for that place at the front of the line to hurt or disappoint us because these are the people we have opened our hearts to let in.

As crowded as that field might be I realized not too long ago that I had failed to identify someone with tremendous capacity to affect me with her choices. You see, as I lay in bed at 2:30 one morning, thinking about this part of Ruth's story, though I desperately needed to go to sleep, my nearer kinsman refused to allow me to do so. When I needed her to just quiet her brain so that I could get some rest, she was inadequate. The minute I crawled out of bed at 6:45 a.m. to get ready for work, she stared straight at me as I glanced into the bathroom mirror. She let me down that night when I needed her to come through for me and she has let me down in many other ways on many other occasions. I have come to identify that the person most responsible for shooting my destiny in the foot has always been me.

Even though Ruth had probably never met this nearer kinsman, he was close enough to hurt her. Though she did not go anywhere near the gate, this was a moment of tremendous vulnerability for Ruth. Her future seemed to rely on the choice of a man who might not even know her name. The decision that could determine the course of the rest of her life was being hashed out in public in front of the most important people in the town. The law gave her the right to be there. Any self-respecting woman would more than likely take advantage of a chance to face that man so that, should he reject her, she could take off his shoe, spit in his face, and make a public declaration that there would be no second chances for him to take her as his wife. Yet Ruth had been counseled by her precious friend to sit down and wait to see how the matter would be resolved, and she did.

Ruth is not the only one who must have felt wide open to potential hurt because of this encounter at the gate. What about Boaz? It must have been obvious, to anyone who knew Boaz well at all, that he had an attraction to Ruth, that, in fact, he had chosen her for love. So much so, that he was willing to make himself vulnerable, to open himself to heartbreak, in order to spare her the pain, shame and embarrassment of this moment. As he stood toe to toe with his rival, I think Boaz was painfully aware of the nearer kinsman's capacity to wound him. Yet as Boaz stepped up for Ruth he placed himself in the line of fire, subjected himself to humiliation, so that she would never have to go there.

> *Boaz took ten of the elders of the town and said, "Sit here,"*
> *and they did so. Then he said to the guardian-redeemer, "Naomi,*
> *who has come back from Moab, is selling the piece of land that*
> *belonged to our relative Elimilek. I thought I should bring the*
> *matter to your attention and suggest that you buy it in the*
> *presence of these seated here and in the presence of the elders of*
> *my people. If you will redeem it, do so. But if you will not, tell*
> *me, so I will know. For no one has the right to do it except you,*
> *and I am next in line." "I will redeem it," he said. Then Boaz*
> *said, "On the day you buy the land from Naomi, you also*
> *acquire Ruth the Moabite, the dead man's widow, in order to*
> *maintain the name of the dead with his property"* (Ruth 4:4-5
> NIV).

Do you think this nearer kinsman felt vulnerable too? He was simply on his way, in the middle of an ordinary day, when Boaz stepped out to stop him, putting him on the spot, in front of the elders of the town no less. This nearer kinsman was presented with an opportunity to buy back a field that Naomi had been forced to sell in order to provide for her and Ruth's basic needs. According to the law of the Hebrew people, if anyone became so impoverished that they had to sell a piece of their land, anyone in the family, beginning with the closest relative, had the right to buy it back in order to keep it within the family. Otherwise one would have to wait until the year of Jubilee, which was the fiftieth year, for that property to be returned to the original family. This kinsman was being offered the chance to buy this field that had once belonged to Elimilek because he was the closest relative. At least in the initial hearing of this, to purchase this field seemed like a great opportunity for the nearer kinsman to extend his land holdings. Then Boaz said, "There's also a young woman involved." It was quite likely that this man could have known Naomi because she lived in Bethlehem before her family sojourned to Moab. She had been married to someone closely related to him. Now she was old, beyond childbearing age. So he most likely knew that he would not be asked to marry Naomi. It was distinctly possible that he was unaware of the existence of Ruth. Even if he had heard about this girl, she was a Moabite, from a people who long stood in opposition to the Hebrew nation. Perhaps he thought no one would expect him to marry her, considering her background. Simple reasoning could have prompted this kinsman to jump at this chance to purchase the field, or perhaps this was simply an instantaneous reaction. We have no way of knowing. Whether by deliberate calculation or a spontaneous whim, this decision seemed to place the nearer kinsman in the driver's seat, determining not only the course of his own future but that of Ruth and Boaz as well.

Yet Boaz had more information to bring to this discussion. Boaz said, "There's a young woman involved here, Mahlon's bride, and if you want to buy the field you have to take her as your bride. You have to have an ongoing intimate relationship with her. You have to have a child with her. And you have to hold that field in trust as a part of that child's inheritance." So now, fully aware of this added information, the nearer kinsman realized that this was no longer simply a one time investment. This was a lifelong commitment. Buying the field, probably at a bargain price since Naomi was impoverished, could have only enriched his holdings, but marrying Ruth, raising a child so that he could give that field to that child, not to mention taking on the responsibility of Naomi's well-being, was going to cost him a lot more than he first bargained. It was a price he was unwilling to pay.

Nearer kinsmen come in all shapes and sizes. Haters, bullies, manipulators, and abusers can leave those within their orbit feeling unloved, forgotten, powerless and out of control, victims of someone else's unhealthy choices. A parent that was impossible to please or incapable of showing affection, leaves the lasting legacy of an aching emptiness in the soul of a child. Mean girls, young and old, intimidate others to mask their own insecurity. Yet not every nearer kinsman is malicious in his or her motive. They are simply impoverished, unable or unwilling to bear the cost of loving you well. You may be standing toe to toe right now with someone that seems to stand in the way of your deepest desires, convinced that they have the power to ruin everything. You and I have not only been to our share of gates, we have met some nearer kinsmen, and still tremble in the wake of what these would-be redeemers' choices might say about who we are and what the future may hold. So much so that each of us most likely carries an arsenal of coping mechanisms, that have a lot more to do with spit and name calling than waiting, not to mention a well-established reluctance to try again.

A significant season of rejection came for me at the hands of a group of church women, who loved their power and were extremely invested in holding onto it. These grownup mean girls never learned to share. Their words and actions made it crystal clear that there would be no place for me in their circle. I was not one of them. I had not been shaped to fit their mold of thinking, nor had I been brought up on their brand of theology. I lived, in their eyes, on the wrong side of town. Unlike them, I spoke with the accent of a native East Tennessean. From the time I expressed an interest in teaching a study of the book of Ruth for some of the women within their sphere of influence, they put up barriers. They held meetings to question my motives, pointed out every real or perceived misstep. At last I chose to step away from teaching at that church altogether because of the constant barrage of accusations and innuendos. After months of standing at the gate, hoping to win their approval, I was done, no more putting myself out there, no more trusting. My heart once broken, I vowed to make it unbreakable, as I set out to reposition it as unreachable. I picked up a brick and a trowel and started construction on a big thick wall.

It seems only natural to set out on a course of isolation and avoidance, after we have been betrayed. We become quick to move away from anyone who shows signs of inadequacy, the potential to disappoint or the possibility of rejecting us. The first whiff of vulnerability and we go into hiding. The problem with this approach is that most wounds take more than time to heal. Some require a touch of fresh wind, an openness to new love, the compassion of a Good Shepherd who very well may lead us to safer pastures next time but Who is also so confident in what He can make out of any situation that, right in the midst of our enemies, He will spread out a lavish feast for us to enjoy without fear in His presence. Our greatest purpose will never be found in saving our lives but in our willingness to lose everything in the reckless abandon of pure trust. We can be still because we know Him, we know He will not be still. While we wait, He is heading to the gate where our destiny will be decided.

Everything true about us resists confinement. No matter how deeply we bury ourselves in our bunkers of self-protective strategies, our souls scream at those walls that surround us, our hearts long for freedom, not a cage. We can not deny that we need more than isolation. What we ache for is redemption, to get everything back, all that is authentic. We long to come out of the shadows, from behind the walls, to somehow become fearless!

The individual strategies that Boaz and Ruth each implement in this vulnerable moment, are so incredible, so radical, so inspiring because what they do is holy, unusual, completely supernatural, other than anything we have tried. Their examples should lead us to question every coping mechanism we have ever employed, every go-to plan of action we run to in fear. God is calling us to an even deeper trust than what brought us to seek His favor. God is asking us a brand new question, as we stand here with Ruth at the gate, "Will you believe, oh, not just believe, but believe to the point that rejection is robbed of its power?"

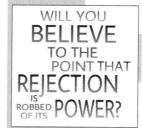

There must be a place at the gate where we can say, because of My Redeemer, because of His confidence in His own abilities, because of His confidence in me, I will no longer run in fear, I will no longer build walls. I can walk straight toward the possibility of rejection, disappointment, and hurt knowing that my Boaz can get me through it, and beyond it, dream still alive, destiny still unfolding on schedule. If I can embrace that level of deeper trust, that greater freedom, I can sit down and be still, no longer attempting to control every outcome. God has ordained gate-vulnerable experiences for me, to strengthen my spiritual muscles, conditioning them to release fear so that I can grab hold of His hand.

To relate this to our earthly experiences think about it in terms of raising children. An overprotective parent actually weakens the confidence of the child. If a parent follows a toddler everywhere saying, "Oh, honey, don't do that. Oh, you mustn't try to crawl. Oh no, I don't want you to walk. Really you can't try to ride a bike. Oh, please! I don't want you to drive. Oh no, no, no!" Is that loving them well? Healthy parents give their children the space to try, even at the risk of failure, because failures hold invaluable lessons. Wisdom tells us to teach them to take baby steps, then to walk, then to run, ride a bike and drive a car. A child will become fearless if they are given the space to try. That courage, gained as they were allowed to put their muscles under enough stress to build them up, can release them to embrace the lives God dreamed for them and do greater things than anyone could imagine.

God, your Father, my Father, is not an overprotective parent. He never says, "Oh no, don't go to the gate where that nearer kinsman is! What if she embarrasses you! What if he rejects you! What if you get hurt!" We see God as the Good Good Father He truly is in this self-portrait He paints in the life of Boaz. Boaz refuses to run away from this challenge. Boaz runs toward it. In fact, he moves Ruth toward it without hesitation. When Ruth comes to him on the threshing floor and uncovers his feet to say "I want you to redeem me," he refuses to sidestep the truth. He immediately reveals the existence of this nearer kinsman and, unintimidated by what might happen there, Boaz heads right to the gate.

It was a supernatural response for Ruth to lie down after first hearing this news and lie there until morning. Who could blame her if she was awake all night pacing the floor? Yet Ruth stayed at his feet when this potentially devastating news came. Then Ruth headed home to sit still and simply wait. Hers is a response born in the soul of a woman who has looked deeply into the eyes of her redeemer and found herself there. No one else gets to define her by their choices or their words, by their willingness to embrace her or their determination to shun her. She knows who she is. Yes, she knows where she came from, but she also knows God's vision of her future destiny is already true and cannot be undone by the decision of a man who does not know her at all. She is fearless, not because she welcomes rejection, but because she knows she cannot be ruined by it.

Ruth had no need to race down to the gate to confront this guy. Wait, what was his name? How interesting it is that his name is never mentioned. This man is such a minor detail in Ruth's story that we do not even need to know who he was. It was unnecessary for Ruth to even acknowledge him, much less tremble in his presence or be intimidated by his power to choose. Ruth knew this anonymous relative could neither determine nor deny anything about her, not her destiny, not her true identity. His name does not even roll by in the credits as her story concludes. Can you grasp that? Will you embrace that concept for yourself? When the story of your life is written in its entirety that one who walked away, that bully that made you absolutely miserable, the haters, the mean girls, that angry, abusive parent, that husband who said he could not love you anymore, that one who broke your heart, the instrument of your most bitter rejection, will barely matter. Your rejectors will become nothing more than a footnote to your destiny, a parenthetical detail. The title of this beautiful love story, tucked away within the story of all stories, that bears the very image of our God, has come to be known by the title, "The Book of Ruth." Her saga bears that image of God that was born on her piece of the puzzle that reveals Who He is, how she saw and experienced Him in her life. Yet, if you read it from cover to cover, if you study it for years and pour through every commentary written that delves into every minute detail, you will never discover this nearer kinsman's identity. Likewise when your story on earth is through, those nearer kinsmen, who did not choose you or want you or celebrate who you are, will be so insignificant, that those who hear it, or read it, or see it unfold will almost forget they ever had any part in it. No one will even remember their names.

While we wait, God does not wait. Naomi seems to be channeling that principle as she spoke to her precious daughter in the faith,

> *Then Naomi said, "Wait, my daughter, until you find out what happens. For the man will not rest until the matter is settled today"* (Ruth 3:18 NIV).

Naomi knew exactly what would empower Ruth to be still in the face of such vulnerability. Ruth could sit still, holding on to her spit, because Ruth was so satisfied with Boaz. Both of these women were letting their hope rest in what they believed this man of kindness, this man of standing who was predisposed to love and accept them, would accomplish on their behalf. Naomi was not urging Ruth to put her faith in the nearer kinsman, she was encouraging her to put her faith in that one who had promised to handle it, the one who was strong and courageous enough to sleep on the threshing floor and guard the harvest, who had said he was willing, who had chosen to love her, who was willing to make a covenant with her and bring everything he had to see her dream come true. Their trust was in someone unusual and rare, who had invited Ruth in and urged her to stay. Boaz had set her free to sit still, because he would not sit still. Boaz had given her the courage to wait because he would courageously step forward to do what needed to be done. Naomi said, "For the man will not rest until the matter is settled today." Boaz had freed Ruth from the threat of rejection, of disappointment, of hurt, with his willingness to love her passionately and to stand up for her in her most vulnerable moment. Ruth could trust him now, when so much was on the line, because he had already shown her that he was trustworthy in so many significant and insignificant details of her days.

This picture of how their relationship evolved is a gift and an invitation to us. You see, none of us just wakes up in the middle of a crisis with a heart at rest, ready to trust deeply in the character and capability of Our Redeemer, any more than Ruth would have been able to sit still had she not first basked in this beautiful relationship with Boaz. You learn who God is on the days when you are not in crisis, when no one is standing there making up their mind about you, when no threat hangs overhead. You learn to trust God when you stay in his field day after day. You learn to trust deeply in God when you intentionally position yourself to hear His voice and say in a response developed over time, "I am whoever you say that I am." Ruth had learned who Boaz was as he, by sheer grace, revealed himself to her little by little, day after day. Ruth's capacity to trust Boaz was established by simply walking with this beautiful man through her ordinary days. The powerful truths she gleaned about his character and his capabilities empowered her to be still.

Ruth could sit at home and wait, instead of running to the gate to demand her rights, because she knew she would be okay no matter what happened there. The generosity of Boaz sent her home, not only well fed, but with overflowing provision. If no man chose to redeem her she would live her life in abundance as she returned every day to bask in the extravagance of the favor she had found the first time she looked into his eyes. The consistency of graciousness she had already experienced with Boaz gave Ruth every reason to wait with confidence in his loving care.

Ruth had also come to know how Boaz felt about her. Perhaps it was the worst kept secret in Bethlehem that Boaz had given his heart away. The Hebrew wording in chapter two indicates that Boaz shared openly, revealing his soul to her. I can just imagine seeing his eyes dance at her exuberance, hearing the harmony of their shared laughter. It was passion that sent Boaz to that gate, not obligation. Ruth could rest assured that Boaz would not let someone less capable of loving her step between her heart and his own.

Ruth had seen Boaz's competence demonstrated in the field as well as on the threshing floor. She had watched him lead with a gentle wisdom. Nobody had a field like Boaz where every person connected to him could count on him to provide ahead of time for each need.

Strangers could come there and find safety. This man was a force. Ruth had seen him in action.

Finally, Ruth knew of his willingness. No one had to coerce Boaz to get involved in her situation. With neither prejudice nor judgement he reached out to her knowing every thing that should have disqualified her from receiving his kindness. Even in his promise to go to the gate to confront the nearer kinsman he assured her, "But if he is not willing, as surely as the Lord lives, I will do it." If you examine this phrase in the original Hebrew, he was saying to Ruth, "if there is any part of this the nearer kinsman refuses to do, I will do it all!" Ruth could sit down and be still, she could wait without knowing exactly what would happen, because she knew the willingness of this man who had made that promise!

Ruth's hope was not in the graciousness of the nearer kinsman. She was not waiting breathlessly to discover if this man had the capacity to fall in love with a Moabite girl. Her confidence never needed to rest in the nearer kinsman's competence or willingness to redeem her. Her confidence was in the one whose love was already decided. Boaz, whom God has provided for us as a picture of Himself, shows us a God with skin on, foreshadows the One Who would willingly step forward to redeem His bride with unusual passion. When you know your Redeemer intimately, you can wait for Him to act in the most vulnerable moments of your life, to protect and provide everything you need. Rejection may come at the hands of a nearer kinsman, but if he will not do any part of what you need, God will provide it all. Ruth could sit down because she knew Boaz would not sit down until she was released to live her destiny!

Think about how different Ruth's story would be if Boaz was left out of the narrative. This is what it would look like to live your story apart from God. Without God we have to face our most vulnerable moments alone, desperate for things to work out, manipulating to achieve the best outcome through whatever means we have to employ. We can easily end up begging people not to reject us or devastated when they do. When our hearts get broken, when someone close to us crushes our spirits, when a nearer kinsman is unable, or simply unwilling, to come through for us, we carry the shame of those wounds away. The accusations and the actions of others define us. We become desperate for the dreams we have given them the power to deny. Your destiny is far too important to God for Him to leave it in the hands of a nearer kinsman. No matter how well intentioned, that person will always be inadequate to pay the price of your dreams.

That's what God warns of in Psalm 49,

No one can redeem the life of another or give to God a ransom for them—the ransom for a life is costly, no payment is ever enough (Psalm 49:7-8 NIV).

Without our Boaz, our Kinsman Redeemer, Who has given us His promise that, if any nearer kinsman is not willing to do any part of what we need from them, He will step up and do it all, we are doomed to lives of desperation. Yet you and I are daughters of the King of Kings, the objects of His incredible affection! We will not be relegated to a cage! Rejection and desperation will not be our destiny! Listen to these words from Isaiah 62 as paraphrased in The Message:

Regarding Zion, I can't keep my mouth shut, regarding Jerusalem, I can't hold my tongue, Until her righteousness blazes down like the sun and her salvation flames up like a torch. Foreign countries will see your righteousness, and world leaders your glory. You'll get a brand-new name straight from the mouth of GOD. You'll be a stunning crown in the palm of GOD's hand, a jeweled gold cup held high in the hand of your God. No more will anyone call you Rejected, and your country will no more be called Ruined. You'll be called Hephzibah (My Delight), and your land Beulah (Married), Because GOD delights in you and your land will be like a wedding celebration. For as a young man marries his virgin bride, so your builder marries you, And as a bridegroom is happy in his bride, so your God is happy with you. I've posted watchmen on your walls, Jerusalem. Day and night they keep at it, praying, calling out, reminding GOD to remember. They are to give him no peace until he does what he said, until he makes Jerusalem famous as the City of Praise (Isaiah 62:1-7 MSG).

Why did Boaz get up early that morning and go straight to that gate to come face to face with the inadequacy of that nearer kinsman? He knew what would be born in that process—Ruth's freedom. God is unafraid in those moments that might seem to hold the undoing of your destiny. He will boldly walk you right toward heartbreak and disappointment, that person who might be inadequate, who might reject you, who might let you down in profound ways. Your God, Your Kinsman Redeemer, believes that strongly in that dream He has placed in your heart. He wants you free from everything that hinders you or holds you back from your already decided destiny. In walking you right to the gate where you encounter an inadequate nearer kinsman, God is releasing you to run with abandon in all the truth of who He created you to be.

Consider these words from Isaiah,

> *The Sovereign Lord has opened my ears; I have not been rebellious, I have not turned away. I offered my back to those who beat me, my cheeks to those who pulled out my beard; I did not hide my face from mocking and spitting. Because the Sovereign Lord helps me, I will not be disgraced. Therefore have I set my face like flint, and I know I will not be put to shame. He who vindicates me is near. Who then will bring charges against me? Let us face each other! Who is my accuser? Let him confront me! It is the Sovereign Lord who helps me. Who will condemn me? They will all wear out like a garment; the moths will eat them up* (Isaiah 50:5-9 NIV).

The Hebrew word translated as "flint" means "the hardness of a rock."[66] Yet, interestingly, this Hebrew word comes from a root word that means "to dream."[67] You see, when you come to a place where what you know about your Kinsman Redeemer releases a rock-like strength in you that enables you to sit still in the most vulnerable moments of your life, in simple, quiet trust, well, that is where your dreams meet your reality. To be fearless is to be confident that His perfect love can never let you down. God may choose to walk you right toward that person, that situation, that threatens to destroy everything you have hoped for. Yet just the other side of your greatest heartbreak waits a love you can never lose. Boaz promised that if there was anything this nearer kinsman refused to do, he would do it all. Ruth could sit down and wait while her future was being decided at the gate because she believed him. Will you believe the way Ruth believed? Will you believe to the point that rejection is robbed of its power? The time has come to take back our power and live the lives our haters have denied us for far too long. Our Redeemer, our Boaz, loves us with a love so completely satisfying that, even in the face of rejection, believing in that love will make us fearless, will set us free.

Chapter 8

Grace is unconditional acceptance given to an
undeserving person by an unobligated giver.

— *TULLIAN TCHIVIDJIAN, ONE-WAY LOVE*

CRASHING THE GATE

Do you remember what it felt like to get your first taste of real freedom when, at sixteen years old, you held your driver's license in your hand? I loved it. I could hardly wait to get out there, to experience that new independence. Our youngest daughter had no sense of urgency when she became old enough to drive. In fact, she waited until she was seventeen to get her license and we practically had to beg her to do it even then. Not me. I was ready and waiting on the very first day I was legally of age. Since my birthday falls right in the middle of summer this meant that I could get myself to the Alice Bell/Spring Hill Aquatic Center on a daily basis from the third day of July throughout the rest of the season. I had been set free and was thrilled to relish in my newfound opportunity to own the road. Thrilled, that is, until the day of my first driving disaster.

I was coming home from the swimming pool on a warm and sunny summer day as I drove into our driveway in my mom's green Pontiac Catalina station wagon. Not exactly my idea of a sweet ride but any vehicle that facilitated my teenage autonomy was as good as a fancy sports car to me. We had a fence that surrounded our backyard with a gate across the driveway. The driveway continued past that gate, circling right and leading right past my basketball goal into our carport that adjoined the back patio of our home. The space between the natural progression of the driveway and the house was also covered by asphalt so that we could actually park an additional two cars in that area. The carport was reserved for my dad's car. So in order to park the station wagon I had to navigate a sharper right turn as soon as the car passed safely through the open gate. The thought of making that turn brought little, if any, anxiety to me. I had done it successfully a number of times, even when I was driving with a learner's permit. However, that task became a bit more challenging because, just as I drove through the gate on this particular day, I was surprised by the sight of my grandmother driving toward me on her riding lawn mower.

My grandparents had lived in the house right across the street from us for my entire life. So seeing them in our yard, or us in theirs, was nothing unusual. They had a huge influence on my life. They were my first heroes, my strongest allies, my only fan base and the people I most wanted to please. One of the things I loved most about them was that they did everything together. Before they retired, they rode to work in the same car every day. When the windows of their house needed to be washed, Papaw would clean the outside while Nanny cleaned the same pane from within. When Papaw bought a boat and took up fishing, Nanny became his fishing buddy. When fishing was no longer how Nanny wanted to spend her free afternoons, Papaw sold the boat. Their enduring marriage, and the constant companionship that characterized it, was almost like a choreographed dance. Yet nothing exemplified their passion for togetherness like watching these two lovebirds do yard work. Nanny always mowed the middle of the yard on her riding mower, while Papaw used a push mower to trim around the trees and the fencing.

So the only unusual thing about seeing my grandmother on that riding mower was the fact that she was in our back yard, not her own. Just as I drove that big old station wagon through the gate, she startled me by popping her mower right up onto the asphalt driveway in front of me. Though she was still quite a distance away, as a result of her sudden and unexpected appearance combined with my inexperience, I jerked the steering wheel too soon and too severely, taking that right turn toward the parking space behind the house a bit too sharply. Before I knew it, I felt a sickening jolt and heard the crunch of metal on metal, as the right back panel of my mom's green station wagon crashed into the gate post. I was mortified. So I did what all of us do, when our vulnerable moments threaten to unmask us as the fools that we are, I ran. I got out of that car and never looked back. I had no desire to see the damage I had done, nor the looks on the faces of my grandparents who were the eyewitnesses to this whole calamity. All I wanted to do was hide. So, with head down, I ran as fast and as far as I could from that crash, taking refuge behind the locked door of the bathroom, vowing never to show my face outside of that tiny room again.

When it comes to our freedom, we can so easily mess it up, crash right into the gate with everyone watching. So one would assume that

Boaz would want to proceed with caution as he came to the place where such life-altering decisions would be made. We might advise him to keep his cards close to the vest, to approach the nearer kinsman with a certain amount of trepidation. It would just be human nature to adopt a self-protective stance until it seemed safe to come out of hiding. One wrong turn could find Boaz wrecking not only his dreams but all future prospects for Ruth, and Naomi as well.

Yet that is not at all how Boaz handles his freedom. Consider what he does next.

> *Boaz took ten of the elders of the town and said, "Sit here,"*
> *and they did so. Then he said to the guardian-redeemer, "Naomi,*
> *who has come back from Moab, is selling the piece of land that*
> *belonged to our relative Elimelek. I thought I should bring the*
> *matter to your attention and suggest that you buy it in the*
> *presence of these seated here and in the presence of the elders of*
> *my people. If you will redeem it, do so. But if you will not, tell*
> *me, so I will know. For no one has the right to do it except you,*
> *and I am next in line." "I will redeem it," he said. Then Boaz*
> *said, "On the day you buy the land from Naomi, you also*
> *acquire Ruth the Moabite, the dead man's widow, in order to*
> *maintain the name of the dead with his property"* (Ruth 4:2-5
> NIV).

What Boaz did for Ruth, as he stood at the gate in her place, is truly shocking, completely unconventional, and unmistakably altruistic. Boaz stepped into the path of this man, whose name we do not even know, who stood between Boaz and his dreams, and, with everybody who was anybody in Bethlehem societal circles watching, Boaz got naked. He really did, in a manner of speaking. When Boaz said, "I thought I should bring the matter to your attention," that particular Hebrew phrase carried the idea of "stark exposure, nakedness, an uncovering of the ear."[68] How radical is that? What did you do the last time you stood before the one person who could bring about your undoing? I would venture a guess that your answer would not have anything to do with taking off your clothes. Would I ever get naked at the gate? Absolutely not! Getting naked, is one of the circumstances that makes me feel the greatest vulnerability. It is most certainly not the cure!

Boaz looked right into the eyes of his rival, the one who had the power to wreck everything, and starkly exposed himself to potential heartbreak. He not only told this guy that there was a field, and that there was a girl, he went ahead and publicly laid out his own desire to step in to redeem it all, should the nearer kinsman decide to opt out. Boaz held back nothing. In starkly exposing his truth, he made no attempt to protect himself by hiding the way that he felt. When he could have crafted a speech intended to manipulate the nearer kinsman's decision, he employed no deception. In declaring his intentions, before this man had made his decision, Boaz added value to the things this kinsman had the first option to reach out and take for himself. Boaz let his rival know that he had the advantage, that he was uniquely positioned to take everything Boaz wanted away.

That is the fearless authenticity of our Redeemer. When all you or I want to do is hide how we feel, protect ourselves from hurt, manipulate every circumstance to facilitate our own desires, or, better yet, run for our lives in sheer panic from any situation that makes us feel vulnerable, our God adopts a much more radical strategy. He just gets naked in front of His rivals, everything to lose, yet nothing to hide. Your Redeemer went to the gate in your place, opened up His arms and said, "Hit me with your best shot!"

Calvary's hill was that gate, the place of your most dramatic vulnerability, and mine. It could have been your undoing. It should have been the place of your greatest embarrassment, the moment when you lost it all. Left to your own devices you would have crashed into that gate for sure. At that gate, it was your destiny that was threatened, not His. No one could touch His destiny, nor find any fault in anything about Him. Yet He went there willingly so that you would never have to go. He hung naked on that cross for every mistake you made, every wrong turn you have taken, every wreck you ever caused in immaturity or pride. He stood in your place in that gate simply because He loves you that much. He starkly exposed his heart, knowing it would be broken. He laid His life down to set you free, to give you an amazing opportunity to believe to the point that rejection is robbed of its power. Now, and for always, you can sit still because He did not sit still, He ran to meet your adversary. Knowing every single thing about you that should most certainly disqualify you, He went there to buy back back your freedom. That is the passion of your Boaz, the ridiculous extravagance of the way He loves you.

There is an incredible principle illustrated in Boaz's nakedness, in this picture of our Savior's willingness to embrace vulnerability in such an unconventional way: when hearts are exposed, destinies are released. You see, because Boaz got naked, Ruth got free. Her liberation was facilitated by his unabashed revelation of his impassioned intentions. Boaz did not go down to the gate to stick his toe in to merely test the water, he dove right in without reserve. This was not a moment to be cagey, to be careful or self-conscious. This could be his only chance to love her. If he was ever going to get to take her as his bride he would have to risk daringly, speak boldly, leave it all at the gate.

For Boaz to starkly expose the secrets of his heart with no guarantee of the outcome required incredible courage. It was a courage that quickly proved contagious. You might say there was an epidemic of nakedness that broke out that day because Boaz was not the only one who got naked at the gate. Pretty soon, you see, Ruth got naked at the gate as well, even though she stayed away. Boaz, as her representative, accurately portrayed her desperate need for redemption. He made no attempt to sugarcoat the situation, or explain away her poverty. The truth was she was no more than a beggar, picking up leftover grain behind the reapers in someone else's field. She had not even had sense enough to carefully choose where she gleaned. As the story goes, she simply stumbled into the field of this one who was predisposed to love her. Ruth's need was real and Boaz boldly declared it, knowing that there was freedom to be found in acknowledging the truth about why they were there. Her destiny would never unfold behind a wall, inside a cage erected to safely contain her real story. Nothing could be accomplished on Ruth's behalf until her need was exposed. So Boaz led the way. His courageous nakedness about his intentions led to a fearless unveiling of everything about Ruth's situation. Boaz brought the truth about Ruth's need to the gate.

Boaz was also completely candid concerning Ruth's loss, a loss Ruth had been fully open about as well. I guess she could have come to Bethlehem pretending Mahlon would follow. She could have kept the fact that she was a widow hidden to avoid being taken advantage of or mistreated. She could have tried to explain away her hunger, deny that her husband's death was a factor in every decision she had made since that day. Yet it was that hunger, precipitated by that tragic loss, that motivated her to go to glean in someone's field. She never would have met Boaz, never would have experienced the favor she had found in his eyes, a kindness that she had been craving for a lifetime, had Mahlon's death not left her a widow who was forced to go out and fend for herself.

Often you and I are reluctant to open up about circumstances that have crushed us, losses we may have survived but which have left us with internal bruising that affects us every single day. Yet without getting real about our losses we will never set out on the road to redemption. They were only standing at the gate that day because Ruth's husband had died. Boaz could be completely open about it. Because Boaz had every intention of making sure that Ruth was well provided for, he had no reason to explain away the truth of what she had lost and what she now needed in order to thrive.

Boaz was even straightforward about Ruth's name, a reputation any girl might try to hide, if possible. Yet have you noticed how often even Boaz referred to Ruth as a Moabitess? What was he, crazy? If anything, owning her heritage only made her more vulnerable, more open to possible rejection. Folks from Moab were persona non grata among the Israelites, and for good reason. The Moabites had been anything but hospitable to the Israelites on their wilderness journey. Boaz was aware of the resentment his people harbored, but still he was completely open about Ruth's backstory. Ruth was who she was and her only path to freedom would be to own it, rather than run from it. We have no way of knowing whether or not her race was a factor in the nearer kinsman's decision. He never explained why he felt his inheritance would be marred if he took her as his wife. Prejudice could have provided a plausible reason for his rejection. What we do know is that Boaz was not repelled at all by where she had been or what she had been through. He could handle it. In fact, His heart was predisposed to love her, just as God's heart is wide open and ready to love you, no matter where you have been or what you have done while you were far from Him. As Boaz stood at the gate in front of the elders of the town, as well as the one man who stood between him and his heart's desire, he was not only real about his own feelings and intentions, he exposed Ruth's need, her loss, and her Moabite heritage.

Yet another element of Ruth's story, and Naomi's as well, had to be starkly exposed in order to release her to run with abandon in the safety of His affection. As Boaz gathered the elders of the town as witnesses, as he stepped into the path of his rival, Boaz was straightforward about the reasonableness of this request. It was perfectly acceptable for Ruth and Naomi to ask their nearer kinsman to marry Ruth, to have a child, to buy the field, to take them into his home. This provision might seem crazy to us today, but it was the common practice in Hebrew culture. This strategy for protecting posterity and alleviating poverty was planned for Ruth and Naomi before they ever found themselves in this situation. They were standing at that gate by proxy, placing themselves in such a vulnerable situation, because they believed that this was a reasonable transaction.

In contrast, in the face of any possible reluctance of someone to meet even our most reasonable expectation, we quickly deny that what we hoped for was reasonable at all. Perhaps we desire for someone to be present when we need them, to say the words we long to hear, share their life with us in a way that makes us feel valued and wanted. This was all that Ruth was hoping to find at the gate. Yet when we find ourselves standing there, hearts in our hands, we have a tendency to explain away our desire, saying, "I didn't need that anyway. I should never have even expected it." We tell ourselves this lie that what we hoped for was unreasonable. If Ruth was unwilling to admit that she believed that what she wanted was not too much to ask, then she would never receive her redemption. She had to allow herself to look for it, hope for it, even admit that she wanted it. She had to be open to the possibility.

In starkly exposing Ruth's need, her loss, her name and the reasonableness of what she wanted, in openly declaring his own desire to step up to redeem each loss, Boaz exhibited the courage to boldly stare into the face of vulnerability, naked and unashamed. As we return to the freedom of the garden, as we find our home in God's presence, we can be honest, totally open about who we are right where we are because we know that nothing can ever separate us from His willingness to love us like we have always needed to be loved. So in this moment God is whispering another question, wooing us to take this to the next level of our intimacy with Him. He is asking at this moment, "Will you believe, not just believe, but will you believe to the point that you will abandon pretense for authenticity?"

WILL YOU **BELIEVE** TO THE POINT THAT YOU WILL ABANDON **PRETENSE** FOR **AUTHENTICITY?**

Ruth's need, and the desire of Boaz to provide for it, could only intersect if the nearer kinsman stepped out of the way. The nearer kinsman had to be dealt with, even if this encounter revealed an inadequacy to provide for her need. Boaz knew that even in the face of rejection by this nearer kinsman, this moment at the gate would not end in Ruth's humiliation. The culmination of this final stark exposure would be Ruth's dreams coming true! Only when every heart was exposed, would Ruth's destiny be released. So facing the potential inadequacy of her nearer kinsman was nothing to fear. His rejection could actually be the gift that would set her free to experience everything she had hoped for before making her journey to Bethlehem.

That dream that lives in your heart, though long buried, that hope to live a story that freely expresses the truth of who you are, was first born in the heart of your Vision Caster, God Himself, the One who gave birth to that dream before you were ever born. It is perfectly reasonable for you to seek to be all God created you to be. It is acceptable for you to think that He would want to buy back everything you have lost in the war that broke out to defeat you. Though people in our lives may fail us, you and I must not abandon who we are. If we live in fearful avoidance of the rejection of those who are too impoverished to love us well, if we pretend to be someone we are not in hopes of manipulating their acceptance, if we explain our need away, Our Redeemer will be standing at the gate but we will never ask Him for the love we have waited a lifetime to experience. The path to your freedom will only be found in the presence of His perfect love. This is the ultimate dream you crave and the unlocking of every other dream. Ask Him to immerse you in His extravagant affection, to make your home right next to His heart. Never let the past inadequacies of imperfect people nor the dread of future rejection rob you of the destiny your God is willing and ready to release in you.

Boaz understood, not only the law, but the spirit of this law as he presented this opportunity to the nearer kinsman.

> *Then Boaz said, "On the day you buy the land from Naomi, you also acquire Ruth the Moabite, the dead man's widow, in order to maintain the name of the dead with his property"* (Ruth 4:5 NIV).

When you look up the law concerning land redemption in Leviticus 25:25 you will not find it specifically stated that the field and the bride had to go together. Some scholars have debated that this may have been a stipulation Naomi added. Perhaps she would only allow the purchase of the field if the redemption of Ruth, and by extension Naomi, was included. However, since there is no evidence of a conversation or any sort of negotiation between Naomi and Boaz, I tend to think this requirement flowed from his desire to make sure their every need was met. Either way it was perfectly reasonable for either Naomi or Boaz to expect such complete redemption. What would be the use of simply buying a field? Doing so would only provide a temporary remedy for the poverty Ruth and Naomi faced as a result of their widowhood. They needed someone who would take them in, love them well and provide for them for a lifetime. This is what Boaz was willing to do and it was perfectly reasonable to expect it from any other man who would take on the right to redeem. Remember the promise Boaz made in chapter 3, "if he won't do any part of what you need, I will do it all."

Boaz was unwilling to settle for less than Ruth's complete redemption and God is not willing to settle when it comes to yours. He is not willing for you to merely trail along behind his servant girls, taking whatever crumbs they drop behind them. He desires nothing less than an intimate relationship with you. He wants to be there day in and day out, helping you separate the truth from the trash that you pick up along the way. He wants to tell you precisely who He saw before He formed you and to release you to fulfill your one-of-a-kind purpose in this world, to live out your destiny of telling Who you have found Him to be from your own unique perspective. You are His Ruth. God calls Himself your Redeemer throughout His beautiful saga. He pictures what that looks like in the life of Boaz. Believe Him for it. Ask Him to do everything Boaz was willing to do, to be the Redeemer He has pictured for us in this beautiful story.

Our gates, our moments of vulnerability, are mere vehicles that carry us to everything we desire. You may have spent a lifetime attempting to outrun rejection, building walls without doors so that you can hide from all possible disappointment, but Ruth's story shows us that the exposure of Ruth's reasonable need and her true identity, the rejection of this nearer kinsman, and the willingness of Boaz to take her as his bride, were all steps that led her closer to her happily ever after. The brilliance of God to fearlessly allow the inadequacy of every nearer kinsman to be exposed rather than avoided, is so that you and I will know that this lesser love was never meant to be enough. All that we hoped this inadequate person would provide, will never measure up to the perfect love that we crave. The poverty of a nearer kinsman can never fill you, it will never give you your destiny. Yet it is a most precious gift. You see, your disappointment will be the threshold you step across into everything you have ever dreamed!

In this atmosphere of stark exposure, the contrast between the rejection of the nearer kinsman and the wholehearted willingness of Boaz to redeem is boldly put on display. Boaz was asking, "Are you willing to redeem, say so now, because if you are not willing I am standing here ready to love her and make her my bride." Now the nearer kinsman reveals his decision,

> *At this, the guardian-redeemer said, "Then I cannot redeem it because I might endanger my own estate. You redeem it yourself. I cannot do it." (Now in earlier times in Israel, for the redemption and transfer of property to become final, one party took off his sandal and gave it to the other. This was the method of legalizing transactions in Israel.) So the guardian-redeemer said to Boaz, "Buy it yourself." And he removed his sandal* (Ruth 4:6-8 NIV).

Ruth could sit down, sit still and simply wait. She did not even need to go to the gate to take the sandal off of the nearer kinsman's foot. He removed it willingly, saying, "I give up my right to even set foot on that land. I no longer want it. I relinquish all my rights to it. Go ahead and take Ruth as your bride. I have no desire for her. Marrying her would cost me too much. I cannot pay the price."

This nearer kinsman bares a striking resemblance to our nearer kinsmen as well. He was more than willing to enter into a transaction that was to his benefit. As long as his connection to Naomi would simply expand his own land holdings in a way that would profit him in the future his answer was, "Yes." However, when he was made aware of Ruth's availability the script quickly flipped. Levitical law mandated every fiftieth year as a Year of Jubilee in which the ownership of property, purchased as a result of another's poverty, would revert back to the family of original ownership provided there was the existence of a rightful heir. To marry Ruth and raise up a son as an heir to the dead would mean that this tract of land would ultimately be given back to that heir in the year of Jubilee, which would result not only in the eventual loss of the land but also the loss of the nearer kinsman's purchase price. Knowing that Boaz stood ready to marry Ruth and produce an heir in the name of Elimelek, if the nearer kinsman was unwilling to do so, would have the same effect on this man's purchase should he simply buy the field. This man was unwilling to pay the price of a transaction that would only benefit others. His decision was determined purely by self-interest.

You see, God teaches us in the gospel of Luke that *"the mouth speaks what the heart is full of"* (Luke 6:45 NIV). So this man's words could not say a thing about Ruth. His words came from within him, they could only reveal what was within his own soul. This nearer kinsman was inadequate to love Ruth the way she deserved to be loved. That is simply all he revealed in saying, "No" to this offer. His choice to refuse to provide for her revealed his own poverty, be that a material poverty or an emotional one. His choice simply exposed the inadequacy of his own resources.

Likewise, when some impoverished person refused to love you, hurt you with cruel words or thoughtless actions, when a nearer kinsman lied about you, betrayed or even abused you, those acts said nothing about you. Those deeds exposed the condition of that rejector's heart. When you simply presented a reasonable need, they were unable or unwilling to supply it. If you and I desire to have our wounds healed and our losses redeemed, if we are ready for God to step up and say "if they have failed you in any part, I will do it all," then we have to open our hands and let those things go. We must see rejection for what it really is and stop carrying its shame into our future. We must intentionally refuse to be defined by someone else's poverty.

As it was in Ruth's experience, sadly, rejection is not always confined to private places. Sometimes it happens at the gate, at the most significant time, when the world is watching, when we desperately want some person to come through for us but, instead, they let us down. Ruth had to be willing to accept the nearer kinsman's decision and stop standing at the gate waiting for him to change his mind. She had to stop waiting for this man to be someone he would never have the capacity to be. She had to stop hoping her kinsman would turn around and love her. Most importantly, she had to refuse to allow his decision to define her. As his decision exposed what was within this man, Ruth could neither change his heart, nor excuse it. Those were not decisions for her to make. What Ruth had to do was accept it. Otherwise Boaz could never step up and redeem. If she stubbornly stayed stuck in that spot, refusing to accept this nearer kinsman's choice, if she walked away mischaracterizing it as defining something about her, then all she longed for, all that was waiting for her at the gate, was never going to happen.

The inadequacy of her nearer kinsman was totally exposed, yet notice, Ruth's destiny was completely unaffected by his poverty. In fact, Ruth's freedom could only be attained through boldly staring into the face of the insufficiency of this man whose name has been left out of her story. Through courageous vulnerability, complete openness, as each man's capacity to provide for her release was honestly exposed, Ruth was released to run after everything she ever wanted. In squarely facing the poverty of the nearer kinsman, Ruth was freed to embrace the unequalled passion of Boaz. A lesser advocate would never have had the courage to starkly expose his intentions to his rival. Yet doing so proved instrumental in releasing Ruth to run with abandon after the one heart who was prepared to love her like she longed to be loved. The brilliance of Boaz to stand naked and unashamed in the presence of his rival illustrates how God employs truth as the weapon that will win our freedom. When every heart is exposed, destinies are released, and we have nothing to fear in that. What if, just the other side of your greatest heartbreak, waits the life you were always meant to experience immersed in a love you can never chase away?

Boaz boldly exposed his truth that day. Ruth had to get real about some things before all of this could unfold well for her at the gate. She openly owned her own poverty, as well as the possible ramifications of the nearer kinsman's choice. Yet, at this point in her story, how hard could that really have been to admit? As we have discovered the richness of Boaz's character and the beauty his heart, as we have fallen in love with this magnanimous man right alongside Ruth, this is the answer we hoped to hear.

Just as Ruth's fearlessness in the face of possible rejection set her free to approach this moment without pretense, we are set free to live authentically, even in the face of possible rejection, because of our awareness of the unfailing love of The One Who stands ready to be our Redeemer. How might the imprint of a mother who was incapable of loving you well and impossible to please, or a father who was distant and detached, perhaps even absent, fade when we see those rejections painted against the backdrop of the extravagant passion of the One Who has promised to buy us out of that poverty? How is the impact of a best friend's betrayal, or an employer's decision to fire you without just cause, diminished because it sent you on a journey to find the destiny you were made to fulfill on this planet? Can you cherish these gifts that freed you to grasp that God is willing to be everything they could never be? In any other context, rejections would feel like they are about us. You or I might walk away from such experiences asking, "What kind of loser am I, if that person refused to love me, would not believe in me, pushed me away?" Yet the nearer kinsman's decision could never make Ruth question her own heart because of the powerful presence of Boaz in her life. Boaz could not wait to love her. This nearer kinsman's decision, his exposure as inadequate and unwilling, only cleared the path for Boaz to do just that, to love her the way she had longed to be loved for a lifetime.

We hold in our hearts the gifts of every lesser god and would-be redeemer who has ever failed us. With complete confidence in His own ability to buy back everything we ever lost in those moments, God walked us straight toward each rejection and now has empowered us to fearlessly look back at each person's inadequacy, knowing it said nothing about us. Each of us has stood at the gate and held out our heart, only to hear someone voice an honest refusal to be what we need, and we are better for it. Those moments we would have done almost anything to avoid have kept us thirsty for the only Drink that could ever satisfy us. So ultimately every nearer kinsman sent us on the road that has led us here.

Yet, if we want to be completely honest, each of us has also stood where that nearer kinsman stood that day. Each of us has been starkly exposed as inadequate, unable to love with a love that is perfect or unfailing. We may have tried, or pretended we could, knowing we could never meet even our own expectations, never have enough to give with a pure unselfishness, until we were finally exposed as the frauds we always knew we were. What a gift we give to those we love by living authentically. Sometimes God gives through us the very things our loved ones and friends need but, at other times, He boldly allows our inadequacy to be starkly exposed, sending them searching for what can only be found in Him. Our greatest gift to those we love can be to own our imperfection and poverty, to say authentically that we are sorry, but not sorry, that we cannot be what only He can. As long as I pretend otherwise, I stand in a space that was meant for only God to fill.

As I reflect on the beauty of how God stepped up to rob rejection of its power in my life and empower me, as a result, to live authentically, I am reminded of an incident in my childhood. I was a third grader at Alice Bell Elementary School, where recess was, without a doubt, my favorite subject. However, my teacher for that particular school year had the nasty habit of depriving us corporately of time on the playground if even one student misbehaved. If you have ever had any exposure to how easily third graders can become distracted, then you know how quickly time in the sun became a rare commodity of unusually high value for every kid in that class. Only after we managed to muddle through multiplication tables and reading group without anyone losing it, and survived the school cafeteria's mystery meat of the day without throwing food or throwing up, could we run, screaming all the way, to our beloved "blacktop." The "blacktop" was a large square of asphalt where probably hundreds of thousands of epic kickball games were enjoyed by kids like me throughout the school's history. As awesome as a good old kickball game can be, and, for this tomboy, that is pretty awesome, nothing particularly memorable normally happened out there until one spring day when something happened to me on the "blacktop" in the middle of a kickball game that I have never been able to forget.

I have no idea what the score was or which team was winning. All I know is that I was standing at my favorite position just to the left of second base hoping the ball would come straight to me, waiting, without fear, for my chance to make a big play. That is when the life-changing incident I am about to describe took place. A classmate's foot made sweet contact with that red playground ball, kicking up a pop fly that was headed in a perfect trajectory to fall right into my hands. So I planted my feet, reached my hands up into the air and waited for my moment of glory. As I stood poised, a voice from behind me yelled, "I've got it!" I knew that voice, it was my classmate, Conley, the biggest guy in the whole third grade. Despite Conley's size and the risk of impending doom, I refused to budge an inch. Frankly, I had no idea why he was shouting, "I've got it!" when clearly that ball was coming to me. No matter what he thought he had, the truth of the matter is that I had it, or I would have it in a matter of seconds. So the best thing for Conley to do would be to back off and stay out of the way. Which is exactly what I hoped to achieve by responding in kind, "I've got it," but Conley was undeterred. He kept barreling ahead, ground shaking with every man-sized step, while I refused to yield, eyes keenly focused on the "joy set before me!" That is why I failed to see it coming. I was completely blindsided when, without warning or explanation, Conley tripped, hurling his body up into the air in another perfect trajectory to violently invade my personal space. The next thing I remember I was no longer watching for that big round playground ball to fall out of the sky. Instead I was watching the "blacktop," which seemed to be speeding by beneath me, taking all the skin from both of my elbows and knees with it in the opposite direction. By the time Conley and I came to a stop I was a bloody mess. Somehow I managed to struggle to my feet and limp pitifully over to my teacher who unsympathetically offered the standard, and always inadequate, comfort prescribed for every elementary school malady from a stomach ache to a hangnail: a wet paper towel.

Each time I recount the dramatic details of my worst day on the playground the same question invariably comes up. People always ask me "What happened to Conley?" As far as I know I have never once told this story to anyone even remotely connected to this boy. Still everyone wants to know and I find great joy in revealing it. You see, the answer to that question holds the beauty of this story, the reason I can relive it with such vivid detail today. The answer concerning what happened to Conley is "Nothing. Nothing happened to Conley!" Conley fell but I took the pain he should have experienced from that disaster. I bore the wounds of his bad decision. My body was torn, my skin was ripped, because when Conley fell, he fell on me. I was strategically positioned between Conley and, at least in the third grade playground context, his worst nightmare.

You know, the same is true when it comes to what our Redeemer did for you and me. The one big difference is that Jesus saw it coming. He saw what was ahead, the disappointment we would experience at the the hand of every impoverished nearer kinsman. He saw how we would develop strategies and coping mechanisms meant to render us invincible, as we played god with our own lives. He was fully aware of the ineffectiveness of every fear-driven selfish choice that could never protect us from the consequences of our heartbreak over the choices of others. Seeing it all as it was about to come crashing down, He went to the gate and willingly stepped in the way. For Him, it was no blind side. His was an act of extravagant passion, a gift of incredible grace! He stared into the face of your enemy, open about His unashamed devotion. If even one need exists that a nearer kinsmen has not, cannot or will not provide, He stands ready to love us perfectly and with extravagance. That thing you fear the most can be simply a vehicle to get you to your freedom. He will meet you in every moment of rejection with His beautiful embrace. He has gone to the gate and He got naked there. Knowing it would demand His very life, involve unequalled suffering, He threw Himself out there to break your fall and mine. So we are released to run with complete abandon. We can be fearless, knowing we have nothing to lose.

Do you know what can happen to your destiny at the hand of your rejector, that person close enough to break your heart, your nearer kinsman? The same thing that happened to Conley, nothing at all. You have a Boaz, an extraordinary Kinsman Redeemer, who stripped off His destiny to take every punch, every slap, every heartbreak on his back in your place. Next time you find yourself in a vulnerable moment, you can sit still and wait. You can take Him at His word. Nothing can touch your destiny because you are His. Now all that remains is your answer to this question, "Will you believe, oh, not just believe, but will you believe to the point that you will abandon pretense for authenticity, standing naked, yet unashamed, set free to live fearlessly by your Kinsman Redeemer's perfect love?"

Chapter 9

A woman in her glory, a woman of beauty, is a woman who is not striving to become beautiful or worthy or enough. She knows in her quiet center where God dwells that he finds her beautiful, has deemed her worthy, and in him, she is enough.

—JOHN ELDRIDGE, *CAPTIVATING: UNVEILING THE MYSTERY OF A WOMAN'S SOUL*

AND THEY LIVED

When my kids were in elementary school my husband, David, was a territory manager for a large paint manufacturer, covering a geographic area that included as many as seven states. As a result he often traveled away from our home from Monday morning until Friday afternoon. I have to admit I formed a few bad habits while he was away. I often stayed up way too late, I commonly let the kids sleep in my bed, and I arguably ate far too many strawberry pop tarts. In my defense, as far as my pop tart issue was concerned, I had not yet discovered the beauty of starting each day with a couple of strong cups of coffee. So, at that time in my life, sugar was the only alternative I had to turn to for the extra jolt, if not the incentive, I needed to get up and ready to face all the demands of a mom's busy day.

So, very late one night or, more accurately, in the wee hours of the morning, I decided to change my clothes in the living room before heading in to join my daughters who were already asleep in my bed. After changing into my pajamas I carefully laid my clothes on the couch in a neat and orderly fashion. Then I quietly tiptoed into my bedroom and carefully slid under the covers without making a sound.

When the alarm went off a few hours later, I felt my usual reluctance toward rolling out of bed to get the girls ready for school but, on this particular morning, that inherent challenge quickly became even harder as I discovered that we were completely out of strawberry pop tarts. This horrifying realization presented me with quite a dilemma. I could either go without my pop tart, which, even now, seems like a ridiculous option, or I could stop by the store on my way home to purchase a box. However, one quick glance at the clock confirmed that there was no time for me to shower and get ready before we headed out.

If you have been paying attention, you already know that this was going to put a severe strain on my hard and fast rule of never being seen in public without my makeup. This unforeseen shortage seemed to promise a disastrous outcome either way but, at the risk of foregoing that frosted strawberry goodness perfectly paired with a glass of chocolate milk, I glanced in the mirror and hastily told myself, "Make it work, girl!" Dabbing on a little foundation, hitting my lashes with a brush of mascara and putting on my lipstick, I frantically ran a brush through my hair. I was sure that if desperate times demand desperate measures, then, truly, there is nothing more dire than a pop tart shortage on a groggy midweek morning. I easily opted for taking the risk of an emergency dash into the grocery store in the hopes of getting in and out without even being recognized. This would be the make or break moment of my entire day.

After doing what little I could to ready my face and hair for my rule-bending pre-shower pop tart run, I literally threw on the clothes that I had taken off the night before, which were, if you will remember, conveniently waiting for me in the living room. I pushed the girls out the front door ahead of me and, miraculously, got them to school on time without even running off the road or getting a ticket. Then I made my way to a nearby grocery. In order to detract from my disheveled appearance I decided on the way that I would have to carry myself with extra confidence, put on a happy face, and take on the friendliest demeanor I could muster, as if I had always had every intention of shopping that early in the morning. I thought if I could project my appearance as being every bit as put together as usual, then hopefully the other shoppers would still be too sleepy-eyed to notice anything was off.

As I walked into the store I spoke first to each individual I encountered. I greeted the bread man who was stocking the shelves on aisle one with a huge smile and an exaggerated "Good Morning!" He responded in kind with a hearty "Hello!" With that, I became convinced that he, along with the few other shoppers in the store at the crack of dawn, had no idea that I had just rolled out of bed and run by in a pop tart panic without first taking a shower. I felt liberated! As a girl who was always extremely self-conscious about her appearance, I was finding new freedom! So I felt exhilarated as I turned the corner into the aisle where my beloved pop tarts were awaiting my delighted embrace. Then, just as I turned that corner I had this funny feeling as I realized, at least I thought, that my shirt tail was not tucked in very smoothly in the back. No problem, I simply reached a hand behind me to tuck it in a little better, never missing a step until I realized that my shirttail was not tucked in at all. This puzzling revelation forced me to stop and further examine a significant bulge I had just discovered protruding under my jeans in the back. So imagine my horror to realize that this unsightly bulge, that I had mistaken for a bunched up shirttail, was actually the pair of underwear I had taken off and laid inside my jeans the night before. I was mortified. I looked around in every direction like a cornered cat but there was nowhere to run. If I was going to get out of that store with my precious pop tarts, which were the cause of this whole fiasco but also the cure, it was obvious that my only escape route would be through the checkout line, where I would most assuredly face an invasive inquisition by a nosy cashier who would undoubtedly ask me how my morning was going so far. Needless to say, I was not prepared to give an answer. So with head down I drove that buggy like a runaway freight train, full steam ahead without even pausing for a second as I swept a box of strawberry pop tarts into the cart and headed straight for the shortest checkout line. I was markedly less friendly with the shoppers I encountered there and said almost nothing to the girl who rang up my minimal purchase. I simply swooped up that box of pop tarts fresh off the conveyor belt, plucked my receipt from her hand, and was out the door, vowing to never be caught in public, showered or unshowered, again.

I have to admit this whole disturbing incident takes the idea of getting one's panties in a wad to a whole new level. Apparently I had walked through that store, speaking to everyone enthusiastically, while wearing a pair and carrying a spare and, at that moment of freak discovery, I had to face the embarrassing realization that I was quite possibly the last one to know. For some crazy reason I am so often reminded of these words spoken by a hero Bible teacher I met in my early days of walking with the Lord, Marge Caldwell, who often explained, "Self-confidence is that feeling you get right before you know better." That is so true. It is in my life anyway.

The funniest part of this story is that, although this was the first time, it would not be the only time, I would get wrecked by this very same fashion emergency. This actually happened to me again a few years later. However, on the second occasion I was not simply making a mad early morning dash into a practically deserted grocery store. Oh no, I was teaching a Bible study, after which I walked down the hall and enjoyed a lively conversation with the senior pastor of the church. On that day I had no idea I was packing extra heat, if I might coin a phrase, until I stopped at my mother-in-law's house on the way home. Yes, after the Bible study, and the conversation with the pastor as well, it was not until I was standing in her driveway, bubbling over with excitement about one of my funny teaching illustrations, that David's mother happened to notice, and bring to my attention, a stray pair of peach panties that had worked their way down my pants leg and were now playing peek-a-boo around the vicinity of my ankle.

Believe it or not, as I think about you reading these words right now, I have no greater hope than that this same thing might happen to you. Never fear, I am not praying for your total public humiliation, that your unmentionables will become the talk of the grocery, or even worse, the church! I am asking My Father that you will not leave these pages, not walk away from the time you and I have spent together immersed in Ruth's incredibly beautiful story, without carrying something away. I hope that something unmistakably personal clings to you from this unveiling of the dreams of God for your life. In fact, nothing would please me more than to find that some truth, a revelation, some sort of Oprah-esque "Ah-ha moment" would stubbornly stick with you, tucked away for you to find in the middle of your next moment of desperation, disillusionment or self-doubt.

God has taken His time, He has been wooing you with the aroma of His unusual passion, making His case, laying truth upon truth to convince you that you were made with a longing for home, a yearning to find your way back to the garden, an insatiable ache to be intimate with Him. He knows how to love you like no one else can and the best part is that He wants to! He wants to! So much so that He has intentionally positioned Himself so that He can. The very Son of God, Creator of the universe, took off His kingly robe to put on skin and walk His passion right up to your door, so that He can personally give you back every single thing that has been stolen away from you in the war that broke out to destroy your destiny. He knows you, knows everything that should rightly disqualify you for His love. Yet He has boldly chosen you to be the object of His extravagant affection! As David wrote in Psalm 18:35 He has stooped down to offer you greatness. He has taken a knee, made His proposal, and He is waiting for your response.

It is almost as if all this comes right out of the movie, *Runaway Bride*.[69] You can almost hear the news teams gathering somewhere nearby, speaking the question that is on each heart into their microphone, "Will she or won't she?" My desperate plea is that you will not run, will not stare Perfect Love in the face and turn to leave unchanged. The one intimate relationship, that will make all the ones that have let you down or left you flat no longer matter, has been offered to you in this Old Testament gospel story.

So we come to this moment in Ruth's story asking, "Will she or won't she?" She made the journey, chose the road that simply moved her toward God. In the face of opposition she relentlessly held on with a death grip to her only friend who knew the way, a friend who had been outspoken with her opinion that this would never happen for Ruth in Bethlehem. Even as they walked into town, Naomi told anyone who would listen that they had no hope. Still Ruth kept reaching out to a greater destiny. Not accidentally, but rather by Divine design, Ruth wound up gleaning in the field of a man of standing, a man who was literally a force in her world. From across that field their eyes met and the magic began to unfold. He invited her to sit with him at his table. He took special care to do those little things that let her know that he cared about her. He even sent her home with a boatload of barley and a to-go box from lunch. No wonder all she could talk about that night was this one she met in that field. With each new detail Ruth shared, Naomi's hope began to be rekindled. With Naomi's encouragement Ruth went alone, in the dark, down to the threshing floor to let Boaz know she was interested too. Then Boaz sent her home to sit still and wait while he went to face her nearer kinsman, the one man who stood between them and the destiny each longed to embrace.

Boaz blew our minds with the way that he approached his rival. He came starkly exposed, laid it all on the line, let this guy know that, if he rejected Ruth, Boaz stood ready to embrace her as his. It truly astounds me how Boaz foreshadowed Christ for us at that moment. Having no idea, this unguarded man pictured Jesus in the most vulnerable place any of us could ever go. There our sweet Redeemer made Himself naked, facing the rejection that should have been ours. He took the sting out of every rejection, every heartbreak and betrayal, with His costly sacrifice. He got there first, went before us, openly, boldly declaring His passion in the face of our poverty, His sufficiency in the face of our failure, His acceptance in the face of every nearer kinsman who said, "I don't want her." Rejection was robbed of its power in that moment when the One Who wanted you, Who loved you like crazy, faced those rejectors for you and stood just the other side of your worst heartbreak, ready to choose you for love. How devastating is the threat of any heartbreak, of the most brutal rejection you or I might ever experience, once we have seen such unusual passion boldly put on display, knowing it was all for us?

Like Ruth, there are some things we have to get past, the inadequacies of our lesser gods must be exposed, before we are free to grab hold of that passion. Yet our Redeemer's extravagance will so overshadow our disappointments that, in the end, no one will even remember the names of those who played such bit roles in our stories as we have been swept up into His. We can get past the gate now. Everything is out of the way. Ruth and Boaz, you and God, have come to that moment where the question demands an answer, "Will she or won't she?"

As we return to chapter 4 of Ruth, as we examine the few remaining verses, we come hoping that Ruth's story, your story, my story will end just like the ones they make into movies, just like every great story we read when we were little girls. We come fully expecting to find the words "and they lived happily ever after." After all, that is the phrase that sends every prince and princess riding off into the sunset. That phrase puts the punctuation on any love story that up until then could have gone either way. This is what we have expected, what we have hoped for, all the way through this story of Ruth and you and me. So as we now come to Ruth 4:13 in the very first part of the verse, that phrase is pretty much what we find. Okay, wait, this verse is not exactly going to say those words, but it is pretty close, maybe a little closer than any of us realize at first glance.

So Boaz took Ruth and she became his wife (Ruth 4:13 NIV).

What better ending could we hope for? You see, it did not matter to Boaz if she showed up in flannel, if she got all tangled up in her veil, if she tripped coming down the aisle, if she had her panty hose safety pinned to her underwear, or even an extra pair accidentally wadded up to create an unsightly bulge that mystified every witness that was present. If Ruth was nervous at all, I just imagine that Naomi was right there to remind her, "He's the one! He really is the one!" Boaz had not only caught her eye, but surely he had won her heart. So much so, that she uncovered his feet, saying "yes" to his unspoken invitation. At that moment, he eagerly made his decision, positioned himself to take care of everything, rushed away to handle every detail. Only after he stared down her most bitter rejector, not until he showed her the fullness of his passion at the place of her greatest vulnerability, was she free to give her whole heart completely to him, so that he might be her husband, her provider, her lover, her friend, her everything that she had ever dreamed. So I absolutely think these words could easily be paraphrased, at least in the Melissa translation, "And they lived happily ever after."

There is one little problem though. The problem I would have is with the reading of that phrase. I think most readers put the emphasis on the wrong word. When you hear it in your mind, or see it up on the big screen, it usually sounds something like this, "And they lived *HAPPILY* ever after." Am I right? Did you just leap right over those first three words on your way to the "happily," almost as if those words are merely stepping stones put in place to get you to the "happily" in a hurry? That describes precisely the way I have always heard it in my mind. That phrase is all about the happily, at least I thought it was until I came to Ruth 4:13. That verse convinced me that I had been saying that phrase, thinking of what my happy ending would look like, in completely the wrong way. As we come to understand the true meaning, the real meat, the whole point of verse 13, then I believe you will conclude with me that we really ought to say "And they *LIVED* happily ever after," because truly the most significant element in Ruth's happiness from that point on was that she finally, genuinely got to live the life she was meant to experience. Ruth's story teaches us that we will never be able to grasp what "happily ever after" truly means, much less experience it, until we step across that threshold to passionately embrace intimacy with the Lover of our souls.

As we take His outstretched hand and enter into this true intimacy that is like no other, that is the moment when life to the fullest, the live-it-up life of truly living out what we have always dreamed, simply begins. What I am trying to convey is that after reading through eight chapters of my observations, the culmination of over fifteen years of meditation and study, as we have been saturating ourselves in Ruth's story for a significant amount of time, as we come to this verse right in the middle of the last chapter of the book that bears her name, we have finally come to the beginning. Can you believe it? All the rest of this has just been the prelude, the introduction, to everything her life was meant to be about. The same is true for you. How you choose to live out your believing when this study is through, how you choose to move forward from here is undoubtedly the real adventure. Throughout the pages and the verses of Ruth so far, she has been dreaming, praying, moving toward, hoping for all that is about to happen, but the living, it starts in Ruth 4:13, *"So Boaz took Ruth and she became his wife"* (Ruth 4:13 NIV).

This whole idea of what it looks like to live intrigues me. Have you ever stopped to think about what it means to truly live? According to *Merriam-Webster's Collegiate Dictionary* to live means "to be alive, to maintain oneself." Sounds a bit like knowing whether you are a water ballerina or a lap swimmer, and selling out to that, knowing exactly what your puzzle piece looks like, what it means to simply do you. The dictionary expands that definition to add these words, "to occupy a home," just finding your space and filling it up, but there is more. The definition continues with "to dwell, to attain eternal life, to remain in human memory or record, to leave a legacy, to have witnesses, to pursue a dream, to have a life rich in experience, to cohabit, to exhibit vigor, gusto and enthusiasm, to be thoroughly absorbed by or involved with."[70]

You see, after all this time, after all the words we have picked apart and examined, we have come to the beginning of Ruth's magnificent story, and your story, and even my own. If we will accept God's beautiful invitation to follow in Ruth's footsteps, then the beginning is "And they lived...they truly lived."

For Ruth, this dream was so real to her that it compelled her to transcend her circumstances and every bit of opposition she would face to believe to the point that she continued to move toward it, no matter what, refusing to be denied, until at last it had become her reality. Though she had once dreamed of love we have now come to the point in her story where she finds herself immersed in a love, more extravagant and rare than anything she ever imagined. Though once she had only hoped to belong, her redeemer had made it possible for her to become part of a people, his people. He had set the stage and now this was her moment, the beginning of Ruth living out her destiny, the beginning of all the happily ever after that Ruth could pack in from this point forward. This was Ruth's chance to live that vision God first deposited in her heart when she was living in a place where He was nothing more than a distant God of a far off people. She had found a place within the context of one intimate relationship that held passion and freedom, energy and richness of experience and, yes, it held life, the chance to be that woman she was created to be, to fulfill the purpose God created her to fulfill before she was ever born.

Would you like to come to the beginning of your destiny? Are you ready to live the life that was once only a dream? What if everything that has happened to you so far was simply the prelude? I am not asking, "Do you know God?" Ruth knew Boaz prior to this moment. She walked with him every day. I am not asking, "Have you seen expressions of God's beautiful heart?" Unquestionably you have because His creation surrounds you and miraculous provisions are placed before you every day. I am not even asking you if you have gleaned some precious truths from those who have been walking in His field even longer than you. I would assume that your eyes have fallen on these pages because you have come to value the opportunity to know more about Who He is. I am asking, more accurately I believe God is asking each of us a new question, "Will you believe to the point that you are living the life that He first dreamed for you? Are you truly living your destiny?"

You and I stand poised with Ruth for our own "and she lived" moments and the key is found in the first four words from Ruth 4:13, *"So Boaz..."* Never forget that Boaz is a picture of our God, the pathway for us to fully understanding what our Redeemer is holding out for us to grasp. This verse explains from the very outset, *"So Boaz took her..."*

Before you think that this story just jumped the shark into a kidnaping tale, let me explain that the Hebrew wording used in this verse means "he accepted her, carried her away, received her."[71] Willing to pay whatever it cost, Boaz flung open the doors of his heart to say "Come in, just as you are! You don't have to fix yourself up, you don't have to change a thing. You don't have to be anything but who you are, right where you are. I already love you, already want you. All you have to do is receive my love and live immersed in it for the rest of your days." Life never really began for Ruth until she came to the place that she understood her redeemer's beautiful acceptance. A foreigner, a Moabite, a widow, Ruth arrived in Bethlehem impoverished and barren. Boaz met her as a beggar. Yet he was not ashamed of her, nor put off by her obvious need. He intentionally moved toward her, opened himself up freely to her and carried her away in his arms to more than she could have ever imagined.

Just as this was true for Ruth, I am convinced that your life, the fullness of life that is your destiny, your happily ever after, can only begin when you grasp the truth that your Redeemer, your God, feels the same way about you. He is completely blown away by your simplest desire to know Him. You do not have to do a thing to get ready to experience the fullness of His passion. Your God accepts you. He receives you. His love is not conditional, nor expressed in only general terms. He loves you, in particular. Not in spite of everything, He loves everything about you. So if you feel like you have lost something of yourself along the way, if the pain of rejection, abuse or heartbreak caused you to leave a part of your heart behind, that is no hindrance to Him, it can never separate you from His love. He is rich enough to buy back every single thing you have ever lost, brilliant enough to see the beauty in you that has never been allowed to emerge. He is artistic enough to fashion your life into the beautiful masterpiece He first conceived. Even if no one in your life has ever had the capacity to recognize it, He sees it, stands poised to release it. To Him, in Him and all because of Him, you are an incredible work of art!

A few years ago I saw a photograph of a painting, entitled *Ripening Pairs.*[72] I need no additional words beyond those two to describe it. It looked exactly like its name suggests. If you have spent any time at all in a produce section or an orchard you have seen the subject of this artist's quite literal interpretation. As the story goes, this masterpiece by American painter, Joseph Decker, was wrapped up in a blanket in a lady's garage in Los Angeles for sixty years until the day that woman decided to have a garage sale. At the sale a 29-year-old saw the painting and thought it was kind of cool. So he paid her price of five dollars and carried it away. When he arrived at home he hung his newly purchased art piece on his kitchen wall and thought no more about it. He surely glanced at the fruit as he came and went from that kitchen each day but it garnered no more particular attention than that, until out of curiosity he decided to research the artist online. His astounding research findings ultimately led to an offer from the National Gallery of Art to purchase the still life rendering of a few not yet perfect pieces of fruit for one million dollars.

When it comes to art, opinions can be so subjective. One person might see a thing of beauty in what another rejects as total garbage, but not so for the artist. To the creator of the art work, to the one who put brush to canvas, every stroke is packed with meaning, each splash of color, every shadow has a special beauty deliberately placed by his hand. So no matter how long you have gone unnoticed or neglected by those who do not understand your true worth, no lack of appreciation can devalue your inherent preciousness to God. He is no ordinary artist for He created the masters. He taught them how to paint. Everyone from Leonardo da Vinci, Georgia O'Keefe, Peter Max, Michelangelo, Norman Rockwell, Pablo Picasso, and, my personal favorite, Charles Schultz, was given their gifts to create lasting beauty by the Greatest Artist, the One who painted you into the world! You are and will always be beautiful to Him. He delights in the light and shade of everything about you. You display the colors of an unseen God in your own special brand of beauty, just as that reflection of the sun in the water, rippled and imperfect, is undeniably connected to that source it can only reflect.

That is what Jesus expressed in what is referred to as His sermon on the mount. I love how His words are paraphrased in the modern language of The Message,

> *Let me tell you why you are here. You're here to be salt-seasoning that brings out the God-flavors of this earth. If you lose your saltiness, how will people taste godliness? You've lost your usefulness and will end up in the garbage. Here's another way to put it: You're here to be light, bringing out the God-colors in the world. God is not a secret to be kept. We're going public with this, as public as a city on a hill. If I make you light-bearers, you don't think I'm going to hide you under a bucket, do you? I'm putting you on a light stand. Now that I've put you there on a hilltop, on a light stand—shine!* (Matthew 5:13-16 MSG)

You are exquisite to God! Boaz shows us that. Boaz was not only confident enough to go to the gate where he would come face to face with his rival for Ruth's heart, brash enough to go toe to toe with that one person who had the goods and the opportunity to reject her, disappoint her, be inadequate for her, but he would be so sure of his capacity to love her that he would boldly, unashamedly, without any reservation, or need for guarantees, accept Ruth as she was, right where she was.

Boaz stood at the gate and defiantly declared "I want her," calling her "Ruth, the Moabitess," blurting out the truth of her name and everything attached to it. What words would he have spoken if you had been that girl? If Boaz stood in your place that day, what label would he use to describe where you came from, what you have been through, or the mistakes you have made?

Just imagine, Jesus at the gate, on the cross, boldly declaring, "I Am here because I love her, just the way she is!" That is the sound of His grace, neither your name, nor a single thing that comes attached to it, could ever extinguish his passion, his willingness to give everything He had to buy you out of your poverty and carry you away in His arms. To continue now to live as if His love is based on your performance or perfection, is to choose a life of poverty when the riches of the grace of your Redeemer are within your reach. It would be like storing a masterpiece in the garage wrapped in a blanket for sixty years and then selling it for five measly dollars to a stranger.

The unrestrained acceptance of Boaz's passion released Ruth to truly, fully, freely live, unshackled and unashamed the minute she received it. He loved her with a love that saw the fullness of her beauty while it was still in its raw, unpolished form. With eyes wide open he relished joining her in the midst of the process that would unleash her as the force she was created to be. God picks up the brush of kindness, dipping it into the colors of His generosity, acceptance and grace in creating this portrait of his heart on the canvas of this beautiful story.

You may have come to these pages thinking of God as distant or harsh. You may be reading these words while muffling the fear that He might have only meant a story like this for someone else. Perhaps you feel forgotten, convinced such passion could never be meant for someone as messed up as you are on the inside. My God is big enough to overcome all your fears and every misconception. He wants you to hear His laughter, see His eyes dripping with favor, and discover your name on his lips, on his mind and at the very center of all that He does. He is different. The word, "holy" means just that, "set apart, like no one you have ever known, unusual, other than anything or anyone else."[73] God is truly the One and Only. He is magnificently set apart in so many ways, not the least of which is His extraordinary capacity to love you. You may stand at this moment of beginning looking for proof, some kind of sign, scared of not being enough, while He cannot wait to love you, to take you as you are. As your matron of honor, a friend of your bridegroom, I can say without reservation, "He's the One! He really is the One!"

Looking back at this verse we read on,

So Boaz took Ruth and she became his...(Ruth 4:13 NIV)

She was no longer alone, no longer an outsider, no longer far from home, no longer a beggar. She was no longer just Ruth, she was his Ruth, his choice, his girl, his love. She was the object of his affection. He was willing to pay any cost for a chance to love her. For her, he had been willing to go to the gate. At that gate he stood starkly exposed, to publicly declare his passion for her. She was the one he was willing to marry so that they might share the most intimate of relationships. If there is a label attached to her name from that moment on, it would simply say that she was his. I long for that too. I long for Someone

Who is completely set apart in comparison to every love I have ever known, Who will say without embarrassment or shame, "I want her with me! She can be mine!" I want to be known for nothing more than the fact that I am His.

This moment is the beginning of Ruth's story because Boaz accepted her just as she was, he was willing to take her just as she was at that moment. Still there is more...

So Boaz took Ruth and she became his bride. (Ruth 4:13 NIV)

Let me make sure that you understand that the invitation Boaz was offering Ruth was not to a weekly or monthly corporate gathering. It was not to a ministry project, nor to a community outreach event. This was not an invitation to join a social club or a sorority. Boaz was not even inviting Ruth to a church service, a Bible study, a worship night or a massive arena crusade. Ruth had been invited to be his bride. That is, without a doubt, a unique invitation. Such an invitation requires an eternal commitment. It meant that Boaz was going to stay. Ruth would never wake up one morning to discover he had changed his mind. Even in the middle of her worst day he would stand beside her and weather that storm. This was not only an eternal commitment, but a very personal one, to know him intimately, one on one. Ruth could come away with him to his chambers, finding her name on his lips, hearing his love spoken in a gentle whisper. She would hear him consistently affirm the beauty he saw in her and always know that she was his favorite. She would feel his arms wrap around her to shelter her from the cold. This invitation was not to some activity or even a circle of friends. This was a marriage proposal, a sacred promise, the oneness consummated in the truest form of intimacy. Ruth's story begins right here. She began truly living when she was willing to take his hand and give her heart fully to him. God is inviting you and I to come home, to journey back to the garden. Only when each of us accepts this beautiful invitation will we ever begin to live the destiny we were made to experience, live this dream that was first born within His heart.

I will never forget that moment when this guy, who was given to me to give me a taste, just a glimpse, of God's incredible love, said, "Will you share my life with me?" Those were the very words he chose to say as he fumbled for a little square box tucked inside the pocket of his suit jacket. He looked at me as if no one else was in the room, though we sat at a table in a crowded dining area of Regas restaurant.

He had to wait for just the right moment, as one waiter after another interrupted him again and again to offer more bread, more tea, more butter. Finally, in an exasperated tone that shooed every one of them away, he gave one final answer saying, "We have everything we need!" My heart pounded in my chest, believing he was about to ask the question I had waited a lifetime to hear. So, how weird would it have been if I just never answered, never made a decision either way, just left him waiting? How bizarre would it seem if I responded to his beautiful invitation to intimate relationship by just stopping by that place once every week or so to sing songs to him or ask him for things, just temporary things, not the everything always that he had offered to me on that day?

So, you see, this has all been the prelude, the courtship, the question, your invitation to go deeper, to no longer be a beggar picking up what someone else leaves behind, to be completely His, beautifully intimately His, making your journey, your dream, your destiny to love and be loved by Him. Can you leave Ruth's story, your story, this incredible proposal without an answer? Can you walk away without carrying something different inside of you, without being ruined for the life you have settled for until now? Can you truly believe without this changing your story?

We may not know the precise details, exactly how or when or what circumstances surrounded them at that moment, but at some point, in some way, Ruth had to decide, to say "Yes" in response to Boaz's willingness to take her as his own. Perhaps she simply took his hand as he sat at Naomi's table describing those moments at the gate. She possibly felt his tender kiss touch her cheek as he turned to leave and she kissed him back. God did not choose to give us the details of how Boaz delivered the news of the outcome of his encounter with the nearer kinsman but we can know that his actions on Ruth's behalf were met with her willingness to respond to his commitment with her own. Nothing less would get her to the beginning of her story. Anything short of a whole-hearted, life-altering "yes" would be walking away, choosing to stay the same as she had always been, Ruth, the Moabite from Moab, a beggar content to pick up the crumbs left by the servant girls in a rich man's field, when she had the chance to own that field and walk it on the arm of the one who had offered her his heart. Her "yes" set the wheels of her destiny as his bride in motion.

There is one more word in this verse that completes this description of the dawn of Ruth's destiny and yours.

Boaz took Ruth and she became his wife. (Ruth 4:13 NIV)

That word translated, "became," in this verse is the Hebrew word, "hayah," which means "to exist, to be, to become, to come to pass, to be done, to happen, to be finished."[74] You may not be familiar with that Hebrew word but you have probably read how God answered a question asked by Moses in Exodus 3.

Moses said to God, "Suppose I go to the Israelites and say to them, 'The God of your fathers has sent me to you,' and they ask me, 'What is his name?' Then what shall I tell them?" God said to Moses, " I am who I am. This is what you are to say to the Israelites: ' I am has sent me to you' " (Exodus 3:13-14 NIV).

The name that God used to identify Himself to Moses is the Hebrew phrase, "ehyeh asher ehyeh," translated "I AM Who I AM."[75] "Ehyeh," is another form of this verb in Ruth 4:13, "hayah."[76] Both describe a simple action that is a part of so much more. Every revelation of God is a true expression of His nature, a genuine taste of all that He is, a facet of His complexity. He has no need to pretend to be anything but Who He is. A more exact translation of God's words to Moses would be, "I will be who I will be."[77] The name Yahweh or Jehovah has its roots in this phrase. This name of God carries the idea that God does not have to get up and decide to be God tomorrow or check to see if He is still God on Saturday afternoon. He was God, He is God, He will always be God.

In the same way, at the moment of her "yes," Ruth's true identity was unleashed as a part of something so much bigger, a continuing revelation of all God created her to be. All those things that never seemed to fit her were completely overshadowed by the freedom that emerged in response to the unvarnished acceptance of Boaz. Where she had once lived, what she had endured there, now faded into the background in light of who she became the minute she gave her answer. Believing his words, embracing this chance, ushered in the destiny she saw by faith before she ever set out for Bethlehem. Now, because of her courageous willingness to believe, her story was dramatically changed as God's beautiful plans began to unfold. Released by Boaz's desire, empowered by Boaz's acceptance, all that remained was for her to live.

As much as this verse signifies the beginning of Ruth's happily ever after, on many levels it also brings some things to an end. Ruth's searching was over. She had found the Love that her heart had always craved. The hunger that drove her to Bethlehem was now satisfied. She had found her home with her redeemer. Her very existence from that point on was rooted in their intimate relationship. Every purpose, every passion, would now flow from what they shared. That beautiful love relationship had become so much a part of who she was that nothing could ever separate her from it. Ruth was now part of a story bigger than the one she could have ever told alone.

Uniting her life with Boaz also fully established once and for all Ruth's new name. Wherever she went she was no longer known as the "Moabite from Moab." Now she was known as Boaz's bride. She carried with her an identity that empowered her to live her own story to the fullest, an authority that expanded her influence in the culture that surrounded her. When she spoke people knew Boaz would stand behind her words. The way people felt about Boaz now impacted the way she was received. Her longing to be accepted among God's people was fulfilled the day she gave her heart to him.

The tense of this word, "hayah" translated "became" indicates that it is a part of a bigger whole, just one element of a bigger story.[78] We also learn from Hebrew scholars that any verb that precedes a verb of this tense, indicates a completed thing.[79] Therefore if we back up in this verse we discover that when Boaz took or accepted her, this act was complete. Boaz's acceptance was not a work in progress, nor was it subject to change. It was decided. Boaz accepted all she had been and done, all she was on that day, and everything she would be or do in the future. God's acceptance of you carries that same finality. His decision about you was finished on the cross. Unconditional love became the backdrop for the unfolding process of Ruth becoming the woman first conceived in the heart of God, fully filling her space, faithfully telling her part of God's beautiful story. God's acceptance of you, my love, holds that same freedom. You can move forward fearlessly authentic, secure in a love you can never lose, immersed in a grace that you will never be powerful enough to ruin.

When you trace this same word, "hayah," back to its root it comes from a word that means, "to breathe."[80] In order for you to fully grasp what that means, I need you to join me in a little experiment. Take in a deep breath and hold it. Continue to hold your breath until I tell you to breathe again. If I were with you in person, of course, it would be easy for you to tell me when you have had enough. A simple wave of your hand could signal me that you feel like you are about to turn blue. Since I cannot see you, I am placing you on the honor system, trusting you to hold that breath until you absolutely cannot hold it another second. Assuming you have not collapsed or anything, if you have not taken another breath since I asked you to stop, breathe now. Which was easier, to breathe or not to breathe? Which was more natural, to breath or not to breathe? You may have always thought that it was a whole lot easier to just live your life however you choose, but the truth is that it is easier to give God your "yes," to live your story as it was conceived, as a part of God's bigger story. That is where you find your life, your breath, your rest, all you were made to do, the essence of who you are. For Ruth to become his wife was like breathing. Their intimacy was this perfect gift that would sustain her every minute of every day that she lived. It was her sweet spot, something that just came naturally for a woman like her. I believe, without a doubt, that it would have been so much harder not to be with Boaz. She was made to be his bride. He loved her like no one else ever had and she found her purpose in loving him back. To walk away from that love would be like holding her breath and never taking another one.

God designed your relationship with Him to be so natural, so right, to fit you so well, that you would no more decide to miss out on this beautiful chance to be intimate with Him than you would decide to try to hold your breath for the rest of your days. You were made to hear His voice whispering your name, telling you who you are, moment by moment, day by day, all day long. He should be in and through everything in your life, like breathing, finding your home in His presence, relaxing in the embrace that releases you to live your beautifully authentic story. Maybe all your life you have been holding your breath. Surely you have grown tired by now. Your life was not meant to be that hard. When you hold your breath it takes all of your energy and attention just to keep that going and, if you go long enough without breathing, quite literally what happens? You die. Let go of all that stuff that was never made to fill or define you, that only keeps you in chains. Say "yes" to what is completely natural. His acceptance is finished. His love is decided. You can choose to relax now and breathe.

This root word that means "to breathe" can also mean "to fall."[81] It is used in Job 37:6 to describe falling snow. What an exquisite image! Have you ever seen snow try? Can you even imagine snowflakes straining to reach the earth, or grabbing hold to stay in a cloud? To fall like snow is effortless. Snowflakes just pile up into incomparable piles of softness and beauty. The particles do not strain to fulfill their purpose. Once only a tiny speck of dust, as water clings to that dust, it freezes. The resulting crystal bumps into other similarly formed crystals, gathering more ice from those interactions, until eventually the snowflake falls from the weight of what it has collected to find its eventual home on the ground. Does that description sound familiar? Just an ordinary girl, chilling out, until one day the water of His Word touches her, so much so, that she carries the truth gathered there away. It clings to her, sticks with her, feeds her in a way that makes her hungry for more. So she returns to get another piece and yet another. She comes together with a small group of friends and she shares what she is learning. Just like those snowflakes they exchange what they have learned and it grows. Until that woman who first heard His voice speak her name starts getting fat, getting full, until at last she begins to relax and just be, just breathe. Like falling snow she is beautiful without even trying.

So this story began with a young woman who knew nothing of God, and who lived in a place where no one else knew God, who was awakened by a flicker of light she found in another woman's heart and the rest of this story is not even about Ruth or Boaz. This story is not about Naomi or the witnesses or anybody else. The rest of this story is all about a God who pursued her until He won her so that she could finally begin to breathe, so that she could finally live her story, so that her beautiful destiny could unfold. And at the end of the prelude of this life Ruth was destined to live God asks each of us another question, "Will you believe to the point that living the life that God dreams for you is as natural as breathing?"

Chapter 10

The builder lifted his old gray head:
"Good friend, in the path I have come," he said,
"There followeth after me today,
A youth, whose feet must pass this way.

This chasm, that has been naught to me,
To that fair-haired youth may a pitfall be.
He, too, must cross in the twilight dim;
Good friend, I am building this bridge for him."
— WILL ALLEN DROMGOOLE, THE BRIDGE BUILDER

I'M PREGNANT!

I know what it feels like to be pregnant! Even though the first sensation of a tiny life's beginning within me happened late in the fall of 1982, I can still remember it vividly. What I remember most is that pregnancy is nothing like what I thought it would be or could have predicted. It is definitely a you-had-to-be-there experience.

My pregnancy journey did not begin the morning that David and I watched for a sign, anxiously waited for one entire hour to see if that early 80's home pregnancy test would give a positive response. Just like with Ruth, there was so much prelude that preceded that moment. Our becoming parents started with that look across a crowded room at a guy who seemed so quiet and gentle, yet strong enough to handle me, and sensitive enough to love me the way I dreamed of being loved. When I walked in, he was already there. I was completely unaware that inwardly I had been seeking him. What I did know was that I was hungry to be loved and hoping for something magical to happen in my life. Then, as I looked into his eyes, I knew instantly that they held my kind of magic. Our relationship began rather slowly...first only a word or two, here and there, that led to casual conversation. Finally, as I have already described, he called to ask me out. After that date, the play and the pig, I was captivated. We dated for a while and then, on a particular

Tuesday night that proved to be a turning point in my life, he opened up and shared his heart. In doing so he spoke his love to me, in words and with no words at all. From that moment I was like a big puddle of melted ice cream, completely undone whenever he smiled in my direction or whispered my name. I longed to stay in that moment, in those arms, forever. Then came that Saturday in August, that beautiful proposal. Three months later we were married and it was, well, amazing and weird, all at the same time.

In many ways marriage was awkward at first. I was inexperienced in love, not always sure of how to have a healthy relationship. Needless to say, I made some mistakes. Though the place we lived was now my home, it still felt a bit strange to me. We had to sort through some stuff, separate truth from lies, and learn how to speak each other's language. We each had to find the courage to stand in our vulnerability when we wanted to run, because as scary as it is to put yourself in a position where your heart can be broken, that is the only way to open it up and let love in. In all the learning and sorting, our love deepened. In the midst of our shared vulnerability we learned how to be true. Our understanding and intimacy grew. Our lives began to blend until it seemed that we were no longer even two people anymore. We were one couple. It was getting harder to ascertain where one of us left off and the other began because we had such an intimate connection, as if all of life was an inside joke we could share with no more than a glance.

One evening as we sat around the dinner table in the home of some friends I held someone else's baby for the very first time. As hard as it might be to believe, I was in my early twenties and married before I ever held an infant in my arms. As I held that baby boy, like babies have a tendency to do, he turned his little head to see if he could find something to latch onto for nourishment and comfort. I did not have what he needed. I was not yet ready to offer myself to sustain another life. As I cuddled and held that little guy in my arms, offering the next best thing by way of a pacifier, I glanced over to see a dream sparkling in my husband's eyes. It was unmistakable that this image he saw in that moment awakened a desire for something he longed for us to share. Though I knew nothing about "birthin' no babies," and could hardly imagine taking responsibility for a baby of my own, before long that sparkle I first saw in my husband's eye spread. I began to dream his dreams for me, to picture myself the way he imagined. I was starting to see babies in my future, thinking maybe someday that could happen to me.

I think I somehow knew the very first morning of my first pregnancy that something was different. It may not even be possible, could be purely my imagination, but I felt a little weird. I was almost, well, not exactly, but sort of nauseated, right off the bat. Saltine crackers were soon my early morning friend. Then one afternoon, sitting at my mother's kitchen table, all I could think of was apples. To be honest, I never really cared that much for apples. Apparently, out of nowhere, my appetites had changed. I was completely unconscious of it until I sat there almost tasting an apple, compelled to ask if she had one. My mother was standing at the sink, with her back turned to us, when she heard my request. Without even turning around she reached over to open the refrigerator door, blurting out, "I craved apples when I was pregnant." Without a moment's hesitation she just spoke our dream out loud. Our desire for something more had been a secret only David and I had shared. So as you can imagine we had to quickly recover our composure when our mouths flew open with our mutual shock at her announcement. Did it show? Was this merely a coincidence or was something happening inside of me that was about to become apparent to everyone? Was my mother simply the first in a long line of people who would soon begin to recognize that I was changing?

Soon the test was taken, the announcement was made and, before anyone could do another thing, I got really hungry. I mean, I was famished all the time. I could hardly take in enough food. My cravings were no longer about just my satisfaction. I was feeding the dream, nurturing a life that was growing within me. So naturally the change that had taken place within me began to show. I started getting fat and feeling full and people began to notice. Then, as I lay across the bed on a lazy Sunday afternoon, I felt the strangest sensation. Something I had never experienced before, as if I had swallowed a caterpillar in all of my eating that had transformed into a butterfly in secret and was now fluttering around, trying to find its wings in some secret place inside of me. Before long, that was no butterfly, it was a crazy sea otter doing flips and turns and pushing on my rib cage with the force of, not an otter, an elephant. I had some pain, as I was stretched and prodded, as I carried the weight of what was growing inside of me.

At last, on a Sunday morning, June 19, 1983, Father's Day, that little life within me found an independent life of her own by way of an emergency C-section. When I woke up from the surgery I missed her, I could hardly wait to hold her in my arms. I had such an immediate longing to see her little face. We were bound by an indelible connection that was intense, yet indescribable. She had come from inside of me. I could hardly imagine myself ever being without her again. This tiny beauty, this incredible blending, giving birth to a miracle entrusted to my heart and my hands by my God was a far cry from anything I had expected and so much more than I had ever dreamed.

One thing I learned during my first pregnancy is that a great number of people seem compelled to engage with expectant mothers in ways that would generally be categorized as socially unacceptable in any other situation. Everyone from distant relatives to mere acquaintances will make comments on your figure and even inquire as to how much weight you may have gained. Complete strangers will share the gory details of their 46-hour labor, as well as the life-altering side effects that now plague them as a result. People will even put their hands on your belly with little or no warning. Who does that in any other season of your life without swift retribution? Yet somehow that baby bump belongs to the world collective.

I will never forget one particularly unfortunate incident. Having reached my peak perimeter, I was waddling through the parking lot toward a Kroger not far from where we live, hoping to quickly pick up just a few items and head back home with no complications, knowing in my condition even that was a pretty big ask. Still, I was minding my own business, trying to get from point A to B without hurting anyone or doing any sort of property damage, when this woman appeared seemingly out of nowhere. Suddenly, as we were passing each other on the sidewalk, she grabbed hold of my arm, her eyes fell with dramatic emphasis on my greatly protruding abdomen, and she blurted out these ominous words, "Honey, you'll wish you were dead!" Then, as instantly as she seemed to appear, she all but vanished, leaving me standing alone, stunned, and trying to process her uninvited and inauspicious prediction.

Can you imagine? Why would she say such a thing? Where did that come from? What personal agony gave her such an impression? As you can imagine, such an ominous and unexpected forecast scared me a little, it shocked me a lot, but ultimately her prediction just was not true of my experience. I can never recall, not even once, having such a desire. I think what she was saying to me was that she assumed my experience would be just like hers. Apparently she believed that every labor and delivery was a carbon copy of all the rest, which, I can assure you, could not be farther from the truth.

To discover the intricate details of Ruth's story has been an amazing journey, just as it was a pure delight for me to hold someone else's baby for that very first time. Still, that is nothing compared with living your own incredible story, birthing the life that God has placed inside of you and bringing that amazing miracle into a world that has yet to see anything quite like it. This study has never really been just about Ruth. Her story is a picture given to awaken a dream, that intricate, personal beauty that is your destiny and yours alone. You were created to live in such intimacy, such oneness with Your Redeemer, that it reproduces His life inside of you and carries Him into the world. Each of our birthing stories is unique. Yours probably shares some of the same characteristics as mine: a hunger, an attraction, a risk, a decision, a vision, not fully grasping what is to come, but a realization that this One Who chose you for His love is the One your heart has always craved. His life, now being born within you, is meant to come through you, to touch and change the world in a way that no one else's ever has before or ever will. We can learn from someone else's story, be inspired, enlightened, encouraged, but we must always remember that we will never know what it is like to be pregnant until we live it, the pain…the joy…the miracle. What is born from your intimacy with God is your own beautiful light, your exquisite adventure, and that destiny will become your legacy, the beauty mark you will leave on those around you, the unique way you carry His life inside of you, the imprint of how His hand has touched your soul and forever changed your story. So as we examine the last few verses in the final chapter of Ruth, we now get the chance to talk about where babies come from.

God's dreams for Ruth were bigger than her own. Once the hint of those dreams could only be seen in the dying ember that remained in the grown-cold heart of a woman who had long ago left the sweetness of God's provision behind. Then as Boaz stood at the gate proclaiming that he was willing to take Ruth as his bride, the townspeople began to prophesy, calling God's even bigger dreams for Ruth out of the shadows. Just imagine how their words must have sounded when they made their way to Ruth's ears.

> Then the elders and all the people at the gate said, "We are witnesses. May the Lord make the woman who is coming into your home like Rachel and Leah, who together built up the family of Israel. May you have standing in Ephrathah and be famous in Bethlehem. Through the offspring the Lord gives you by this young woman, may your family be like that of Perez, whom Tamar bore to Judah" (Ruth 4:11-12 NIV).

I think Ruth never saw this coming. She may have understood that woven into the purpose of levirate marriage was the hope of conceiving a child, but to compare her to Rachel and Leah, both matriarchs of the nation of Israel, was beyond belief. How could a girl like her ever end up in such company? Such hope would be cast aside as ludicrous back home in Moab. Even Naomi stood in the middle of that road on their way to Bethlehem and basically said, "If you go with me, nothing like that will ever happen for you." Undeterred, Ruth simply left where she was and moved toward God, the Great Giver of Unimaginable Possibilities. Ruth could not see how her story would end as she began that courageous journey. She simply put her trust in a God who could. Like parents on Christmas morning, just imagine God's excitement as the time approached for the big reveal. God made it clear through the prophet Isaiah,

> *I make known the end from the beginning, from ancient times, what is still to come. I say, My purpose will stand, and I will do all that I please* (Isaiah 46:10 NIV).

God conceived the perfect ending for Ruth's story before she ever made a move toward Him. He held this surprise close to the vest, waited through the journey, through the gleaning and even the rejection, to establish the fact that He was the only means by which anything like this could ever come to pass. Then, when the time was right, in that moment, at this crossroads where Ruth's destiny was being decided, He spoke a greater vision than anyone could have imagined through the witnesses that were gathered around as Ruth's redeemer and her rejector met face to face. Boaz stayed true to his promise that if the nearer kinsman was unwilling to do any part of what Ruth needed, he was willing to do it all. Yet the God who wooed her to His heart now unveiled plans to do something even greater, a destiny beyond her wildest dreams. The spontaneous utterances of those gathered at the gate spoke the more of God that always meets us at the point of our deepest trust.

When Ruth first clung to her mother-in-law, she was not only grabbing hold of Naomi, she was clinging to Naomi as her pathway to God. She refused to let go, refused to turn back at Naomi's urging, because she was convinced that the end of the story that Naomi's God could write would be worth it. That belief formed the basis for her answer to the most basic, yet significant, question that you and I have an opportunity to answer every day, all the time, "Will you choose

Moab or Bethlehem? Will you stay where you are or move closer to God? Will you trust Him to write the most beautiful ending to your story, a more amazing destiny than anything you dream?" The wisdom of Solomon counsels us,

> *Better is the end of a thing than the beginning thereof: and the patient in spirit is better than the proud in spirit* (Ecclesiastes 7:8 NIV).

Ruth had chosen Bethlehem every time she had an opportunity to turn back. She had consistently pursued the God of the Hebrew people since she clung to her mother-in-law on the road that brought her there. She had relentlessly run after this dream of finding her home among God's chosen people. So it is no great surprise that we have come to the point in Ruth's story in which folks strategically positioned around her begin to dream dreams for her too.

God has purposely designed your destiny and mine to be lived out intertwined and supported by other believers. The writer of Hebrews calls them the cloud of witnesses, those who gather at our gates, who watch us run and cheer us toward a glorious finish. These are they who have lived their own God stories, who bring evidence of the miracles that unfold when our faith meets His unfailing faithfulness. We need them to fan the flames of our believing, to remind us of what is true. The God Who "calls into existence the things that do not exist," so often speaks our dreams to life through them. Look around you. Who in your life has a deep understanding of the ways of God? Who carries an authentic history of trusting Him in the face of their own storms? Who do you know that is living out a radical believing, immersed in their own beautiful intimacy with God? Those are your witnesses who can testify to His incredible power, the people that God wants you to bring into your most vulnerable moments in which your destiny hangs in the balance. God will use their voices, their stories, to call out a destiny that is bigger than anything you can dream.

God holds your destiny. He sees it. He has it. He dreamed it before you were ever born and only He can lead you there because only He knows the way. Your only hope of living the life you were made for rests in your decision to take His hand and relentlessly refuse to let go. That is really all that Ruth did. God did the heavy lifting. He led her first to a family, then on a journey, into a particular field, to a quiet moment on the threshing floor, to sweet rest in the response to her greatest vulnerability, and beyond her fear. God led her through all that so that He could lead her to her home, a place she could stay, a place that was a perfect fit for the woman He created her to be. That is what we find in Ruth 4.

> *So Boaz took Ruth and she became his wife. When he made love to her, the Lord enabled her to conceive, and she gave birth to a son* (Ruth 4:13 NIV).

The phrase translated in the NIV "he made love to her" is translated in the King James Version as, "went in to her." These words describe an intimacy of relationship that God created for a man and his wife. This is not a one night stand or a fleeting affair that we see portrayed in the movies. It is exclusive and immersive because it is given only to be a picture, an allegorical expression of our lives immersed in His. This is the special oneness that has in it the potential to create new life.

The key word in this phrase is the word translated "went."[82] It means that Boaz was abiding with her, dwelling with her, it has the connotation of a sexual intimacy, but, in looking at the various meanings of this word, this term definitely does not describe a casual connection, something we might refer to as a fling or an affair. He came to live with her and share an on-going intimacy. He came to know her and be known by her in an everyday, all the time way. He came to share his life with her, a relationship like the one my husband, David, invited me to share with him almost 40 years ago.

This is the type of relationship that God wants you to experience with Him. He is not asking you to go out into the world and create something for Him, achieve something on His behalf, organize and produce some elaborate endeavor that will impress Him and be deserving of His admiration. He is asking you to come home with Him. He is urging you to stay with Him, to love Him with a deep and abiding affection. He is wooing you to move ever closer to Him as your relationship grows sweeter and more effortless over time. It is only in such beautiful closeness, where your life is literally hidden in His, that dreams are conceived, that babies are born, that something beyond your wildest imagination is created within you that is meant to come through you to deliver something that bears His image that others can see, touch and experience. He wants to birth something through you that will live on after you have gone. That is the biology of where babies come from, but it is also the theology of how God's image is recreated in you to fulfill the specific purpose you were created to fulfill on this planet.

God calls you His temple. The people of God knew exactly what that terminology meant. The temple of the Old Testament was built for one purpose, to be the designated place where God's presence came to dwell and live among His people. This was the place from which God would speak to those He had chosen for His love. If your life is not the dwelling place of God, if He is not in and through all that you do, if you are not hearing His whispers, saying words that, apart from His divine revelation, you would never even know to say, then you will carry an ache of the soul that will never leave until you find your place with Him. He created you to be His temple, to be His bride, to carry the warmth of His touch, the depth of His being, to speak out what He speaks in, and be a living expression of His beautiful character to a world that is crying out to know Him.

Some of those hungry, yearning people are spouses, children, friends, neighbors, co-workers and family members who may only have one flickering hope of seeing Jesus, of knowing He has chosen them to forever bask in His extravagant passion, if they are willing to choose Him back. God still puts skin on and walks into the world so that they might find their way to Him, but now He puts your skin on, He births His life in you and in me. We carry His life in us, the fruit of our intimacy with Him. All that we give birth to looks like Him but it looks a lot like us too and always will. We reflect His light just like that image of the sun is revealed in the ripples of the water. It will never be our perfection that draws them, it will be our connection, the undeniable fact that, despite our frailty and flaws, they see Jesus in us. Those we love will be drawn to whatever aspect of His inexhaustible beauty they see imperfectly reflected in our lives. We carry His glory, the weight of who He is and how He loves, and it remains on everyone and everything we touch. The poetic language of Song of Solomon expresses it this way,

> *My beloved is to me a sachet of myrrh, resting between my breasts* (Song of Solomon 1:13 NIV).

When Brittany, our first precious baby girl, was born, she arrived seven weeks earlier than we expected. So her first seven weeks of life were spent in the Neonatal Intensive Care Unit at the University of Tennessee Regional Medical Center. David and I would go there every day, take her out of the little isolette that kept her warm while we were away from her, and hold her up against us, so that she would know who she belonged to, who she came from, who loved her more than words could ever say. We would whisper "I love you's" in her tiny ear. Dave would sing his favorite Beatles songs quietly over her. We would tell her who she is, over and over, whispering her name. Then reluctantly the time would come for us to unwrap her little pink blankets and lay her gently down in her little plastic fish bowl world, always pausing to hold her tiny fingers a little longer through the holes on the side after we closed the door, and all the way home we would miss her. At home I would often lay my head on David, sort of bury my face into his shirt because I could still smell her little Brittany smell, lingering there from when he had held her close.

The essence of God's presence lingers on you when you have spent sweet time in His embrace. As you return again and again, the fragrance of His perfume begins to permeate your soul until it mingles with every little thing He loves about you and you carry that aroma away. It clings to you, penetrating the fabric and the flavor of all He brings to life through you. As you remain in that beautiful intimacy, so close that you can feel His breath and hear His faintest whisper, you get lost in it, absorbed by it, drenched with the aroma of His Spirit. More than anything, that is why God put on skin and positioned Himself as your Kinsman Redeemer, to bring you home to the garden and wrap you in the fragrance of His presence.

John's gospel records these words of Jesus, *"Apart from me you can do nothing"* (John 15:5b). That verb translated "do" means "to create something that has an independent life of its own."[83] Only authentic intimacy, beautiful oneness, gives birth to Spirit-filled words, Spirit-led prayers, and Spirit-drenched plans. Without Him, you or I can build many things. Like the workers of Babel, who attempted to construct a tower to heaven with their man-made bricks, we can build something humanly conceived, lacking spirit and life, leaving confusion in its wake. Lasting legacies are the fruit of intimacy. As the Apostle Paul so clearly put it *"Christ in you, the hope of Glory"* (Colossians 1:27 NIV). This is the mystery that is the only pathway to your destiny and mine.

That apple, the one I consumed in the midst of my craving, came right out of my mom's refrigerator. I could get in my car and drive to the store and get another one very similar to it, any time I choose. So it would be easy for me to assume that apples come from refrigerators or grocery stores, but that is not exactly true. Apples are certainly not "born" in refrigerators. You could never trace an apple's origins back to a produce bin in grocery store. If you want to discover where apples come from you have to begin with a seed, planted in a fertile place, where it is watered and warmed by the sun until, without even trying, life springs out of that single seed, before long becoming a tree. As that tree matures it begins to flower, expressing beauty and fragrance that emanates out into the world around it. Yet in the midst of that beauty and fragrance something is beginning to change. It starts at the very heart of the flower and, at first, remains unseen. That which is still hidden beneath its beauty matures. The fruit that existed inside a tiny seed and was hardly visible within the flower, then grows to the point that it can no longer be contained. It is ready to break free and begin nourishing those around it, hungry ones like me who consume that fruit without even stopping to consider all the glorious prelude that preceded that moment. Not so, with God, when it comes to the life He plans to birth through you. He relishes the prelude, refusing to hurry love past the twists and turns that strengthen it for the birth pangs of fruition.

Perhaps God has been stirring a holy hunger in you as we have made this journey through Ruth's incredible story? Your hunger is an invitation, it is a place in the fertile soul of your heart that has been made ready to receive the seeds of truth that God has been gently planting in you. Once that seed meets the fertile soil of a heart made ready, it impregnates you with His vision and passion, giving birth to dreams that look a lot like Him but undeniably reflect your own personality and passions. These words, birthed in me, flowed onto this page so naturally, right out of my unhurried journey in secret with Him. They are meant to plant seeds of light and life that will become your own and grow within you. This book may be approaching its end and yet, like Ruth's story, it is just getting started. This is merely seed, meant to bring life, to invite you to something more, to increase your appetite and expectation, to woo you to a deeper, more intimate union with God than you have ever experienced.

The thing is, you can eat apples at someone else's table or go to any grocery store and pick up a delicious piece of fruit there. You can go back from time to time and pick up more fruit, grown in someone else's orchard and you can carry that fruit home, but you can never produce your own fruit just by going to the produce section, even if you go there on a regular basis.

What you can do is take the seed, this truth, the extraordinary gospel lived out in the context of Ruth's story, and you can own it. You can make it your own and begin to live your happily ever after with the One your heart was made to crave. You see, it never was the fruit you wanted, it was the intimate journey on the way that is your destiny. That realization releases the beauty of Ruth's story that extends beyond anything we could have anticipated. The reach, the impact of Ruth's story, lived on in you and me and those we entrust it to, stretches farther than our spiritual eyes can see.

You see, if you cut open a single piece of fruit, you discover there is more there than meets the eye. Every piece of fruit is pregnant, in a manner of speaking. That fruit always carries the seed of future fruit already inside of it. Can you grasp the implication? You see, when God gave birth to this story in Ruth's life it already carried within it the seeds of what would come to life in my spiritual womb and yours as well. God's dreams for you are so much bigger, immeasurably beyond what you could ask or even imagine, but you will never find the destiny you were made to crave by chasing a dream. God's brilliance is to release your destiny within you, where seeds of the fruit that will come to life in the spiritual sons and daughters that will follow you back to the garden. are already waiting to be born. We carry babies in us that we will never see, more numerous than we could ever count, more beautiful than we could ever dream. Ruth really has become like Rachel and Leah who gave birth again and again, birthing a people of God who would pass on the story of his goodness and grace from generation to generation.

Now this story, this seed, is entrusted to you for your generation and every one that will follow. The seeds of truth we have gathered are in your hands and in your heart. You must bring water, to flow through a root system you intentionally put into place as you keep reaching out for Him, listening for His voice to speak fresh revelation from His Word. Before you know it, His perfumes will be on your garments and you too will be like Rachel and Leah and Ruth who each carried life within her, until it was birthed through her, to become a people of God.

> *So Boaz took Ruth and she became his wife. When he made love to her, the Lord enabled her to conceive, and she gave birth to a son* (Ruth 4:13 NIV).

There is a profound miracle and a powerful message in those words. You see, Ruth was married before she came to Bethlehem. Before she ever came in pursuit of this God Who was pursuing her heart, she was married to Naomi's son until the day he died. We know Elimelek and his family lived in Moab for ten years but we have no way of knowing exactly how long Ruth was married to Mahlon. Yet we do know this, no life was created through that marriage, no babies were born out of that relationship. So when Ruth came to live among the people of God she not only carried the mark of being a woman from an enemy nation, she carried this mark of having an empty womb. In her culture, a woman who was childless was considered rejected by God. Barrenness was even viewed as a punishment for sin, an indictment on the way that woman had lived or some sin that she had committed. So, you see, God, in birthing something through Ruth, healed what was broken in Ruth.

I wonder if you have silently questioned whether this story could ever really be yours. Maybe hidden within your soul is a deep sense of shame embedded in some self-inflicted wound of a choice that can never be unmade. Perhaps your brokenness came from the hand or heart of an abuser you could not escape or a haunting memory that you have never been able to outrun. Can you see what God is showing us here, in this part of Ruth's incredible story? God will choose the place of your greatest disappointment, your biggest failure, your worst heartbreak and, by His touch, transform it into a birthing canal for His glory. God refuses to let your destiny be denied by anything you have done or any way in which you have been wounded or abused.

Ruth's dream seemed completely hopeless. For Ruth to believe that she would have a child with Boaz, to be raised up in the name of her dead husband and father-in-law, was truly outrageous. To think of her as she sat at home while Boaz went to the gate for this, just amazes me. How could she do anything but sit there questioning her own ability? She may have even given voice to her doubts, asking Naomi, "What if Boaz goes to the gate and tells everyone there that we will have a child and then I never get pregnant?" Do you think she may have worried, "What if something is wrong with me?" I probably would have wrestled with those kinds of thoughts. In fact, I wrestle with thoughts like those all the time. She probably questioned whether something like this could even be possible for a girl like her. That must be why God chose her. She is just like us. We can identify with her brokenness and yet we share her dreams, her desire to live a life only God could design and bring to pass. At this moment, like no other, she seems to be a perfect heroine for folks like us, who struggle to believe.

No matter where you have been or what you have come through on the way to this moment in your story, this is not a time to turn back and give up. This is your time to hang on to every word that God has spoken to you through Ruth. God has always known that this story, not just Ruth's, but yours and mine, had a miracle coming. This verse should become our mantra, our motivation to keep believing when the odds seem stacked against us. God enabled Ruth to conceive! This young girl from the wrong town who was raised to believe in the wrong

god, and, in most people's eyes, had the wrong dream, would soon give birth to something beyond her wildest imagination! If God did this miracle for Ruth, will He do anything less for you and me? He is inviting us to believe beyond our circumstances. Can you hear it? God is asking, "Will you believe, not just believe, but will you believe to the point that your brokenness is transformed into a birthing canal for His glory?"

The way I have come to understand it, the God I believe in, Who is powerful enough to do anything He chooses, will only do one of two things with your wounds, with the characteristics and experiences that you consider to be your weaknesses. He will either unleash His supernatural power into that area of brokenness in your life, providing total healing and restoration, or He will recast that weakness in such a way that it becomes a place of such miraculous provision and revelation that you will no longer consider it a weakness at all. This was Paul's experience. I just love the way his words are expressed in The Passion Translation,

> *But he answered me, "My grace is always more than enough for you, and my power finds its full expression through your weakness." So I will celebrate my weaknesses, for when I'm weak I sense more deeply the mighty power of Christ living in me. So I'm not defeated by my weakness, but delighted! For when I feel my weakness and endure mistreatment—when I'm surrounded with troubles on every side and face persecution because of my love for Christ—I am made yet stronger. For my weakness becomes a portal to God's power* (2 Corinthians 9:11-12 TPT).

Maybe you have always tried to hide every weakness by concocting an elaborate cover up or by compensating so that no one has a clue. How crazy would it be to come out of the shadows, as you realize that if Your Redeemer does not choose to remove it, He will infuse it with such power that you will begin to celebrate it as this incredible pathway in which you have experienced His divine presence like never before.

Absent His supernatural healing, your deepest wound, your greatest disappointment, your own barrenness will become a portal for His incomparable power!

I have no idea how you have been hurt and would never want to minimize your heartache in any way. My own heart breaks to think that my metaphorical words would ever add in any way to the pain of a woman who has experienced infertility when these words are only intended to offer the hope of a redemption only God could orchestrate. Whether your heartbreak came by way of an inability to conceive a child, betrayal, sexual abuse, abandonment, or any of the seemingly limitless ways in which evil casts its hideous gaze in our direction, I know that your heartbreak can feel like a bottomless pit of pain, beyond remedy, outside of the miraculous work of Jesus. Only a God who would leave heaven to find you, can bear the cost of buying back every single thing this heartbreak has ripped out of your hands. This story is in no way intended to brush away your wound as inconsequential but to tell you that your story will not leave you here, your Redeemer has come! I may not know how your story will end but He saw the end from the very beginning and if you will just believe enough to take His hand right where you are, your journey toward restoration can begin in this very moment.

God knew. He always knew about that dream long buried deep beneath the rubble of Ruth's repeated disappointment. Ruth never had to say a word because that dream refused to stay in the grave. In fact, God seemed to be intentionally fanning the flames to resurrect Ruth's desire. Though, as far as we know, Ruth never said a thing, everyone else could not stop talking about the possibility. Naomi hinted at it when she asked, *"Is not Boaz a kinsman?"* with complete understanding of what a kinsman's responsibilities would include. Naomi had babies on the brain. Boaz echoed the idea in Ruth 3:11 saying, *"All the townspeople know that you are a woman of noble character."* The Hebrew word, "chayil" was used to describe Ruth as a force, a woman of influence and power. It comes from a picturesque root word that means, "to twist and writhe in the pain of labor, to be able to bear children."[84] Boaz was saying, "I know you can do this!" Even in his words of rejection the nearer kinsman acknowledged the inevitability of Ruth's fruitfulness. He saw her expected offspring as a threat to his predetermined intentions to have children of his own who would one day inherit everything he would spend his life accumulating. While Ruth was waiting, most probably wondering if she would be able to pull this off, what God knew, what Naomi and Boaz and even that nearer kinsman had become convinced of, even total strangers on the street were talking about, as if it were already true.

The witnesses at the gate compared Ruth to, of all people, Rachel and Leah who participated in what turned out to be the biggest baby-making contest in the Old Testament, even pulling their hand maidens into the fight before they were through. The Hebrew word translated "built" in reference to these fierce competitors has within its meaning the idea of "obtaining children."[85] So the elders at the gate were describing Ruth, this woman who was barren, this woman who had never had anything come out of her womb, as being like two women who were famous because they "built by birthing." God's original design has always been for us to increase and multiply, to make disciples who make disciples, one generation of believers birthing the next. God grows His people through reproduction, conceiving His very life in us through intimacy, so that we can be the Rachel's and Leah's of our generation, giving birth to spiritual sons and daughters. The fruit of your spiritual womb already has, within it, an unimaginable harvest, the future fruit that will come to life in the wombs of those believers who will follow you into the chambers of your King.

These witnesses also had something to say about Boaz. They foresaw that he "would have standing in Ephrathah." Ephrathah, meaning "fruitfulness,"[86] was another name for the town of Bethlehem. The "House of Bread" was destined to be a place of great abundance and the people would be known for their uncanny ability to bear fruit. These elders did not see Boaz as one kept out of that promise. They saw him as having a distinct reputation among the fruitful ones. In other words, these elders were praising Boaz for what they saw unfolding in Ruth's womb as a result of his presence in her life. They were anticipating the intimacy that Boaz and Ruth would share, believing that this young woman, now redeemed out of her poverty by this magnanimous man, would give birth to a life that would carry his seed into the future.

Finally these witnesses foresaw the family that would be born to Boaz and Ruth as like that of Perez. Perez is a very specific and interesting choice to complete this prophetic triad. He was an ancestor of Boaz, the product of a levirate marriage, except, in his case, the kinsman was an unwilling participant. His mother, Tamar, used deception to get pregnant and the son conceived through her deception was Perez. His name meant "a breach or break."[87] Perez was a twin. Though his twin brother's hand reached out of the womb first, Perez managed to push past him on his way out of the womb. Though he was not technically the firstborn, he was still the one chosen by God. In Nehemiah we learn that Perez had more than four hundred sons and all of them were able men (Nehemiah 11:6 NIV). The word "able" is the same word spoken of Ruth when she is called "a woman of noble character," and used to describe Boaz as "a man of standing."[88] Born out of his mother's sorrow, loss, anguish and even sin, Perez broke through to become a mighty man of valor, a force, having strength like that needed to be able to labor in child birth. In saying that their family would be like that of Perez, God was once again emphasizing His propensity for grace over the law, His willingness to manifest His powerful presence in this world in unexpected ways through unconventional vessels.

The captive ones described in Psalm 126 came back home after 70 years spent as slaves under the oppressive rule of their enemy in a foreign land carrying dreams in their hearts. The Hebrew word literally means they were "pregnant, fat, full"[89] at a time in their lives when the hardness and cruelty of their circumstances should have drained every last dream out of them. Yet consider this eyewitness account of one of these travelers toward home,

> *When the Lord restored the fortunes of Zion, we were like those who dreamed. Our mouths were filled with laughter, our tongues with songs of joy. Then it was said among the nations, "The Lord has done great things for them." The Lord has done great things for us, and we are filled with joy. Restore our fortunes, Lord, like streams in the Negev. Those who sow with tears will reap with songs of joy. Those who go out weeping, carrying seed to sow, will return with songs of joy, carrying sheaves with them* (Psalm 126:1-6 NIV).

Ironically these people were fruitful, even before they were free. In the phrase translated, "carrying seed to sow," the Hebrew word for seed is "zera" which can mean "offspring or children."[90] For 70 years the people of God had been oppressed. It would not have surprised anyone to find them cynical and embittered from the hardness of their years in captivity. Yet they came home singing. Their mouths were filled with laughter. No circumstance had been able to deny them their destiny. They had seed in their pockets and their offspring were in their arms and in their wombs. As God released them, as He brought them back home where they belonged, He had more than freedom on his mind for His chosen people. God's plans to reproduce His life in them were undeterred by the sin that precipitated their captivity or the abuse they suffered at the hands of their oppressors. Their destiny to be fruitful and multiply outlasted their captivity, as God brought them home carrying the seed of that destiny in their hands, in their hearts and on their lips.

As we return our thoughts to Ruth we find that the life conceived in Ruth, came through her. She gave birth to a son. The Hebrew word for son is "ben" which comes from the word in Ruth 4:11 that indicates "intimate relationship."[91] This refers to offspring, life that comes, not just from you, through you. If I bake you a cake that would be a lovely gesture, but if I have you a baby that is a completely different thing! That cake may be a gift that came from me but that baby would have to come through me. A baby is an intimate creation. God has set us apart to be reproductive in this world. I think too many believers are baking cakes, when we ought to be birthin' babies! Life is not about the work you can do for God, it is about the fruit of your womb conceived as your life becomes intimately intertwined with His.

Just imagine you and I are both pregnant and, for the sake of argument, imagine our babies are both due on the same day which just happens to be today. If by some crazy miracle we both go into labor and each baby is born right here and right now, would you expect your baby to look like mine? If they were born at the exact moment would they not be twins? Of course not, the babies would not be twins. Genetics demands that each child would bear a resemblance to its own father and mother. You and I could bake the same cake from the same recipe and come pretty close to creating cake twins, but if we give birth, the new life that comes through us carries our DNA and, therefore, each baby will bear some resemblance to the one through whom it came. It would be craziness to expect otherwise.

Ruth gave birth to a son. I cannot say definitively what this baby boy looked like, whether he had curly dark hair and blue eyes with dimples in his round cheeks, or dark eyes and auburn locks that curved around a tiny slender face. I simply imagine that if you could look into the face of the son that she bore, you would see glimpses of Ruth. The fruit of her womb carried her DNA within him, carried characteristics of his mother, and his father as well.

Knowing this, you need not fear that God's purpose for your life is going to be some grand departure from anything you would ever want. Whatever is birthed through you should look like the Father but bear a striking resemblance to you. Far too often we feel like we must chase a dream that will never fit us in order to please God. We compare our story to someone's that we admire, or even envy, and end up walking away from our true destinies feeling like failures. God wants to birth a dream through you that carries your DNA and highlights the best of who you are right where you are. Comparison is always a trap meant to distract you from the unique race that God has called you, and you alone, to run. Ruth gave birth to a son that came through her and came out looking like his mother. That is a picture of what God wants to bring to life through each of us, a destiny that is ours. Still there is more that God had planned to birth through this amazing story and, again, God brought witnesses to announce it.

This time they were the women who surrounded Ruth and Naomi. When they began to speak, His praise was on their lips.

> The women said to Naomi: "Praise be to the Lord, who this day has not left you without a guardian-redeemer. May he become famous throughout Israel! He will renew your life and sustain you in your old age. For your daughter-in-law, who loves you and who is better to you than seven sons, has given him birth." Then Naomi took the child in her arms and cared for him (Ruth 4:14-15 NIV).

One of the things that strikes me the most in this powerful portrait of God is the selflessness of the kinsman redeemer. Boaz was willing to give up his son to redeem the name of a dead man. He could have held onto his son, caring only for his own reputation, but this beautiful man gave the child that he surely loved for those who could not remedy their situation, for a family who had run away from home and walked away from God. When, like the nearer kinsman, Boaz could have put his needs first, allowing this family to reap the harvest of their bad choices, Boaz refused to leave them with what they deserved. He gave them more again and again, until he gave his very own son for their redemption. That is grace in its purest form, such a picture of our good and generous God who gave His Son for our redemption.

So perhaps it should come as no surprise to see Ruth's selfless act of placing her child in the arms of her mother-in-law. She was simply doing what she saw her sweet Boaz doing. What a redemptive moment she created with this selfless gesture. What a sight it must have been to see that baby boy in Naomi's arms. The words Naomi spoke when she first came home to Bethlehem were, "I went out full." Do you want to guess what that Hebrew word translated "full" means? It means "pregnant."[92] Naomi left Bethlehem pregnant, a dreamer full of expectation, brimming with hope. Yet, like the prodigal who would have settled for the food he fed to the pigs so intense was his hunger, Naomi came home hungry and humbled. She came home empty and hopeless. This bitter woman was now reborn and the women living there said "Naomi has a son."

Up until that moment Naomi must have thought this story was for someone else. Though she was content to stay on the sidelines, her God would not leave her there. Naomi may have thought it was too late for her story, too late for her to find love, so Love Himself came to find her. Each time Ruth had an encounter with Boaz, as much as he had Ruth's welfare on his heart, he never failed to mention Naomi and send home something for her benefit as well. At the gate it was not only Ruth's name Boaz spoke but Naomi's too. That beautiful baby boy was not only born into this world to redeem Ruth, he came to buy back every single thing Naomi had lost while she was living in the land of the enemy. Ruth's story of release had become Naomi's story of restoration. As the women around her testified, her Lord had not left her out, He had written them both into His story.

So this is the story of a Jewish woman, who thought God had abandoned her, who came to a foreign land carrying only a flicker of the light of God that once burned brightly within her. Though living in a land where the One True God was completely left out, this woman brought Him with her. Though she had left His presence, His presence never left her. Without any effort she bore the fruit of that unusual presence, offering a Gentile girl a taste she had never known. That taste planted a seed of believing in Ruth, a seed that already carried the promise of fruit that was to come. So the characteristics of God that Naomi carried in her, though imperfectly reflected, planted the seed of a dream that God could love a girl from Moab and make her a part of His chosen people. When Naomi turned to go back home, Ruth clung to her, refusing to let her go back home without her. So this tired Jewish woman, now broken, was broken open and something was birthed that day, at that moment on the road, as these two women simply made their individual decisions to move toward God and to move toward Him together. What was alive in Naomi was now alive and growing in Ruth. Naomi's God was Ruth's God, Ruth's passion, Ruth's hope. Out of their love for God these two women from different cultures had grown to love each other. Naomi had taken Ruth to places Ruth had never been before and guided her on the journey. I can even imagine, when the time came, Naomi was holding Ruth's hand as she endured the pains of labor, wiping her brow, reminding her to breathe. No wonder it almost seemed like Naomi had a baby, because she had been there every step of the way.

This is also the story of a Gentile girl from Moab who had no idea who God was until that Jewish woman came to town, but the fruit of God's presence in Naomi's life was so contagious it set a fire in Ruth's heart, giving her the courage to cling to it when it would have been easier to turn away. This young Gentile woman found favor in the field of her redeemer and became intentional about hearing his voice and pursuing his heart. Ruth, the Moabitess, should have been rejected, should have been left out, yet she audaciously believed that this man of standing would spread the corner of his garment over her and take her as his bride. All Ruth asked was that he tell her who she was. Yet he took her place at the gate, the place of her greatest vulnerability, and put his unusual, extravagant love on display. Their beautiful intimacy birthed a brand new life through her and when the baby was born they chose to name him, Obed, meaning, "servant,"[93] the very same word Ruth had used to describe herself. The life that was birthed in her was without a doubt his father's son, but he looked like his mother too, carried her heart as well. This young woman from Moab, who had no right to even be there, went chasing after love, and God's dream for her was bigger than anything she ever imagined would happen to her.

A Jewish woman who had given up on love and a Gentile woman who had lived her whole life in a place where Love was completely left out, found themselves written into God's story, painted into this beautiful self-portrait of God. The fruit of His presence in them would carry within it the seed of future fruit they would never even see or dream. One woman birthed that baby and another woman held him in her arms, and this child did not simply grow up to inherit the land once owned by a man who died in a foreign country, Obed grew up to be fruitful like his father. He grew up to have a son whose name was Jesse. Jesse had a son whose name was David, who against all odds, became a king because he was chosen by God. From that king's line another child, another Son, would come carrying redemption, to buy back every single thing the enemy had stolen, everything that had been lost through sin and death. He came not only for that Jewish woman but also for that young girl from Moab, and all of us who have found ourselves written into His story as well.

Do you think Ruth ever dreamed or Naomi could have imagined that this baby that they took turns holding in their arms, this fruit of their womb, already carried within him the seed of Our Savior Who would someday usher in the very life of God with skin on, the

Redeemer we all were made to crave. Jesus intentionally made Himself a man, a servant, our kinsman, so He could give back everything we have lost in the war that broke out long before we were born.

This whole story has never been just Ruth's story, this story is about you, it has always been about God's passionate, extravagant, unusual love for you. This is a love story, not just a baby story. The baby is the gift that flows so naturally out of the intimate relationship that is your destiny. The dream God dreams for you is that you will believe, oh, but not just believe, that you will believe to the point that it forever changes your story into the story He dreamed for you before time began. This is the story of a girl who knew nothing about love, nor seed, nor "birthing no babies," who simply left where she had always been and moved to where she knew God was. She was the reason He gave everything He had to buy her out of her poverty. She was so satisfied with the way He loved her that she became fearless in the face of every rejector. She never had to pretend to be anything other than what was true about her because she came to realize He accepted her for who she was right where she was. She found her home with Him, a home where she was content to stay. So, they lived, in that beautiful garden He planted, where He told her the stories of His dreams for her that were beyond anything she could ever imagine until, at last, each one came true.

Epilogue

Our theology must become biography.

—*Tim Hansel, Holy Sweat*

WILL YOU BELIEVE?

Ruth's incredible story is still being written in the lives that continue to bear the fruit of her courageous decision to believe to the point that it radically changed her story. As you have followed in her footsteps on this journey, one that began in a place where God was completely left out and led to a destiny that far exceeded her dreams, God has been inviting you to embrace this story as your own. He has woven your story into His. He simply asks that you take Him at His Word. The unfolding of this story in your life continues as you identify where you find yourself in this story. That is the beautiful beginning of everything God has in store for you. He has chosen you for His love and extravagantly accepts who you are right where you are, but He will not leave you there. Your authentic answers to the questions God has posed within these pages hold the key that will release you to move beyond everything that has ever held you back from the soul-satisfying intimacy that has always been your destiny. So I need to ask you one last time...Will you believe, not just believe, not will you simply offer your intellectual agreement to a statement of faith, but will you truly put all your trust in Him to this extent, in these specific ways?

Will you believe to the point that it changes your story?

Will you believe when believing gets hard?

Will you believe that God already loves you like no one else has ever loved you?

Will you believe to the point that you will stay?

Will you believe to the point that you will go alone to be with Him and wait to hear His voice?

Will you believe to the point that rejection is robbed of its power?

Will you believe to the point that you abandon pretense for authenticity?

Will you believe to the point that living the life that God dreams for you is as natural as breathing?

Will you believe to the point that your brokenness is transformed into a birthing canal for His glory?

This is the spiritual road map to your destiny. Ruth simply believed, put her total trust in her redeemer at every crossroads, took him at his word in the face of every opportunity to turn around, and it set her free from everything she had been through and the only life she had ever known, to make way for a life and a legacy beyond her dreams. What about you? Your story too has been beautifully woven into the exquisite story of your Kinsman Redeemer. Your destiny awaits you. Will you believe?

WORKS CITED

[1] King, M. L., Jr. (n.d.). I Have A Dream. Speech.

[2] Boom, C. T., Sherrill, E., & Sherrill, J. L. (1974). The hiding place: By Corrie ten Boom, with John and Elizabeth Sherrill. New York: Bantam.

[3] Boom, C. T., Sherrill, E., & Sherrill, J. L. (1974). The hiding place: By Corrie ten Boom, with John and Elizabeth Sherrill. New York: Bantam.

[4] Boom, C. T., Sherrill, E., & Sherrill, J. L. (1974). The hiding place: By Corrie ten Boom, with John and Elizabeth Sherrill. New York: Bantam.

[5] Boom, C. T., Sherrill, E., & Sherrill, J. L. (1974). The hiding place: By Corrie ten Boom, with John and Elizabeth Sherrill. New York: Bantam

[6] "Unknown Quotes." BrainyQuote, Xplore, www.brainyquote.com/quotes/unknown_133991.

[7] Zodhiates, S. (1992). The complete word study dictionary: New Testament. Chattanooga TN: AMG Publishers.

[8] Zodhiates, S., & Strong, J. (1992). The complete word study New Testament: King James Version (2nd ed.). Chattanooga: AMG.

[9] Zodhiates, S., & Strong, J. (1992). The complete word study New Testament: King James Version (2nd ed.). Chattanooga: AMG.

[10] Strong, J. (1984). The New Strongs Exhaustive Concordance with Dictionary of Hebrew Bible. Nashville: Thomas. Nelson Publishers.

[11] Strong, J. (1984). The New Strongs Exhaustive Concordance with Dictionary of Hebrew Bible. Nashville: Thomas. Nelson Publishers.

[12] Strong, J. (1984). The New Strongs Exhaustive Concordance with Dictionary of Hebrew Bible. Nashville: Thomas. Nelson Publishers.

[13] Baker, W., & Carpenter, E. E. (2003). The complete word study dictionary: Old Testament (1st ed.). Chattanooga, TN: AMG.

[14] Strong, J. (1984). The New Strongs Exhaustive Concordance with Dictionary of Hebrew Bible. Nashville: Thomas. Nelson Publishers.

[15] Jackson, P., Osborne, B., & Walsh, F. (Producers), & Jackson, P. (Director). (2002). The lord of the rings: two towers [Motion Picture]. USA: New Line Cinema.

[16] Jackson, P., Osborne, B., & Walsh, F. (Producers), & Jackson, P. (Director). (2002). The lord of the rings: two towers [Motion Picture]. USA: New Line Cinema.

[17] Nelson, J., Zwick, E., Herskovitz, M., Solomon, R., & Hall. B. (Producers), & Nelson, J. (Director). (2001). I Am Sam [Motion Picture]. Burbank, CA: New Line Cinema.

[18] Strong, J. (1984). The New Strongs Exhaustive Concordance with Dictionary of Hebrew Bible. Nashville: Thomas. Nelson Publishers..

[19] Baker, W., & Carpenter, E. E. (2003). The complete word study dictionary: Old Testament (1st ed.). Chattanooga, TN: AMG.

[20] Baker, W., & Carpenter, E. E. (2003). The complete word study dictionary: Old Testament (1st ed.). Chattanooga, TN: AMG.

[21] Baker, W., & Carpenter, E. E. (2003). The complete word study dictionary: Old Testament (1st ed.). Chattanooga, TN: AMG.

[22] Nelson, J., Zwick, E., Herskovitz, M., Solomon, R., & Hall. B. (Producers), & Nelson, J. (Director). (2001). I Am Sam [Motion Picture]. Burbank, CA: New Line Cinema.

[23] Zodhiates, S., & Baker, W. P. (1994). The Complete Word Study Old Testament. Amg Pubs.

[24] Zodhiates, S., & Baker, W. P. (1994). The Complete Word Study Old Testament. Amg Pubs.

[25] Woolf, H.B. & Webster, N. (Eds.).(1977). Webster's New Collegiate Dictionary

[26] Ephron, N. (Director). (1993). Sleepless in Seattle [Motion picture]. USA: TriStar Pictures.

[27] Ephron, N. (Director). (1993). Sleepless in Seattle [Motion picture]. USA: TriStar Pictures.

[28] Ephron, N. (Director). (1993). Sleepless in Seattle [Motion picture]. USA: TriStar Pictures.

[29] Baker, W., & Carpenter, E. E. (2003). The complete word study dictionary: Old Testament (1st ed.). Chattanooga, TN: AMG.

[30] Zodhiates, S., & Baker, W. P. (1994). The Complete Word Study Old Testament. Amg Pubs.

[31] Zodhiates, S., & Baker, W. P. (1994). The Complete Word Study Old Testament. Amg Pubs.

[32] Baker, W., & Carpenter, E. E. (2003). The complete word study dictionary: Old Testament (1st ed.). Chattanooga, TN: AMG.

[33] Zodhiates, S., & Baker, W. P. (1994). The Complete Word Study Old Testament. Amg Pubs.

[34] Zodhiates, S., & Baker, W. P. (1994). The Complete Word Study Old Testament. Amg Pubs.

[35] Zodhiates, S., & Baker, W. P. (1994). The Complete Word Study Old Testament. Amg Pubs.

[36] Walvoord, J.F., Zuck, R. B., & Dallas Theological Seminary. (1985) The Bible Knowledge Commentary: Am exposition of the scriptures. Wheaton, Ill. Victor Books.

[37] What is an ephah, (n.d.). Retrieved from http://www.answers.come/Q/What_is_an_ephah

[38] Zodhiates, S., & Baker, W. P. (1994). The Complete Word Study Old Testament. Amg Pubs.

[39] Ephron, N. (Director). (1993). Sleepless in Seattle [Motion picture]. USA: TriStar Pictures.

[40] Fleming, V., Cukor, G., LeRoy, M., Taurog, N., & Vidor, K. (Directors). (1939). Wizard of Oz[Motion picture]. USA: Metro-Goldwyn-Mayer.

[41] Scott, R. (Director). (2000). Gladiator [Motion picture]. USA: DreamWorks Pictures.

[42] Zodhiates, S., & Baker, W. P. (1994). The Complete Word Study Old Testament. Amg Pubs.

[43] Zodhiates, S., & Baker, W. P. (1994). The Complete Word Study Old Testament. Amg Pubs.

[44] Baker, W., & Carpenter, E. E. (2003). The complete word study dictionary: Old Testament (1st ed.). Chattanooga, TN: AMG.

[45] Jackson, P., Osborne, B., & Walsh, F. (Producers), & Jackson, P. (Director). (2002). The lord of the rings: return of the king. [Motion Picture]. USA: New Line Cinema.

[46] Baker, W., & Carpenter, E. E. (2003). The complete word study dictionary: Old Testament (1st ed.). Chattanooga, TN: AMG.

[47] Baker, W., & Carpenter, E. E. (2003). The complete word study dictionary: Old Testament (1st ed.). Chattanooga, TN: AMG.

[48] Baker, W., & Carpenter, E. E. (2003). The complete word study dictionary: Old Testament (1st ed.). Chattanooga, TN: AMG.

[49] Solt, Andrew (Director). (1988) Imagine: John Lennon [Motion picture]. UK: Warner Bros.

[50] Ephron, N. (Director). (1998). You've Got Mail [Motion picture]. USA: Warner Bros.

[51] Ortberg, J. (2008). If You Want to Walk on Water, You've Got to Get Out of the Boat. Grand Rapids, MI: Zondervan.

[52] Ortberg, J. (2008). If You Want to Walk on Water, You've Got to Get Out of the Boat. Grand Rapids, MI: Zondervan.

[53] Ortberg, J. (2008). If You Want to Walk on Water, You've Got to Get Out of the Boat. Grand Rapids, MI: Zondervan.

[54] Baker, W., & Carpenter, E. E. (2003). The complete word study dictionary: Old Testament (1st ed.). Chattanooga, TN: AMG.

[55] Baker, W., & Carpenter, E. E. (2003). The complete word study dictionary: Old Testament (1st ed.). Chattanooga, TN: AMG.

[56] Merriam-Webster's collegiate dictionary (10th ed.). (1999). Springfield, MA: Merriam-Webster Incorporated.

[57] Docter, P., & Del Carmen, R. (Directors). (2015). Inside Out [Motion picture]. USA: Pixar.

[58] Baker, W., & Carpenter, E. E. (2003). The complete word study dictionary: Old Testament (1st ed.). Chattanooga, TN: AMG

[59] Hoffman, M. (Director). (1996). One Fine Day [Motion picture]. USA: Lynda Obst Productions.

[60] Zodhiates, S., & Baker, W. P. (1994). The Complete Word Study Old Testament. Amg Pubs.

[61] Simon, P., Beckett, B., Brecker, M., Dixon, J., Gadd, S., Hawkins, R., Hood, D., ... Jessy Dixon Singers. (2004). Still crazy after all these years. Burbank, Calif: Warner Strategic Marketing.

[62] Rascal Flats (Musical group). (2008). Greatest hits: Volume 1. Australia: Universal Music Australia.

[63] Baker, W., & Carpenter, E. E. (2003). The complete word study dictionary: Old Testament (1st ed.). Chattanooga, TN: AMG.

[64] Woolf, H.B. & Webster, N. (Eds.).(1977). Webster's New Collegiate Dictionary

[65] Baker, W., & Carpenter, E. E. (2003). The complete word study dictionary: Old Testament (1st ed.). Chattanooga, TN: AMG.

[66] Zodhiates, S., & Baker, W. P. (1994). The Complete Word Study Old Testament. Amg Pubs.

[67] Zodhiates, S., & Baker, W. P. (1994). The Complete Word Study Old Testament. Amg Pubs.

[68] Baker, W., & Carpenter, E. E. (2003). The complete word study dictionary: Old Testament (1st ed.). Chattanooga, TN: AMG.

[69] Marshall, G. (Director). (1999). Runaway Bride [Motion picture]. USA: Paramount Pictures.

[70] Merriam-Webster's collegiate dictionary (10th ed.). (1999). Springfield, MA: Merriam-Webster Incorporated.

[71] Zodhiates, S., & Baker, W. P. (1994). The Complete Word Study Old Testament. Amg Pubs.

[72] http://artdaily.com/news/9366/Man-Sells-Garage-Sale-Painting-for--1M#.XH1KyxpOlvI

[73] Baker, W., & Carpenter, E. E. (2003). The complete word study dictionary: Old Testament (1st ed.). Chattanooga, TN: AMG.

[74] Baker, W., & Carpenter, E. E. (2003). The complete word study dictionary: Old Testament (1st ed.). Chattanooga, TN: AMG.

[75] Walvoord, J.F., Zuck, R. B., & Dallas Theological Seminary. (1985) The Bible Knowledge Commentary: Am exposition of the scriptures. Wheaton, Ill. Victor Books.

[76] Walvoord, J.F., Zuck, R. B., & Dallas Theological Seminary. (1985) The Bible Knowledge Commentary: Am exposition of the scriptures. Wheaton, Ill. Victor Books.

[77] Walvoord, J.F., Zuck, R. B., & Dallas Theological Seminary. (1985) The Bible Knowledge Commentary: Am exposition of the scriptures. Wheaton, Ill. Victor Books.

[78] Zodhiates, S., & Baker, W. P. (1994). The Complete Word Study Old Testament. Amg Pubs.

[79] Zodhiates, S., & Baker, W. P. (1994). The Complete Word Study Old Testament. Amg Pubs.

[80] Zodhiates, S., & Baker, W. P. (1994). The Complete Word Study Old Testament. Amg Pubs.

[81] Baker, W., & Carpenter, E. E. (2003). The complete word study dictionary: Old Testament (1st ed.). Chattanooga, TN: AMG.

[82] Zodhiates, S., & Baker, W. P. (1994). The Complete Word Study Old Testament. Amg Pubs.

[83] Zodhiates, S., & Strong, J. (1992). The complete word study New Testament: King James Version (2nd ed.). Chattanooga: AMG.

[84] Zodhiates, S., & Baker, W. P. (1994). The Complete Word Study Old Testament. Amg Pubs.

[85] Baker, W., & Carpenter, E. E. (2003). The complete word study dictionary: Old Testament (1st ed.). Chattanooga, TN: AMG.

[86] Zodhiates, S., & Baker, W. P. (1994). The Complete Word Study Old Testament. Amg Pubs.

[87] Zodhiates, S., & Baker, W. P. (1994). The Complete Word Study Old Testament. Amg Pubs.

[88] Zodhiates, S., & Baker, W. P. (1994). The Complete Word Study Old Testament. Amg Pubs.

[89] Baker, W., & Carpenter, E. E. (2003). The complete word study dictionary: Old Testament (1st ed.). Chattanooga, TN: AMG.

[90] Zodhiates, S., & Baker, W. P. (1994). The Complete Word Study Old Testament. Amg Pubs.

[91] Zodhiates, S., & Baker, W. P. (1994). The Complete Word Study Old Testament. Amg Pubs.

[92] Zodhiates, S., & Baker, W. P. (1994). The Complete Word Study Old Testament. Amg Pubs.

[93] Baker, W., & Carpenter, E. E. (2003). The complete word study dictionary: Old Testament (1st ed.). Chattanooga, TN: AMG.

Made in the USA
Monee, IL
10 September 2019